THE CHINESE
FINANCIAL SYSTEM

THE CHINESE FINANCIAL SYSTEM

Cecil R. Dipchand,
Zhang Yichun,
and Ma Mingjia

Contributions in Economics and Economic History, Number 157

GREENWOOD PRESS
Westport, Connecticut • London

HG
187
.C6
D56
1994

Library of Congress Cataloging-in-Publication Data

Dipchand, Cecil R.
    The Chinese financial system / Cecil R. Dipchand, Zhang Yichun,
and Ma Mingjia.
      p. cm.—(Contributions in economics and economic history,
ISSN 0084–9235 ; no. 157)
    Includes bibliographical references and index.
    ISBN 0–313–29282–5 (alk. paper)
    1. Financial institutions—China. I. Chang, I-chün. II. Ma,
Mingjia. III. Title. IV. Series.
HG187.C6D56   1994
332.1'0951—dc20   93–50539

British Library Cataloguing in Publication Data is available.

Library of Congress Catalog Card Number: 93–50539
ISBN: 0–313–29282–5
ISSN: 0084–9235

First published in 1994

Greenwood Press, 88 Post Road West, Westport, CT 06881
An imprint of Greenwood Publishing Group, Inc.

Printed in the United States of America

∞™

The paper used in this book complies with the
Permanent Paper Standard issued by the National
Information Standards Organization (Z39.48–1984).

10 9 8 7 6 5 4 3 2

CONTENTS

ILLUSTRATIONS

FIGURES

TABLES

PREFACE

The Canadian International Development Agency (CIDA) has provided generous financial aid to facilitate the transfer of management technology to China under the Canada-China Management Education Program (CCMEP). Through CCMEP, Canadian universities are linked with Chinese counterparts in an effort to upgrade the delivery and quality of management education in China. Dalhousie University in Halifax, Canada, and Xiamen University in Xiamen, China, are linkage partners under this program.

This book is the result of the joint research efforts of Canadian and Chinese scholars under the auspices of the Dalhousie/Xiamen University Linkage Program. As reforms were undertaken in China, the financial system of the pre-1979 era changed rapidly to accommodate the financial needs of economic reconstruction. This book provides the essential structure of the Chinese financial system as it had evolved by the 1990s. Considering the political, economic and social conditions that prevailed before 1979, the development of the Chinese financial system by 1990 is quite a commendable achievement.

Major funding for the study was provided by CIDA through the Dalhousie/ Xiamen University Linkage Program, the Dalhousie University School of Business Administration, and the Douglas Mackay Foundation for International Banking. Many thanks are due to the Centre for International Business, Dalhousie University, and the Management Education Centre, Xiamen University, for personnel and facilities used for research purposes.

We wish to thank our many research assistants and acknowledge that any remaining errors in the book are ours.

The authors are heavily indebted to Leslie Stockhausen, who prepared the camera ready copy pages of this book.

Cecil R. Dipchand
Dalhousie University

Zhang Yichun
Xiamen University

Ma Mingjia
Bank of China

THE CHINESE
FINANCIAL SYSTEM

1

The Pre-1980 Experience

The Chinese Communist Party (CCP) was established in 1921 with the stated purpose of seizing power from the Kuomintang (KMT) government and to convert China into a socialist state.[1] After the establishment of the CCP, its armed forces, the People's Liberation Army, fought continual military skirmishes with the KMT until 1937, when the Japanese invaded China. In the interest of national security and defense, the CCP and KMT joined forces in the War of Resistance (1937–45) against Japan. However, after V-J day, when the Japanese conceded defeat, the conflict between the CCP and KMT resumed and intensified, and by 1949, the CCP had achieved its objective of seizing political power in China.

This chapter is a summary of the main events that influenced the structure of the financial markets from 1949 to 1979. An appreciation of these events facilitates an understanding of the material presented in chapters 2 through 9. This chapter is not intended to give a detailed account, an assessment, or an evaluation of the events that occurred over the 1949–1979 period; such a presentation has been done in volumes of publications.[2] The intended purpose of this chapter is to present a synopsis of the political ideology, general economic conditions, and structure of the financial markets as they existed by the end of 1979.

A word of caution is needed on the statistics presented in this chapter. Data has been taken from several studies in which the authors cautioned that the statistics might not be completely accurate or consistently compiled. Nevertheless, the statistics are useful as they give some general trends or indicators of events that took place during the period.

CHINA IS ESTABLISHED AS A SOCIALIST STATE

On October 1, 1949, the People's Republic of China (hereafter called China) was established and the CCP proceeded to lead the people from a new democracy to socialism.[3] It is alleged that this process was completed by 1956 with at least three objectives having been achieved (Liu and Wu, 1986: 13):[4]

1. Land was confiscated from the feudal class and turned over to the peasants.

2. Monopoly (or bureaucratic) capital controlled by capitalists or imperialists was confiscated and turned over to the state.

3. Industry and commerce (belonging to the national bourgeoisie) were protected for the benefit of the Chinese people.

In fact, these three objectives were achieved in a piecemeal manner starting in 1946, when Harbin was liberated. As additional cities were liberated, the People's Liberation Army seized land and capital from the KMT bureaucrats. By September 1949, the Chinese People's Political Consultative Conference (CPPCC) enshrined these objectives into the "CPPCC Common Outline," which served as a provisional constitution. As the KMT retreated to Taiwan, the CCP was dismantling Old China's capitalist features through the following activities.[5]

1. Firms in the financial sector were either closed, merged with Chinese institutions or restructured as socialist entities.

    a. Four well-known KMT families (Chaing Kai-shek, T-V. Soong, H. H. Kung, and the Chen brothers) had controlled more than seven of the largest Chinese financial institutions, and these were taken over. These institutions included four banks, two agencies, and one reserve bank: Central Bank of China, Bank of China, Transportation Bank, Farmer's Bank of China, Central Trust, the Post and Remittance Administration, and the Cooperative Reserve. Except for the Bank of China and the Transportation Bank, the operations of the others were merged with branches of the People's Bank of China. The Bank of China and the Transportation Bank were restructured as Chinese banks (discussed later in this chapter).

    b. In addition to the previously mentioned banking institutions, there were an estimated 3,500 banks in the provinces and municipalities which were either closed, merged with branches of the People's Bank of China or turned into joint state-private banks.[6] About 2,400 of the banks had strong KMT connections, and their closure or takeover were almost immediate. Those banks that were owned by national bourgeoisie were given an opportunity to conform to socialist principles, and many of them became state-private banks. However, they did not last long: higher taxes and wage contracts forced them to close or sell out to the state and by 1955, they had ceased to exist.

    c. An estimated 100 trust and insurance companies were taken over by the state and were closed or restructured as socialist entities. Most of these operations were in the larger cities of Shanghai, Beijing and Tianjin.

    d. Mortgages were banned and mortgage companies were given until about 1955 to wind up operations.

2. The securities industry was effectively closed in 1949. Some attempts were made to reopen securities exchanges in Beijing and Tianjin in 1949, but by 1953 these had again closed.

3. In the industrial sector, the larger firms that were under KMT ministries and departments were effectively nationalized. The same was true for firms in communications, transportation, and commerce. These firms were dominant and controlled a significant proportion of the national economy.

4. The special agreements and privileges of foreign countries were abolished and the Chinese took control of foreign trade and foreign exchange.

These actions were not completed overnight, and in the meantime, the confiscated assets had to be protected. This was achieved mainly through changes in the ownership structure of the productive forces in the country. The collective economy replaced the individual economy, particularly in agriculture and, to a lesser extent, in smaller cottage industries. The state economy replaced the capitalist or bureaucratic economy in the dominant industrial sectors and accelerated the trend toward significant state ownership of the productive forces.

While the changes in ownership structure were going on, attempts were made to unify financial and economic affairs. Until 1950, finance and economic affairs were managed separately: each liberated area had its own currency and was responsible for its own revenue and expenses. This situation changed in the mid-1950s when these affairs were unified under the central government and brought under state control. Expenditures were unified in a state physical plan and financial resources to implement the physical plan were unified under a credit plan (Figure 1.1). The credit plan detailed the finances required to implement the projects in the physical plan. All government departments, state-owned enterprises, cooperatives and communes submitted budgets for capital construction and operations to the branches of the People's Bank of China. These individual submissions were then pooled to form a national physical plan. Based on this physical plan, a credit plan was determined. Once approved by the state Council, the physical and credit plans became the blueprints for economic operations for the coming fiscal year.

The procedures for the preparation of the physical and credit plans varied over the 1950–1979 period but the control and organizational principles illustrated in Figure 1.1 remained intact. The People's Bank of China (PBOC) allocated funds to economic units based on the credit plan and acted as auditor to review the final accounts and ensure the funds had been spent as budgeted. Moreover, PBOC had overall supervision and control of cash management in the economy, and its ultimate responsibility was to ensure that idle cash was deposited in a state bank and that payments to enterprises from governments flowed through a state bank as well.

By 1952, a new democratic economy was established with five economic sectors: "the state-owned economy, individual economy, privately owned capitalist economy, co-operative economy and state capitalist economy— existing side by side under the leadership of the socialist state-owned economy."[7]

The move to socialism was done through the First Five-Year Plan Period (1953–1957), and by the end of this period, China claimed to have achieved

Figure 1.1
The State's Physical and Credit Plans

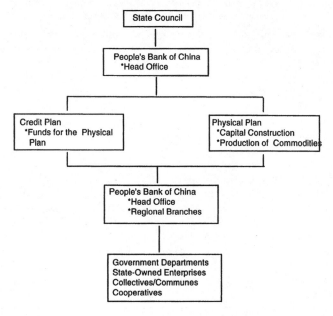

*to be allocated

---

its socialist transformation. By the end of 1956, the state-owned, cooperative, and joint state-private economies accounted for about 93 percent of the national income (Liu and Wu , 1986: 125):

	Percent of national income	
	1952	1956
State-owned; co-ops; state-joint	21.3%	92.9%
Individual/private capitalist	78.7	7.1
	100.0%	100.0%

Considering only the gross value of output from industry, private ownership was almost nonexistent by the end of 1956.[8]

	Percent of gross value of output		
	1949	1951	1956
Private ownership	63%	50%	–
State-private	2	4	32
State-owned	35	46	68
	100%	100%	100%

The socialist philosophy remained intact until 1979 despite attempts to move the country towards full scale communism during the Great Leap (1958–1960).[9] Support for communism continued during the cultural revolution (1966–1976) but these attempts failed (Liu and Wu, 1986: 335–416).[10] The 11th Party Central Committee, at its meeting in December 1978, reaffirmed that China would continue as a socialist state.

REFORMING THE FINANCIAL SYSTEM

In China, the money supply, price levels and inflation were of serious concern (if not in a shambles) by the time of liberation (Young, 1965). From the time of the Japanese invasion in 1937 to 1946, prices had increased by about 2,000 percent; high inflation continued into 1949. For example, using a base of 100 for wholesale prices in December 1948, the index rose to 153 in January 1949, to 287 in April, to 1,059 in July and to 5,376 in November 1949. Speculation was also rampant in currencies. For example, the price of silver dollars quadrupled every 10 to 13 days in early 1949 (Liu and Wu, 1986: 10). The People's Government realized it must take very drastic actions to stabilize the economy.

The People's Bank of China (PBOC)

The People's Bank of China played a key role in the unification of the economy's financial and economic affairs. PBOC was established in Shijiazhuang, Hebei Province, on December 2, 1948, through an amalgamation of three Chinese banks: North China Bank, Beihai Bank, and Northwestern Peasant's Bank. The head office was moved to Beijing in February 1949, and the main duties of PBOC included:

1. Issuance of money and control of the money supply;

2. Supervision and control of the financial operations of government agencies, public enterprises and cooperatives through a specified cash management plan;

3. Supervision and control of foreign exchange; and

4. Supervision and control of banks, other financial institutions, and the financial markets.

In 1949, PBOC established a four-tier level of operation: a national bank at the head office in Beijing; four regional banks in administrative areas (East China, Middle-South China, Northwest China, and Southwest China); and 40 sub-banks and 1,200 branches across China. However, in the interest of centralized administration, the regional banks were closed in June 1954. Moreover (as discussed later in this chapter), PBOC incorporated the operations of other banks until 1979. For this reason, the Chinese banking system was called a monobanking system up to 1979. Figure 1.2 illustrates

Figure 1.2
The Monobanking System and the Ministry of Finance

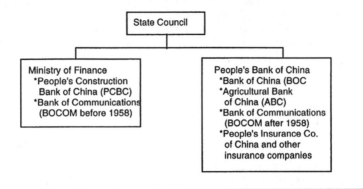

the monobanking system and its relationship with the Ministry of Finance which had administrative control over other financial institutions.

Unification of Chinese Currencies. There was a proliferation of currencies in the various regions in China, and consequently, there were several modes of payment, including gold, silver dollars, foreign exchange, and KMT gold yuan coupons (Xinhua, 1983: 172–188). As a consequence, interregional trade was restricted and, worse yet, there was rampant speculation both in commodity prices and in currencies. There was a need to unify currencies in order to promote monetary control and, on December 1, 1948, PBOC issued the renminbi (RMB) as the unified currency and recalled notes issued in the different liberated areas. However, the RMB was not immediately successful due to low expectations about its value, and speculation continued with gold, silver, and foreign currencies. To curb this speculation and stabilize prices, the People's Government outlawed the free circulation of gold, silver, and foreign currencies, which it authorized PBOC to exchange for RMB. Generally, these measures were successful and RMB continued as the unified currency.[11]

Cash Management Plan. With PBOC and a unified currency in place, the People's Government directed attention to controlling the cash supply in the economy. By the mid-1950s, all government offices, state-owned enterprises, and cooperatives were required to deposit surplus cash with PBOC (usually daily). Also, all settlements among the above mentioned organizations were done through direct bank transfers, not cash. Thus, a limited amount of cash entered the economy, mainly through wages or the sale of goods in the free markets. With the passage of time as public ownership increased, free markets declined and the bulk of the transactions (estimated at about 95 percent) were noncash. By the end of 1952, inflation had fallen to a monthly average of 2 percent. It remained at this relatively low level during 1953–1979.

Availability of Credit. The physical plan (with its associated credit plan) and the cash management plan were effective credit controls. Government offices, state-owned enterprises, and cooperatives could not extend credit to each other. There was nothing similar to accounts receivable or accounts payable since obligations were settled through direct bank transfers on a daily basis. Government offices, state-owned enterprises, and cooperatives received allocations from the credit plan. In addition, enterprises, cooperatives, and communes (mainly in the rural areas) could receive direct grants from the state and state-approved bank loans. Usually, the bank loans were short-term, intended to finance working capital, and were repaid once inventories had been liquidated.

Survivors of the Confiscation Process

The confiscation of financial institutions with bureaucratic capital was relatively swift for some enterprises but lengthy and painful for others. In general, enterprises with strong KMT connections were confiscated and closed or reformed rather quickly. In other cases, however, confiscation was delayed to give the respective owners the opportunity to rehabilitate and conform to socialist principles. With respect to the banking sector, the notable survivors were the Bank of China and the Bank of Communications (formerly the Transportation Bank).

Bank of China (BOC). This bank, established in 1912, specialized in international banking activities under the KMT government. In May 1949, when Shanghai was liberated, the People's Government took over the bank, confiscated its assets, and restructured the management team. In November 1949, the head office was moved from Shanghai to Beijing, and in October 1953, the Government Administrative Council designated BOC as a specialized bank to deal with foreign exchange under the leadership of PBOC.

Bank of Communications (BOCOM). This bank was established on March 4, 1908, and played an active role in financing projects in transportation, telecommunications, and the postal service as well as in industry and commerce. After the liberation, the bank was taken over by the People's Government and reformed with respect to ownership, operation, and management. The bank was placed under the Ministry of Finance to supervise the affairs of joint state-private enterprises. In 1951, the head office was moved from Shanghai to Beijing and in 1958, the bank's domestic operations were consolidated with those of PBOC.

Newly Established Financial Institutions

People's Construction Bank of China (PCBC). This bank was established in October, 1954, by the Government Administrative Council within the Ministry of Finance to handle budget appropriations for capital construction. During the Great Leap (1958–1960), PCBC was turned into the Capital Construction Financial Division of the Ministry of Finance and all of its branches were closed.

Agricultural Bank of China (ABC). This bank was established in March 1955 but closed after 21 months and merged with PBOC. It reopened again in November 1963 and operated independently for 22 months, whereupon it was again merged with PBOC.

People's Insurance Company of China (PICC). This insurance company was established on October 20, 1949, with approval from PBOC. Its head office is in Beijing and, by the end of 1956, PICC had acquired 468 regional companies and 2,542 representative offices. PICC was placed under the administrative control of PBOC.

Rural Credit Cooperatives (RCCs). Credit cooperatives grew in importance after liberation. Prior to 1949, peasants were financed by landlords, other rich farmers, and merchants, a group that disappeared after the revolution. RCCs emerged to fill the gap, deriving their funding from bank loans and deposits from peasants and using it to issue short-term personal loans. Usually, each village or commune had an RCC which was really an extension of banking services to the rural area. By 1955, there were an estimated 159,000 RCCs covering 85 percent of rural villages, involving 65 percent of farmers, and employing about 320,000 people. RCCs are under the supervision of the Agricultural Bank of China.

Abolishment of Securities Markets in China

After liberation, the securities markets in Shanghai, Tianjin, Beijing, and other Chinese cities were closed and remained dormant until the early 1980s. These facilities were viewed as agents of speculation that fostered the accumulation of bureaucratic wealth. However, bonds were issued by the various levels of government. For example, in January 1950, the state issued RMB 90 million in *fen* of *Zheshi* (commodity-linked) bonds, and during the 1954–1957 period, the state had four bond issues worth RMB 2.75 billion.[12] These funds were needed to finance capital construction and were issued to reformed national bourgeoisie and other well-to-do Chinese or allocated to state-owned enterprises. During the Great Leap (1958–1960), 11 local governments (provinces, municipalities and autonomous regions) received state permission to issue RMB 2.35 billion worth of bonds to finance capital construction.

China Refrains from Foreign Borrowing

During the First Five-Year Plan Period (1953–1957), China relied almost exclusively on domestic resources to finance capital construction and did not use foreign capital. Of the revenue of RMB 134.59 billion during this period (Table 1.2), foreign loans accounted for less than 3 percent of the total. However, China was not against accepting technical and other assistance from friendly countries, especially the Soviet Union and the

People's Democracies in Eastern Europe. In 1954, China and Russia signed an agreement under which the Russian government would assist with the development and construction of 156 projects in China.[13] These activities were underway when, in 1960, disagreements between the two governments led to the withdrawal of Russian technicians from China. While most of the projects were completed or near completion, they were not yet operational due to lack of technical skills on the part of the Chinese or the lack of spare parts. Under the agreement extending until 1960, China owed Russia about 1.406 billion rubles, which were repaid by 1964 with exports of primarily mineral products and farm produce. The Russian experience hardened the resolve of the Chinese against foreign aid.

China's Modest Foreign Aid Program

China has never been a significant supplier of financial assistance to other countries. However, to keep up with the Russians and to maintain visibility and credibility with the Third World, China instituted a modest foreign aid program. Usually, Chinese aid was settled with exports of goods and services to the recipient countries. For example, between 1956 and 1965, China committed about US $845 million to 21 countries in the Third World. However, only about US $200 million in goods and services were delivered.[14] The financial demands of the Chinese economy limited the extent to which it could help other countries.

SUMMARY OF ECONOMIC DEVELOPMENT, 1952–1980

The Chinese completed a successful rehabilitation of the economy by the end of 1952 and established a reasonable foundation for the start of the First Five-Year Plan Period (1953–1957). Inflation was brought under reasonable control through a series of measures including aggressive efforts to increase savings at banks, sales of government bonds, and the unification of financial and economic affairs. Monetary policy came under the control of state planners and played an accommodating rather than an allocative role. Commodity prices stabilized, speculation diminished, and criminal elements in the society were effectively controlled. Politically, the country was united and under state control in an administrative sense.

National Income Spent

In nominal terms, national income spent increased by an average annual rate of 7.08 percent, from RMB 60.1 billion in 1952 to RMB 368.6 billion in 1980 (Table 1.1).[15] The periods of relatively high growth include the First Five-Year Plan Period (1953–1957), the Economic Readjustment Period (1963–1965), and the Fifth Five-Year Plan Period (1976–1980). The growth in national income spent suffered declines during the Second Five-Year Plan Period with the Great Leap (1958–1962) and the early years of the cultural

Table 1.1
Selected Economic Data for the Chinese Economy, 1952–1980

| | National Income Spent | | Savings | Agriculture | | Indices of Gross Industrial Production | | | | | |
	(RMB Billions)	Annual Growth (%)	Rate (%)	Index	Annual Growth (%)	Light Industry Index	Light Industry Annual Growth (%)	Heavy Industry Index	Heavy Industry Annual Growth (%)	Industry and Agriculture Index	Industry and Agriculture Annual Growth (%)
1949				67.4		46.6		30.3		56.3	
1950				79.3	17.66%	60.6	30.04%	46.7	54.13%	69.5	23.45%
1951				86.8	9.46%	81.0	33.66%	69.7	49.25%	82.7	18.99%
1952	60.1		21.40%	100.0	15.21%	100.0	23.46%	100.0	43.47%	100.0	20.92%
1953	72.7	20.97%	23.10%	103.0	3.00%	126.7	26.70%	136.9	36.90%	114.4	14.40%
1954	76.5	5.23%	25.50%	106.6	3.50%	144.8	14.29%	163.9	19.72%	125.2	9.44%
1955	80.7	5.49%	22.90%	114.7	7.60%	144.8	0.00%	187.7	14.52%	133.5	6.63%
1956	88.8	10.04%	24.40%	120.5	5.06%	173.3	19.68%	262.3	39.74%	155.5	16.48%
1957	95.5	7.55%	24.90%	124.8	3.57%	183.3	5.77%	210.7	-19.67%	167.8	7.91%
1958	111.7	16.96%	33.90%	127.8	2.40%	245.1	33.72%	555.5	163.64%	221.9	32.24%
1959	127.4	14.06%	43.80%	110.4	-13.62%	299.0	21.99%	822.7	48.10%	265.0	19.42%
1960	126.4	-0.78%	39.60%	96.4	-12.68%	269.7	-9.80%	1035.8	25.90%	279.3	5.40%
1961	101.3	-19.86%	19.20%	94.1	-2.39%	211.1	-21.73%	554.2	-46.50%	192.5	-31.08%
1962	94.8	-6.42%	10.40%	99.9	6.16%	193.6	-8.29%	429.0	-22.59%	173.0	-10.13%
1963	104.7	10.44%	17.50%	111.6	11.71%	198.1	2.32%	488.2	13.80%	189.6	9.60%
1964	118.4	13.09%	22.20%	126.7	13.53%	233.4	17.82%	590.7	21.00%	222.9	17.56%
1965	134.7	13.77%	27.10%	137.1	8.21%	344.7	47.69%	651.0	10.21%	268.3	20.37%
1966	153.5	13.96%	30.60%	147.0	7.22%	394.7	14.51%	830.0	27.50%	314.7	17.29%
1967	142.8	-6.97%	21.30%	151.2	2.86%	366.7	-7.09%	664.0	-20.00%	284.5	-9.60%
1968	140.9	-1.33%	21.10%	147.5	-2.45%	348.7	-4.91%	630.1	-5.11%	270.6	-4.18%
1969	153.7	9.08%	23.20%	149.2	1.15%	436.6	25.21%	906.7	43.90%	337.4	23.77%
1970	187.6	22.06%	32.90%	166.3	11.46%	515.6	18.09%	1290.2	42.30%	424.3	25.76%
1971	200.8	7.04%	34.10%	171.4	3.07%	549.1	6.50%	1566.3	21.40%	475.9	12.16%
1972	205.2	2.19%	31.60%	171.1	-0.18%	855.1	55.73%	1675.9	7.00%	497.4	4.52%
1973	225.2	9.75%	32.90%	185.5	8.42%	644.9	-24.58%	1821.7	8.70%	543.0	9.17%
1974	229.1	1.73%	32.30%	193.2	4.15%	662.3	2.70%	1792.6	-1.60%	550.6	1.40%
1975	142.1	-37.97%	33.90%	202.1	4.61%	748.4	13.00%	2093.8	16.80%	616.2	11.91%
1976	242.4	70.58%	30.90%	207.1	2.47%	766.4	2.41%	2104.3	0.50%	626.6	1.69%
1977	257.5	6.23%	32.30%	210.6	1.69%	876.0	14.30%	2405.2	14.30%	693.7	10.71%
1978	297.5	15.53%	36.50%	229.6	9.02%	970.0	10.73%	2780.4	15.60%	779.0	12.30%
1979	335.6	12.81%	34.60%	249.4	8.62%	1063.8	9.67%	2994.5	7.70%	845.2	8.50%
1980	368.6	9.83%	31.60%	259.1	3.89%	1259.5	18.40%	3036.4	1.40%	908.6	7.50%
Annual average (1953–80)		7.08%	28.37%		3.65%		10.89%		15.66%		8.97%

Source: Liu and Wu (1986: 476–477, Tables 1 and 2)

Table 1.2
State Revenue and Expenditures, 1950–1979 (Value in Billions of Renminbi)

Five-Year Plan Periods	Revenue	Expenditures	Surplus (Deficits)	Annual Growth (%)	
				Revenue	Expenditures
1950–52 (Rehabilitation Period)	38.20	36.66	1.54		
1953–57 (First Five-Year Plan Period)	134.59	134.57	.92	11.0	11.60
1958–62 (Second Five-Year Plan Period)	211.66	228.87	(17.10)	.20	.10
1963–65 (Economic Readjustment Period)	121.51	120.50	1.01	14.70	15.20
1966–70 (Third Five-Year Plan Period)	252.90	251.85	1.05	7.00	6.90
1971–75 (Fourth Five-Year Plan Period)	391.97	391.94	.03	4.30	4.80

Source: China Handbook Editorial Committee (1984: 334, Table 7.1).

revolution (1966–1968). Modest growth was experienced during the remaining years of the cultural revolution (1969–1976).

National income spent was allocated to consumption, the military and investments in fixed assets through savings. Over the 1952–1980 period, the savings (or accumulation) rate averaged 28.37 percent annually (Table 1.1). While the trend was generally upward, the savings rate during the 1961–1969 period declined due to the negative impact of the Great Leap and the Cultural Revolution. It may be argued that the high savings rate deprived the Chinese people of a better standard of living during this period. However, the state would counter this argument by pointing to the fact that the savings were needed to fund capital construction. China's resolve was to fund its projects with domestic funds.

State Revenue and Expenditures

Over the 1950–1979 period, the state had a total revenue of RMB 1,538.38 billion and total expenditures of RMB 1,567.85 billion, resulting in a deficit of RMB 29.47 billion (Table 1.2). The deficits were incurred during the Second Five-Year Plan Period (1958–62), mainly to finance the Great Leap, and during the first four years of the Fifth Five-Year Plan Period (1976–80) to finance reconstruction after the cultural revolution. The state revenue included proceeds from the sale of bonds, and deficits were usually covered by increasing the money supply. This practice had serious implications for inflation and price stability. Another concern was the declining growth in state revenue. The rate of growth of state revenue declined after the Economic Readjustment Period (1963–65), from an annual average of 14.7 percent to 4.3 percent in the Fourth Five-Year Plan Period (1971–75).

One of the immediate results of the declining trend in state revenue was a declining growth in the state's contribution to capital construction. Over the 1950–1980 period, the state contributed RMB 604 billion to capital

Table 1.3
Total Investment in Fixed Assets, 1950–1980 (Value in Billions of Renminbi)

Five-Year Plan Periods	Total Investment	Capital Investment Total	Capital Investment By State	Repairs and Renewal	Annual Growth (%) Total Investment	Capital Construction Total	Capital Construction By State	Repairs and Renewal
1950–52 (Rehabilitation Period)	7.84	7.84	6.63	0.00				
1953–57 (First Five-Year-Plan Period)	61.16	58.85	53.12	2.31	34.34%	33.10%	34.53%	76.37%
1958–62 (Second Five-Year-Plan Period)	130.70	120.61	94.44	10.09	4.60%	3.51%	−0.70%	24.02%
1963–65 (Economic Readjustment Period)	49.95	42.19	37.17	7.76	35.54%	36.40%	39.50%	34.82%
1966–70 (Third Five-Year-Plan Period)	120.91	97.60	87.13	23.31	16.77%	19.49%	18.01%	9.53%
1971–75 (Fourth Five-Year Period)	227.65	176.40	145.45	51.25	8.35%	5.79%	4.47%	19.89%
1976–80 (Fifth Five-Year-Plan Period)	318.62	234.42	180.85	84.20	6.80%	7.16%	2.10%	6.71%
1953–80 (Total)	916.82	737.90	604.79	178.92	17.07%	16.83%	15.21%	26.32%

Source: China Handbook Editorial Committee (1984: 334, Table 7.1).

construction (Table 1.3). However, the rate of growth of the state's contribution declined since 1965 to a point where it was questionable whether the government could generate sufficient revenue to cover all desired expenditures and avoid deficits. Alternatively, the state had the option to scale down capital construction and dampen industrial expansion.

The sources of state revenue underwent some profound changes over the 1949–1979 period (China Handbook Editorial Committee, 1984: 141–142). In 1951, state-owned enterprises and cooperatives accounted for 34.1 percent of state revenue, capitalist industry and commerce for 33 percent, and the individual sector for 30 percent. However, by 1976, state-owned enterprises and cooperatives accounted for 99.5 percent of state revenue, a change that clearly reflects the dominance of public ownership in the socialist economy. Considering state revenue by industrial sectors, heavy and light industries accounted for 77.9 percent of state revenue in 1976, up from 30.2 percent in 1950. Agriculture, as a source of direct revenue, declined significantly from 29.2 percent in 1950 to only 3.7 percent in 1976, while other industries contributed 40.6 percent and 18.4 percent, respectively. Heavy industries were promoted by the state, and in 1976 they accounted for 45.1 percent of state revenue, compared to 8.4 percent in 1950. One of the reasons for the decline in the contribution of the agricultural sector to state revenue was that the state was not inclined to increase the agricultural tax, despite increased agricultural production.

The bulk of state revenue came from two sources, income from state-owned enterprises and tax revenues (China Handbook Editorial Committee, 1984: 343).

	1949–1952	1956–1976
Income from enterprises	25.9%	54.7%
Taxes	59.1	44.3
Others	15.0	1.0
	100.0%	100.0%

Income from state-owned enterprises included profits and the basic depreciation fund and accounted for 54.7 percent of state revenue in the Fourth Five-Year Plan Period, compared to 25.9 percent in the 1949–1952 Rehabilitation Period. This is further evidence of the dominance of public ownership in the Chinese economy. Tax revenues included industrial and commercial taxes, industrial and commercial income taxes, customs duties, and agricultural taxes.[16]

With respect to state expenditures, economic development accounted for an average of 56 percent over the 1950–1976 period (China Handbook Editorial Committee, 1984: 343). By the Fourth Five-Year Plan Period (1971–75), state expenditures were distributed as follows: economic development and cultural activities (culture, education, science, and health), 67.0 percent; national defense 18.4 percent; administration 4.5 percent, and others, 10.1 percent.

Investment in Fixed Assets

Over the 1952–1980 period, investment in fixed assets totaled RMB 916 billion, with RMB 737 billion (80 percent) for capital construction and the balance for repairs and renovations (Table 1.3). Of the capital construction budget of RMB 737 billion, the state provided RMB 604 billion (82 percent). State investment was targeted mainly at industry, especially heavy industry including coal, iron, steel, transportation, and energy.[17]

The growth in capital construction declined during the Second Five-Year Plan Period (1958–62) despite a stated objective to increase fixed assets in order to move China into the Industrial Age. Investment had skyrocketed over the 1958–1960 period, but once the folly of the Great Leap had been recognized, there were drastic cutbacks over 1961–1962. More important, the rate of capital construction had been declining since 1965, from an annual average of 36.4 percent in the Economic Readjustment Period (1963–65) to 7.16 percent in the Fifth Five-Year Plan Period (1976–80). The state's contribution to capital construction fell even more rapidly from 39.5 percent to 2.10 percent, respectively (Table 1.3).

Capital appeared to have lost its efficiency over the years. It is estimated that under the First Five-Year Plan Period (1953–57), an investment of RMB 100 generated RMB 25 of national income. However, during the Fourth Five-Year Plan Period (1971–75), the same investment generated only RMB 15 (China Handbook Editorial Committee, 1984: 340). The negative impact of the Great Leap and the turmoil of the cultural revolution were clearly evident.

Gross Agricultural and Industrial Output

In 1952, agriculture accounted for 66.78 percent of the gross value of agricultural and industrial output, and industry, 33.22 percent. However, by 1980 there had been a structural shift, with agriculture at 30.8 percent and industry at 69.2 percent.[18] This structural change in the economy reflects the state's efforts to boost industrial production. In a country where over 80 percent of the population lives in rural areas and is dependent on agriculture, the state's industrial policy may be questionable. It does not appear that the peasants who engineered and carried out the revolution had much to gain. The index for agricultural production increased at an average annual rate of 3.65 percent over 1949–1980; that for light industry, at 10.89 percent; and that for heavy industry, at 15.66 percent (Table 1.1).

Over the period 1949–1980, output for heavy industry showed the most gains. In 1949, output accounted for 9.74 percent of gross agricultural and industrial production, and in 1980, 36.57 percent. As stated, the state had directed investment to these industries, to the detriment of agriculture.[19] Future continued support for the industrial sector at the expense of the agricultural sector could lead to shifts in population and employment, with unpleasant consequences.

THE CALL FOR REFORM AND THE OPEN DOOR POLICY

Like the Great Leap (1958–60), the initial draft of the "Outline for Ten-Year Planning for the Development of the National Economy (1976–85)" contained unrealistic economic goals.[20] For example, plans called for the construction of 120 large projects during the period, including 10 iron and steel plants, 9 nonferrous metal plants, 8 coal mines, 10 oil and gas fields, 30 power plants, 6 new trunk railway lines, and 5 new harbors. This was a monumental task, and if achieved, it would have made China an industrialized nation by the year 2000. Throughout 1978, there were repeated demands for accelerated construction, additional capital funds, and increased imports of technology and equipment. In the end, the efforts failed. The economy lacked, among other things, the natural resources, the financial strength, the technology, and the manpower to undertake construction on such a grand scale and at such a fast rate. The state suffered massive deficits in 1979 and 1980 due to its need to finance imports of technology and equipment.

There were significant imbalances in the economy, including the following:

1. The volume of capital construction meant that the population had to do with less consumption over time, and standards of living suffered.

2. There was great reliance on heavy industries, to the detriment of agriculture.

3. Capital began to lose its efficiency. Some giant projects were poorly conceived and hastily implemented, to the detriment of their potential efficiency and profitability.

4. Surprisingly, there was unemployment in China: an estimated 20 million in 1978.

The 11th Party Central Committee, held in December 1978, noted the failure of the past two years and decided to make adjustments to the economic policies. Premier Zhao Ziyang outlined ten principles that were to be followed for economic reconstruction in the near future.

1. Agriculture was to be developed using correct principles and scientific management and techniques.

2. Consumer goods industries were to be further developed, and there would be some redirection of emphasis away from heavy industries.

3. The energy and transportation industries would feature prominently in future development.

4. Existing enterprises would be used to their maximum and technological transformation would be implemented as a step-by-step process.

5. Existing enterprises would be consolidated to improve efficiency.

6. Construction funds would be increased, but used wisely.

7. An open door policy with the outside world would be established to enhance

China's capacity for self-reliance.

8. The economic system would be actively reformed with the help of the people.

9. The scientific and cultural level of the people would be raised, and worthwhile scientific research projects would be undertaken.

10. The concept of "everything for the people" would be adopted, and organized production and construction for the people's livelihood would be the primary objectives.

After 1979, the financial system was reformed to help China in "readjustment, restructuring, consolidation and improvement."[21] Chapters 2 through 9 provide an outline of the reform of the financial system, but it must be remembered that this system is only one part of a political, economic, and social environment.

NOTES

1. The CCP philosophy and its influence on two ardent followers are reviewed in Fang and Fang (1986).

2. For a good discussion of these events and for further references, see Huang (1981), Liu and Wu (1986), Shang (1989), and Shang, Wu, and Luo (1992).

3. Chairman Mao Zedong believed that the new democratic stage was necessary to move to socialism. In his view, the new democratic revolution was an antiimperialist and antifeudal revolution undertaken by the people under a proletarian leader. Once the imperialists and feudalists had gone, then real progress could be made to build a socialist state. A socialist state or system is characterized by public ownership of the means of production and the implementation of a mechanism for the distribution or allocation of resources.

4. China was liberated in stages, province by province. This discussion will not focus on such piecemeal liberation and, rather, assumes that all China was liberated on October 1, 1949. This assumption does not limit the focus of discussion.

5. Old China normally refers to China prior to 1949, and New China, to the period after 1949. While the official name of the country is the People's Republic of China, the term China is in popular usage, and will be used in this book.

6. Li (1987) reported lower amounts, at 1,032 private banks and branches and 100 insurance and trust companies.

7. Liu and Wu (1986: 86).

8. King (1968: 184) reported similar percentages for the commercial sector.

9. King (1968: 188–202) contains an economic evaluation of the Great Leap, with the basic conclusion that it was a failure. Similar conclusions were reported by Liu and Wu (1986: 229–251).

10. The 1966–1968 period was the worst time of the cultural revolution and the period during which the economy suffered the most. Economic recovery occurred starting in 1969, despite the fact that the ultra-leftists were still active. However, in 1974, the Gang of Four (Jian Qing, Zhang Chunqiao, Yao Wenyuan, and Wang Hongwen) resurrected the revolution in public and attempted to seize political power. This created turmoil and economic stagnation, and a subsequent decline occurred.

11. The initial issue of RMB in 1948 was in large denominations, which created some inconveniences for trade and also proved easy to smuggle out of the country. Accordingly, a new issue with smaller denominations was printed in 1955.

12. Zheshi bonds were commodity linked, with fen as a unit. Each fen was worth 3 kg of rice, 0.75 kg of flour, 1.33 meters of white cotton cloth, and 8 kg of coal.

13. According to King (1968: 179), the Treaty of Friendship, Alliance and Mutual Aid with China was destined to last for three five-year plan periods and involve 300 projects worth U.S. $3 billion.

14. The Chinese aid was about one-tenth that of Russia during the same period (King, 1968: 198).

15. The data in Table 1.1 is in current prices. The national income spent differs from national income due to differences between imports and exports and statistical errors.

16. For a description of the fiscal and budgetary system of the state in the 1960s, see Donnithorne (1967: ch. 14).

17. King (1968: 182) reported that in 1957, 44 percent of the capital construction budget went to the heavy industries, compared with 30 percent in 1952. To some extent, this was done at the expense of agriculture, where the percentage fell from 14 percent in 1952 to 9 percent in 1957.

18. The statistics quoted in this discussion are derived from data reported in Liu and Wu (1986: 477, Table 2).

19. King (1968: 182) quoted several studies confirming the existence of this trend over the 1950–1957 period. The investment policy of the state resulted in agriculture accounting for a lower percentage of national income over time. Moreover, household consumption was falling as a percentage of national income.

20. This section draws on Liu and Wu (1986: 412–439).

21. Liu and Wu (1986: 439).

REFERENCES

China Handbook Editorial Committee. 1984. *Economy*. Beijing: Foreign Languages Press.

Donnithorne, Audrey. 1967. *China's Economic System*. London: George Allen and Unwin.

Fang, Peter Juoheng, and Fang, Lucy Guinong. 1986. *Zhou Enlai: A Profile*. Beijing: Foreign Languages Press.

Huang Dang. 1981. *Issues on Socialism, Finance and Banking*. Beijing: People's University.

King, Frank H. H. 1968. *A Concise Economic History of Modern China (1840–1961)*. New York: Praeger.

Li Mao-sheng. 1987. *Study on the Chinese Financial Structure*. Shanxi: Shanxi People's Publication House.

Liu Suinian and Wu Qungan. 1986. *China's Socialist Economy: An Outline History (1949–1984)*. Beijing: Beijing Review.

Shang Ming, ed. 1989. *China Today: Money and Banking*. Beijing: China Social Science Press.

Shang Ming, Wu Xialing, and Luo Lanbo. 1992. *Banking Credit Management and Money Supply*. Beijing: People's University.

Xinhua. 1983. *A History of Chinese Currency*. Hong Kong: Xinhua Publishing House.

2

People's Bank of China: The Central Bank

Central banking in China is relatively new and has experienced all the "growing pains" that would be expected of an institution of this nature in an economic and political environment such as in China. The People's Bank of China (PBOC), which was established in 1948 to serve a liberated nation, emerged as the central bank in 1983–1984. This chapter is a review of the activities of the central bank up to the early 1990s; the role of PBOC over 1949–1980 was reviewed in chapter 1. The central bank operates under a socialist philosophy, politics has some influence on its development and operation. In addition, the central bank operates in an economy that is influenced by the actions of myriads of economic units, and consequently a knowledge of the economic performance of China after 1980 is useful. To maintain the continuity of the discussion in this chapter, a summary of the Chinese economy over 1980–1990 is presented separately as the Appendix, for the reader's benefit.

The economic and financial reforms undertaken since 1979 are quite numerous, and a period-by-period review would entail a lengthy discussion and analysis beyond the scope of this book. This chapter will simply give an overall assessment of the reforms and their general results up to 1990. Further details may be obtained from sources identified in the chapter references. Moreover, several topics in this chapter are discussed in greater detail in other chapters of this book. These chapters are identified in the text.

THE ESTABLISHMENT OF THE CENTRAL BANK

The monobanking system, with the People's Bank of China (PBOC) at its helm, dominated the Chinese financial scene after liberation and until 1984. Under this unitary and highly centralized banking system, PBOC functioned as both a central bank and a commercial bank. The head office, branches, sub-branches, and associated agencies handled activities relating to the issuance of currency, deposits, loans, settlements, and remittances.[1] The Bank of China (BOC) was primarily concerned with foreign exchange business, while in the rural areas, credit cooperatives operated under trying circumstances to mobilize rural savings for rural development. Under the unified credit plan, the monobanking system was simply a distributor of funds according to plan and a watchdog supervising the spending of those funds. The decision to go after economic reform after the 11th Party Central Committee in December 1978 was significant for, among other things, financial market reform. The horizontal circulation of capital had to be promoted to boost the planned commodity economy, and in the early 1980s, certain important events occurred that led to the demise of the monobanking system.

With respect to the existing domestic financial institutions, the Agricultural Bank of China (ABC) was reactivated in 1979 to focus exclusively on the funding needs of the agricultural sector. Concurrently, BOC was taken over by the State Council and confirmed as a foreign exchange and foreign trade bank. In addition, the People's Construction Bank of China (PCBC) was placed under the ownership of the State Council, with management responsibilities assigned to the State Construction Committee and the Ministry of Finance on behalf of the council (see chapter 3). The rural credit cooperatives (RCCs) became subject to ongoing reforms starting in 1980 and were placed under the supervision of ABC (see chapter 5). RCCs were viewed as the institutions that could best mobilize rural savings and promote rural development, while urban credit cooperatives (UCCs) emerged in the early 1980s to serve collectives and individuals in the cities and towns (see chapter 5).

In the early 1980s, the State Council permitted governments, financial institutions, and enterprises to establish trust and investment corporations (TICs) in an effort to tap idle funds for investment. China International Trust and Investment Corporation (CITIC), a state-owned enterprise, was established in 1979 and was later to play a leading role for China in the international financial markets. By 1982, there were an estimated 600 TICs operating in China's undeveloped financial market (see chapter 5).

Also on the domestic scene, the state was giving clear signals of its desire to decentralize some of its financing functions for budgetary and other reasons. In 1979, the state changed its strategy for the financing of construction by state-owned enterprises. Budget allocations became classified as loans and were placed under the supervision of the PCBC, and the banking system was called on to play a greater role in allocating credit in the economy (see chapter 3). Local governments and enterprises had access to more foreign exchange and were given greater freedom concerning how these funds might be used. With respect to fiscal matters, the state introduced a tax system, first on a trial basis, in 1979 and then, for the entire country, in 1985. The sources of state revenue were shifting from a dependency on enterprise profits to a reliance on revenues from taxation, which would involve the entire nation, not only state-owned enterprises (Appendix). Finally, the state sector was accounting for less of the country's economy as new forms of ownership were introduced. Over 1978–1987, the share of industrial output of the state sector dropped to 70 percent, while collectives increased to 27 percent and foreign-funded firms to 3 percent (Liu, 1989b: 22–28).

On the international scene, the government kept its promise to open China to the outside world, and the following events comprised some of the main initial actions that were taken. Foreign financial institutions were allowed entry into the country. In December 1979, the State Council permitted foreign banks to establish representative offices in Beijing, and the Export-Import Bank of Japan was the first to do so. By 1985, there were an estimated 63 representative offices in Beijing (Langstron, 1985b: 70–71). In 1982, the NanYang Commercial Bank of Hong Kong was allowed to open a branch in Shenzhen and Nantong Bank from Macao opened a branch in the Zhuhai Special Economic zone (see chapter 8). In 1980, China Oriental Leasing Co. was established as the first joint venture leasing company in China involving foreign banks and Chinese financial institutions (see chapter 5). This set a pattern for similar financial institutions and for joint venture finance companies in the mid-1980s. By 1985, there were approximately 32 joint venture leasing companies and 3 joint venture finance companies operating in China.

Gradually, China abandoned its isolationist policy and courted the international financial markets for foreign currency loans. High profile visits were made overseas by Chinese leaders and financiers, including one to the Chase Manhattan Bank in Washington, D.C., in 1980 (Shrodes, 1980: 108–110). In return, foreign finance experts were invited to visit China, including officials from the Daiwa and Nomura securities firms from Japan in 1980 (Bonavia, 1980a: 85). In 1980, China joined the International Monetary Fund (IMF) and the World Bank and in 1983, the Asian Development Bank. As a member of the World Bank, China was regarded as a member of the Third World, and thus qualified for concessionary loans. Moreover, membership in the IMF and the World Bank facilitated China's access to export credits from the U.S. Eximbank, the Japan Export-Import Bank, and equivalent European agencies. In 1980, China had a declared foreign debt of US $3.4 billion (Bonavia, 1980b: 69); in 1982 in Tokyo, CITIC floated China's first foreign currency bond since liberation (Chen and Zhao, 1990: 74), and by February 1982, China had signed agreements to borrow U.S. $1.275 billion in Euroloans through banks in Japan, the United States, and Europe.[2] Finally, foreign investors were invited to invest in China's special economic zones and were offered various incentives to do so (see chapter 6) and, starting in 1981, China signed international treaties relating to the protection of foreign investments and the avoidance of double taxation (Han Guojian, 1989: 21 and Han Baocheng, 1989: 42).

In the meantime, the economy was not doing well, as the economic optimism of the Ten-Year Plan (1976–85) proved unrealistic. In the early 1980s, the growth of the gross national product (GNP) declined, the trade balance was generally negative, and state revenues declined or stagnated (Appendix). The government deficits for 1979 (RMB 17.06 billion) and 1980 (RMB 12.75 billion) were the highest since liberation. In 1981, the state was forced to issue treasury bonds for the first time since 1957 to finance its deficit; this activity continued throughout the decade (see chapter 7). Traditionally, China had used the money press to finance its deficit, but those days appeared to be over. Within limits, local authorities were allowed greater control over budgets, capital construction, export/imports, fund-raising, and foreign exchange (Appendix). The state was moving away from direct microeconomic management of the economy.

The dismantling of the monobanking system, the proliferation of new domestic financial institutions, the emergence of a primary bond market, the foray into the international financial market, the entry of foreign financial institutions, and the soft economy were compelling factors to suggest the need for serious macro-economic management of the economy. China was changing from a ledger-transaction to a cash society, and monetary control was needed. Credit management was becoming important and interest rates had to play a greater role in the allocation of funds. The State was resorting to the domestic and foreign debt market so the management of government debt and associated market operations had to be given greater attention. Foreign exchange management became important considering the expanded relationships with the international community. Overall, the entire financial system had to be supervised and controlled for orderly reform and further development. Following the typical Western approach, this meant the need for a central bank.

The General Functions of the Central Bank

On September 17, 1983, the State Council issued the "Resolution about the People's Bank of China Acting Specially as the Central Bank," which authorized PBOC as the central bank of China: "The People's Bank of China is a national institution through which the State Council directs and administers financial operations of the whole country, and it is the central bank of China." This stipulation was reaffirmed in the "Provisional Regulations Governing the Administration of Banks of the People's Republic of China," issued by the State Council on January 7, 1986 (PBOC, 1986). The dual nature of both "a national institution" and "the central bank" dictates the functions and the organizational structure of PBOC, which officially assumed central bank functions on January 1, 1984.

PBOC is under the direct administration and authority of the State Council, and its primary tasks are as follows (Chen and Zhao, 1990: 26–28):

1. Given the economic policies set by the State Council, PBOC is required to formulate money, credit, and other financial policies for macroeconomic management of the economy.

2. PBOC is required to promote monetary stability and economic development in the economy through the promulgation of relevant laws and regulations relating to, among other factors, the control of credit and the money supply. In this task, direct economic, legal, and administrative measures should be taken.

3. PBOC is required to promote monetary stability and economic development by indirect measures including levers (deposit reserve requirements, interest rates, discount rates, etc.) and administrative means, such as mandatory planning under the unified physical and credit plans.

4. PBOC is required to promote, supervise, and control all aspects of the operations of China's financial market (banks, nonbank financial institutions, securities markets, etc.) in order to facilitate orderly development of financial activities.

To undertake these four related tasks, PBOC has to perform a multitude of functions, which will be summarized in the next pages. Generally, it makes recommendations to the State Council and, if they are approved, the authority to implement them. (PBOC derives its authority from the State Council and cannot act independently.)

The following is a summary of the functions of the various organizational elements of PBOC as set out in the "Provisional Regulations of the Administration of Banks of the People's Republic of China" of January 7, 1986.

Central Bank. The central bank functions include the following:

1. Formulating and implementing monetary policies, which involves, among other functions:

   a. Setting and adjusting monetary targets;

   b. Issuing the domestic currencies, including renminbi and foreign exchange certificate;

   c. Formulating and implementing the state credit plan, foreign currency credit plan, and social credit program;

   d. Centralizing the management of credit funds in both renminbi and foreign currency;

   e. Exercising unitary management over capital funds of state-owned enterprises;

   f. Setting and adjusting domestic credit;

   g. Setting and adjusting domestic reserve ratios;

   h. Setting and adjusting interest rates on loans and deposits; and

   i. Formulating and implementing policies and programs for refinancing and rediscounting.

2. Formulating and implementing policies relating to foreign reserves, which

involves, among other functions:

  a. Formulating balance-of-payments plans with relevant economic units;

  b. Managing foreign exchange reserves;

  c. Setting and adjusting foreign exchange rates for the domestic currency; and

  d. Administering the foreign debt.

3. Formulating and implementing policies relating to debt financing by the state, which involves, among other functions:

  a. Organizing the issuance and redemption of state bonds;

  b. Repaying debt from and receiving debt proceeds into the state treasury; and

  c. Advising on and assisting with the preparation of state budgets.

4. Formulating and implementing policies relating to the financial market, which involves, among other functions:

  a. Drafting laws and regulations relating to the nature and operations of the financial market;

  b. Approving the establishment, closures, and combinations or mergers of financial institutions and other participants in the financial market;

  c. Approving the issuance and trading of securities;

  d. Establishing clearing and settlement mechanisms;

  e. Supervising, monitoring, and controlling the business activities of participants;

  f. Compiling relevant statistics on market activities;

  g. Investigating, analyzing, and forecasting economic trends and related topics;

  h. Proposing financial reforms and organizing experimental reform programs; and

  i. Recommending candidates for senior positions and for dismissals.

Board of Governors. The board has the following functions:

1. Deliberating problems relating to general and specific financial policies;

2. Deliberating vital issues relating to the unified annual state physical and credit plans, cash budget, and foreign exchange budget;

3. Determining the principles governing the establishment, closures, and combinations or mergers of banks and other financial institutions; and

4. Reviewing and evaluating other matters concerning the overall financial situation in China and abroad.

Head Office, Branches, Sub-Branches and Other Organizations. Within their respective jurisdiction, the functions include the following:

1. Implementing state financial policies, principles, laws and regulations, and basic rules of financial business;

2. Managing the currency storehouse, controlling and transferring the basic funds for issuance, and adjusting currency circulation;

3. Supervising the implementation of the interest rate policy of PBOC across the different types of financial institutions;

4. Formulating and supervising the implementation of the unified physical and credit plans and the cash budget;

5. Supervising the implementation of monetary policy;

6. Acting on behalf of the state treasury to manage cash and foreign exchange;

7. Examining and approving the establishment, closures, and combinations or mergers of financial institutions;

8. Directing, managing, harmonizing, supervising and auditing the business of financial institutions;

9. Evaluating and approving the issue of shares, bonds, and other securities by enterprises and local governments;

10. Accepting reserve and other deposits from the various financial institutions; and

11. Investigating issues relating to the economy and finance, keeping informed of the trend of change in credit and currency issue, and making timely reports to the local governments, higher authorities of PBOC, and other sectors of interest.

In order for PBOC to assume only central bank functions, it had to divest itself of its commercial banking activities. This was done through the establishment of a new state-owned bank: the Industrial and Commercial Bank of China (ICBC) which was established on January 1, 1984 (see chapter 3). The following are some relevant statistics for PBOC before and after the establishment of ICBC (Salem, 1987b: 58–59):

	Before End 1984	After End 1985
Total institutions	23,166	3,889
Total Employment	460,458	130,744
Branches	51	29
Central and sub-branches	336	164
Sub-Branches: Prefectures	362	50
Sub-Branches: Counties	2,247	559
City offices	1,021	12
Small branches	4,494	48
Savings bank offices	11,783	51

The Organizational Structure of PBOC

Figure 2.1 reflects the organizational structure of the central bank. PBOC is under the direct administration and authority of the State Council, and the Board of Governors as the highest management authority resides at the head office. The board decides on the recommendations that should be made for State Council approval. The board is composed of the president and vice-president of PBOC a small number of consultants and experts, a deputy minister of the Ministry of Finance, a deputy director of the State Planning Commission, a deputy director of the State Economy Commission, presidents of all specialized banks, and the general manager of the People's Insurance Company of China. The president of PBOC is the chairman of the board, and the vice-chairman is selected from among the directors. The governing board has a general secretary, a position normally held by a director, and all members of the board are appointed by the State Council. The general functions of the board were listed in the previous section, "The General Functions of the Central Bank."

The head office of the POBC is in Beijing; it is organized on a (functional) departmental basis as shown in Figure 2.1. The relatively large number of departments reflects the multitude of functions that the PBOC must carry out on a daily basis. In addition, there is a main branch in each province, autonomous region, and municipality directly under the State Council, in each city with plan independent of the provincial government, and in each special economic zone. These main branches have the responsibility to carry out PBOC functions within their respective regional or administrative jurisdictions. The main branches are assisted by central sub-branches in the prefectures, sub-branches in the counties, and business offices or agencies in the bigger towns and industrial centers.[3] In addition, there are municipal branches in larger cities and municipal sub-branches in other cities, which are under the provinces. Some municipal branches and sub-branches have agencies, local offices and savings offices in less populated areas (Figure 2.1).

At the end of 1990, PBOC had 46 main branches in the provinces, municipalities, autonomous regions, and special economic zones throughout China. In addition, there were over 2,400 sub-branches and other organizations at the county level. By the end of 1990, PBOC had a total of over 2,500 branches, sub-branches and associated organizations employing over 141,000 personnel. There is a vertical management system and unified administration within the PBOC organization. In principle, branches and other subordinate units must carry out duties as prescribed by the head office. The main branches have regional jurisdictions and are responsible to carry out PBOC activities in their respective jurisdictions. Local governments must ensure that PBOC implements the financial policies approved by the state and protect the legitimate rights and interests of PBOC, but must not interfere with its normal business operations. The

Figure 2.1
The Organizational Structure of the People's Bank of China

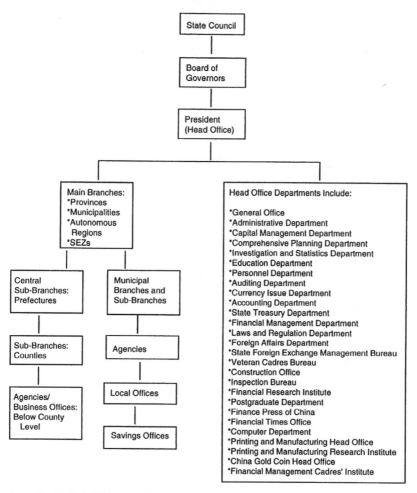

Source: People's Bank of China, Head Office, Beijing, 1991.

general duties of the head office, main branches, and other subordinate organizations were summarized in the previous section.

PROMOTING AND SUPERVISING CHINA'S FINANCIAL SYSTEM

As a national institution, and with State Council approval, PBOC is required to promote the development of a viable financial system to

Figure 2.2
The Chinese Financial System as It Had Evolved by 1990

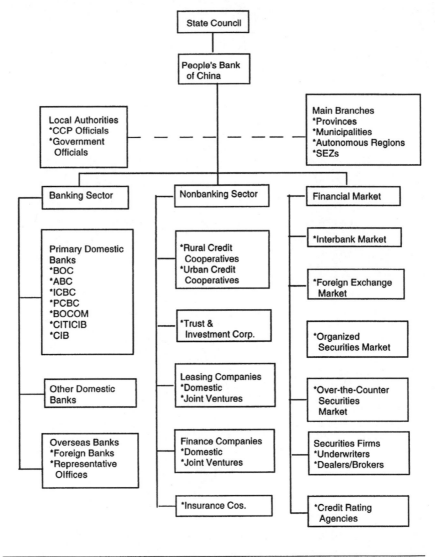

enhance the economic growth of the country. Over the reform era, the concept of financial system was defined to include the banking sector, the nonbanking sector, and the financial market (Figure 2.2). The financial system that is reflected in Figure 2.2 evolved since 1979 with the approval of the State Council and under the guidance and supervision of the central bank.

As a central bank, PBOC has a general responsibility to supervise the business operations of participants in the financial system. This supervisory role includes (a) approval for entry in, consolidation within, and exit from the financial system, and (b) directing, managing, monitoring, and auditing the business activities of financial system participants. There are elaborate reporting procedures, to be completed on prescribed statistical forms and on a timely basis. In particular, financial institutions are required to submit prescribed information relating to the implementation of the unified credit plan, deposits and reserves, loans, foreign reserves, and so forth. Participants in the financial market are required to report on their trading and other business activities.

Most of the administrative functions of PBOC are carried out by the main branches throughout the country under the watchful eyes (and meddling fingers) of the local authorities (Figure 2.2). As explained later in this chapter, this structure has not worked too well to promote the stature of the central bank.

The Banking Sector

Despite the incomplete statistics shown in Table 2.1, it is a foregone conclusion that the banking sector dominates the Chinese financial system. The seven primary domestic banks increased their total assets from RMB 958.46 billion in 1985 to RMB 2,902.47 billion in 1990, reflecting an annual growth rate of 24.81 percent. Asset growth in the reform era was facilitated by at least three factors: the ability to attract deposits which grew at an annual rate of 24.78 percent over 1985–1990 (Table 2.1), the access to funds from a developing interbank market (see chapter 6), and the flotation of financial bonds in the securities markets (see chapter 7).

In addition, there are some smaller regional domestic banks, including Yantai and Bengbu Housing Savings Banks, China Merchants Bank, Shenzhen Development Bank, Fujian Development Bank, and Guangdong Development Bank (discussed in chapters 3 and 4). Moreover, new regional banks are established as needed. In 1992, two such banks were approved to spur development: Shanghai Development Bank, Shanghai ("New Bank 'a Major Step' in Shanghai," 1993) and Hua Xia Bank, Beijing (Sender, 1993: 41). The Hua Xia Bank is a subsidiary of Capital Iron and Steel Corp., Beijing, which was the first industrial enterprise to establish a bank.

The Nonbanking Sector

The nonbanking sector includes the credit cooperatives, trust and investment corporations, leasing companies, finance companies, and

Table 2.1
Selected Statistics for Financial Institutions (Value in Billions of Renminbi)

Financial Institutions	Total Assets						Total Deposits					
	1985	1986	1987	1988	1989	1990	1985	1986	1987	1988	1989	1990
Primary Banks												
ABC	199.10	236.92	273.67	314.30	373.12	473.63	91.20	121.20	148.70	171.40	205.50	264.00
BOC	260.56	345.04	441.97	559.70	677.41	859.11	116.20	151.50	196.00	214.40	276.30	390.50
PCBC	168.80	229.70	277.80	339.45	407.49	517.80	57.60	69.50	82.30	96.70	115.20	158.00
CBC	328.74	419.47	486.82	667.39	772.53	938.37	193.53	253.72	314.46	356.17	413.11	517.35
BOCOM			44.11	42.22	53.00	78.51			9.35	19.63	26.13	44.43
CITICIB			8.76	13.33	15.78	21.43			4.93	5.79	7.32	10.75
CIB	1.26	2.57	3.83	6.70	10.01	13.62	0.01	0.02	0.07	0.85	1.36	1.87
Total	958.46	1,233.70	1,536.96	1,943.09	2,309.34	2,902.47	458.54	595.94	755.81	864.94	1,044.92	1,386.90
r* for 1985-90						24.81%						24.78%
Credit Cooperatives												
RCCs	95.57	122.49	161.85	191.13	230.99	299.95	72.49	96.23	122.52	139.98	166.34	214.49
UCCs		3.19	9.04	18.52	28.42	na		2.95	7.56	15.71	22.08	na
Total	95.57	125.68	170.89	209.65	259.41	na	72.49	99.18	130.08	155.69	188.42	na
r* for RCCs for 1985-90						25.70%						24.23%
r* for UCCs for 1986-89					107.31%						95.61%	
Trust and Investment Corp.												
CITIC	4.61	8.03	14.22	21.75	26.65	33.78	1.35	1.56	2.11	5.30	6.29	10.65
Others		23.89	48.16	73.55	77.44	na		12.98	29.91	49.18	52.17	na
Total	4.61	31.92	62.38	95.30	104.09	na	1.35	14.54	32.02	54.48	58.46	na
r* for CITIC for 1985-90						48.93%						51.15%
r* for others for 1986-89					48.00%						58.99%	
PICC	4.74	6.64	9.73	13.69	17.41	23.84						
r* for 1985-90						38.14%						

Source: See relevant figures and tables in chapters 3, 4, and 5.

r* = annual growth rate for the period specified.
na = not applicable.

insurance companies (Figure 2.2). Credit cooperatives and trust and investment corporations may be regarded as near-banks and, in 1989, their total assets were about one-tenth the total assets in the banking sector. These institutions are relatively small: by the end of the 1980s, there were about 63,000 credit cooperatives (60,000 RCCs and 3,000 UCCs), with over 300,000 associated organizations and about 300 trust and investment corporations (see chapter 5). RCCs mobilize savings in China's rural communities, which account for over 80 percent of the population while UCCs perform a similar function in the urban centers. Credit cooperatives depend heavily on deposits to finance their loan portfolios, and they have done an excellent job in attracting funds from individuals and collectives (Table 2.1). Deposits for RCCs grew at an annual rate of 24.23 percent over 1985–1990, which is similar to that for the banks.

Trust and investment corporations are owned by governments and banks and are a product of the reform era. Their primary task is to tap idle pools of funds from enterprises, institutions, and government departments and channel them to approved investments. Some of these institutions have the authority to borrow overseas. Their assets have grown at about 48 percent per year over 1985–1990, and deposits, at a slightly higher rate (Table 2.1). Like the banking sector, trust and investment corporations raise funds through deposits, loans from other financial institutions, and bonds in the domestic and foreign securities market.

Data is not readily available for leasing and finance companies but these institutions have been increasing in numbers and importance over 1980–1990 (see chapter 5). Some are domestically owned, while others are joint ventures with foreign financial institutions including international banks. Finally, the insurance business has regained a foothold in China, and the People's Insurance Company of China (PICC) dominates the industry (Shang, 1988: ch. 10). Insurance companies have limited authority to invest in securities or fixed assets, and the funds they attract are held mainly as deposits in banks (see chapter 5).

The Financial Market

The financial market includes three main components: the interbank market, the foreign exchange market, and the securities market. The interbank market was developed to facilitate the horizontal flow of short-term funds among banks and other financial institutions, while the foreign exchange market is a market mechanism used to allocate foreign currency in the economy (see chapter 6). The securities market facilitates the primary and secondary distribution of bonds issued by the state, financial institutions, and enterprises, and shares issued by enterprises. There are two organized securities exchanges (Shanghai Securities Exchange and Shenzhen Securities Exchange), as well as over-the-counter securities exchanges in financial centers throughout the country (see chapter 7).

Table 2.2
State Debt: Borrowing and Repayment (Value in Billions of Renminbi)

Year	Sources of Borrowing				Repayment			
	Total	State Treasury Bonds	Foreign Debt	Others	Total	State Treasury Bonds	Foreign Debt	Others
1979	3.53		3.53					
1980	4.30		4.30		2.86		2.44	0.42
1981	7.31		7.31		6.29		5.79	0.50
1982	8.34	4.38	4.00		5.55		4.96	0.59
1983	7.94	4.16	3.78		4.25		3.66	0.59
1984	7.73	4.25	3.48		2.89		2.27	0.62
1985	8.99	6.06	2.92		3.96		3.26	0.70
1986	13.83	6.25	7.57		5.02	0.80	3.45	0.77
1987	16.96	6.31	10.65		7.98	2.32	5.20	0.46
1988	27.08	9.02	13.86	4.00	7.68	2.84	4.26	0.58
1989	28.30	5.61	14.41	8.28	17.24	11.93	4.58	0.73
1990	37.55	9.35	17.82	12.38	19.04	11.38	6.82	0.84

Source: China Finance and Banking Association (1991: 244).

Market intermediaries include the securities firms which act as underwriters, dealers, and brokers. The financial market is another product of the reform era and its activities have important political, ethical, and economic implications.

DEBT MANAGEMENT FOR THE STATE

Except for a small surplus in 1985, the state had budget deficits in each year over 1979–1990 (Table A.5). It was common practice to print more money in order to finance the deficit, but by the early 1980s, the state began to have second thoughts about this action. In 1981, it started to issue treasury bonds to help finance budget deficits, a strategy that was continued for the entire decade (see chapter 7). Additionally, China looked overseas for foreign currency funding for economic reconstruction. Table 2.2 shows that state gross debt financing increased from RMB 3.53 billion in 1979 to 37.55 billion in 1990. China follows the Soviet practice of treating debt proceeds as revenue, so reported budget surplus or deficit accounts for debt financing (Table A.5).

PBOC has at least three major functions in the area of debt management for the State:

1. PBOC participates in the budget process, together with the Ministry of Finance and other government ministries. Where budget deficits are expected, the central bank is required to advise on the likely sources of financing.

2. As an administrator of the state treasury, PBOC has to determine annual debt repayment and ensure that funds are available to meet such obligations.

These payments have to be accounted for in the state budget and, in the case of foreign debt repayment, in the unified foreign exchange credit plan. Table 2.2 shows the annual debt repayment for 1980–1990 to both domestic and foreign creditors.

3. In principle, PBOC is permitted to make short-term loans to the state to cover temporary imbalances in revenues and expenditures. Although overdrafts on a long-term basis are prohibited by regulation, the state has found it convenient to disregard this prohibition. Over 1979–1990, the cumulative net budget deficit after debt financing totalled RMB 90.16 billion, some of which was financed through overdrafts   at PBOC. Interestingly, this cumulative budget deficit was about 40 percent of the net increase in currency in circulation (Mo) during the period (Table 2.3).

ESTABLISHING A STABLE MONETARY POLICY

One of the main functions of PBOC is to "establish a national monetary system with a reformed enterprise system, based upon a market regulatory system" (Liu, 1989a: 20). In essence, this means the establishment of a monetary policy that will maintain price stability and control inflation, restrict unwarranted expansion in domestic credit, and promote orderly economic development. Under the direction of the State Council (and the State Planning Commission), the central bank has used several direct and indirect measures in an attempt to shape a monetary policy for the economy.

Issuance of Currency

PBOC has the sole authority to issue currency: both renminbi and the Foreign Exchange Certificate (FECs). Renminbi was first issued in 1948 and FECs, in 1980. Available statistics indicate that currency outstanding (Mo) grew between 22 and 24 percent per year over 1979–1990 (Table 2.3). This growth rate is substantially higher than that for national income (14.2 percent, Table 2.8) or GNP (14.47 percent, Table A.1). Annual highs of over 40 percent growth rates were experienced in the boom years of 1984–1985 and 1987–1988. Slowing the growth rate of the money supply or the cash flow in the economy has been the primary economic lever that PBOC has used to cool an overheated economy. This strategy was followed in the early 1980s, 1985–1986 and 1989–1990 and is a relatively crude approach to an economy's credit management. Given the statistics, it is reasonable to conclude that a cash overhang exists in the Chinese economy.

Interest Rate Policy

Interest rates on deposits and loan are set by PBOC subject to approval by the State Council, and financial institutions are free to vary these rates in

Table 2.3
Money Supply Statistics: Liabilities (Value in Billions of Renminbi)

Year	Mo	M1	M2	Demand Deposits of Units	Quasi-Money Total	Quasi-Money Personal Deposits	Quasi-Money Time Deposits of Units	Mo	M1	M2	Demand Deposits of Units	Total	Quasi-Money Personal Deposits	Quasi-Money Time Deposits of Units
										Annual Changes (Percent)				
IMF Estimates														
1978	21.20	58.04	88.97	36.84	30.93									
1979	26.77	73.66	114.29	46.89	40.63			26.27%	26.91%	28.46%	27.28%	31.36%		
1980	34.62	91.93	144.16	57.31	52.23			29.32%	24.80%	26.14%	22.22%	28.55%		
1981	39.63	107.04	170.29	67.41	63.25			14.47%	16.44%	18.13%	17.62%	21.10%		
1982	43.91	115.70	193.43	71.79	77.73			10.80%	8.09%	13.59%	6.50%	22.89%		
1983	52.98	137.05	233.44	84.07	96.39			20.66%	18.45%	20.68%	17.11%	24.01%		
1984	79.21	212.59	327.50	133.38	114.91			49.51%	55.12%	40.29%	58.65%	19.21%		
1985	98.78	248.32	399.06	149.54	150.74			24.71%	16.81%	21.85%	12.12%	31.18%		
Chinese Estimates														
1985	98.78	334.09	519.89	235.31	185.80	162.26	23.54							
1986	121.84	423.22	672.09	301.38	248.87	223.76	25.11	23.34%	26.68%	29.28%	28.08%	33.95%	37.90%	6.67%
1987	145.45	494.86	833.09	349.41	338.23	307.33	30.90	19.38%	16.93%	23.96%	15.94%	35.91%	37.35%	23.06%
1988	213.40	598.59	1,009.98	385.19	411.39	380.15	31.24	46.72%	20.96%	21.23%	10.24%	21.63%	23.69%	1.10%
1989	234.40	638.22	1,194.96	403.82	556.74	514.69	42.05	9.84%	6.62%	18.32%	4.84%	35.33%	35.39%	34.60%
1990	264.44	760.89	1,529.37	496.45	768.48	703.42	65.06	12.82%	19.22%	27.99%	22.94%	38.03%	36.67%	54.72%
r*	24.31%	22.45%	23.17%	21.32%	24.42									
r**	21.77%	17.89%	24.09%	16.10%	32.84	34.09%	22.55%							

Source: The IMF estimates are taken from IMF, International Financial Statistics (1987): 280–281. The Chinese estimates are taken from China Finance and Banking Association (1991): 37.

r* = annual growth rate over 1979–85 based on IMF estimates.
r** = annual growth rate over 1985–90 based on the Chinese estimates.

Table 2.4
Personal Deposit Rates Published by Banks (Annual Percent)

Types of Deposits	1985 Apr. 4	1985 Aug.	1986 Mar.	1986 Aug.	1987 June	1987 Aug.	1988 Sept.	1989 Feb.	1989 June	1990 Apr.	1990 Aug.
Demand deposits	2.88	2.88	2.88	2.88	2.88	2.88	2.88	2.88	2.88	2.88	2.16
Time deposits with lump-sum withdrawals											
3 Months									7.56	5.30	4.32
6 Months	5.40	6.12	6.12	6.12	6.12	6.12	6.48	9.00	9.00	7.74	6.48
1 Year	6.84	7.20	7.20	7.20	7.20	7.20	8.64	11.34	11.34	10.08	8.64
2 Years							9.18	12.24	12.24	10.98	9.86
3 Years (2)	7.92	8.28	8.28	8.28	8.28	8.28	9.72	13.14	13.14	11.88	10.08
5 Years (2)	8.28	9.36	9.36	9.36	9.36	9.36	10.80	14.94	14.94	13.68	11.52
8 Years (2)	9.00	10.44	10.44	10.44	10.44	10.44	12.42	17.64	17.64	16.20	15.68
Installment deposits with lump-sum withdrawals											
1 Year	5.40	6.12	6.12	6.12	6.12	6.12	7.20	9.54	9.54	8.28	7.20
2 Years	6.84	7.20	7.20	7.20	7.20	7.20	8.64	11.34	11.34	10.08	8.64
3 Years	7.56	7.92	7.92	7.92	7.92	7.92	9.72	13.14	13.14	11.88	10.08
Lump-sum deposit with instalment withdrawals											
1 Year	5.40	6.12	6.12	6.12	6.12	6.12	7.20	9.54	9.54	8.28	7.20
2 Years	6.84	7.20	7.20	7.20	7.20	7.20	8.64	11.34	11.34	10.08	8.64
3 Years	7.56	7.92	7.92	7.92	7.92	7.92	9.72	13.14	13.14	11.58	10.08
Principal deposits and interest withdrawals											
1 Year	5.40	6.12	6.12	6.12	6.12	6.12	7.20	9.54	9.54	8.28	7.20
3 Years (2)	6.84	7.20	7.20	7.20	7.20	7.20	8.64	11.34	11.34	10.08	8.64
5 Years (2)	7.56	7.92	7.92	7.92	7.92	7.92	9.72	13.14	13.14	11.88	10.08
Interchangeable deposits: time and demand											
Less than 6 months			2.88	23.88	2.88	2.88	(1)	(1)	(1)	(1)	(1)
Over 6 months			5.51	5.51	5.51	5.51	(1)	(1)	(1)	(1)	(1)
Over 1 year			6.48	6.48	6.48	6.48	(1)	(1)	(1)	(1)	(1)
Deposits in RMB by overseas Chinese											
1 Year	7.20	8.28	8.28	8.28	8.28	8.28	9.72	13.14	13.14	11.88	10.08
3 Years	8.28	9.36	9.36	9.36	9.36	9.36	10.80	14.94	14.94	13.68	11.52
5 Years	9.00	10.44	10.44	10.44	10.44	10.44	11.88	16.74	16.74	15.48	13.68

Source: Chen and Zhao (1990: 171).

[1] The interest rate was 90 percent of that for deposits and withdrawals by a lump sum with similar maturity.
[2] On September 10, 1988, matured deposits were indexed to inflation.

either direction by .20 percent. Table 2.4 shows personal deposit rates published for specialized banks at various times since 1985. Interest rates on demand and time deposits for enterprises are similar to those for personal deposits of the same types.

As shown in Table 2.4, PBOC and the Chinese banks have designed a variety of deposit accounts to attract funds in order to assist in meeting the financing requirements for economic reconstruction. They have tracked inflation rates since 1985 and have adjusted deposit rates accordingly. In addition, starting in September 1988, some savings deposits were indexed to inflation (Table 2.4, note 2). The expansion of branch networks, the

Table 2.5
Lending Rates of Specialized Banks (Annual Percent)

	1985 April	1985 Aug. 1	1987 Jan. 1	1988 Sept. 1	1989 Feb. 1	1989 June 20	1990 Jan. 1	1990 Mar. 21	1990 Aug. 21
Working Capital Loans									
General (from 1990)									
3 months							11.34	7.92	7.92
6 months							11.34	9.00	8.64
I year							11.34	10.08	9.36
State-owned enterprises, incl. collectives in industry, commerce, and agriculture	7.92	7.92	7.92	9.00	11.34	11.34			
Foreign trade enterprises	7.20	7.20	7.20	9.00	11.34	11.34			
Construction enterprises	4.32	4.32	4.32	9.00	11.34– 12.06	11.34– 12.06			
Township enterprises	8.64	8.64	9.64	9.00	11.34	11.34			
Private individuals and commercial enterprises	9.36– 11.52	9.36– 11.52	9.36– 11.52	11.70	11.70	[1]	[1]	[4]	[5]
Peasant households	7.92	7.92	7.92	9.00	11.34	11.34	11.34		
Loans for Fixed Assets									
Less than 1 year	5.04	7.92	7.92	9.00	11.34	11.34	11.34	10.08	9.36
1 to 3 years	5.76	8.64	8.64	9.90	12.78	12.78	12.78	10.80	10.08
3 to 5 years	6.48	9.36	9.36	10.80	14.40	14.40	14.40	11.52	10.80
5 to 10 years		10.08	10.08	13.32	19.26	19.26	19.26	11.88	11.16
Over 10 years		10.80	10.80	16.20	[2]	[2]	[2]	11.88	11.16
Equipment Loans									
Township enterprises	9.00– 9.36	10.08– 10.80	10.08– 10.80	10.80– 13.32	[3]	[3]	[3]	[3]	[3]

Source: China Finance and Banking Association (1991: 201).

[1]Loan rates were floating at 30 percent above a base of 11.34 percent.
[2]Negotiated on the basis of a one-year compound interest rate on loans.
[3]Same as loans for fixed assets.
[4]Loan rates were floating at 0.20 percent above a base of 10.08 percent.
[5]Loan rates were floating at 0.20 percent above a base rate of 9.36 percent.

improvement of services, door-to-door solicitation, new products, and similar efforts have paid off through increased deposits. Rates in the banking sector had to remain competitive with those in the securities market, particularly in the bond sector (see chapter 7). As discussed in chapter 7, enterprise and financial bonds with attractive yields were issued in China in the late 1980s and competed with banks for funds from individuals.

Demand deposits of units (enterprises, institutions, government departments, etc.) increased at an annual rate of 16.10 percent over 1985–1990. With this rapid increase, the broader definition of money, M1 (which includes Mo plus these deposits), increased at an annual rate of 17.89 percent over the same period (Table 2.3). Personal deposits and time deposits of units increased by 34.09 percent and 22.55 percent, respectively, over the same period. M2, which includes M1 and these deposits (or quasi-money) increased at an annual rate of 24.09 percent over 1985–1990 (Table 2.3). Like Mo, both M1 and M2 exceeded the growth rates of national income (at 14.2 percent) and GNP (at 14.47 percent).

Table 2.5 shows the lending rates for the specialized banks. Generally,

Table 2.6
Money Supply Statistics: Assets (Value in Billions of Renminbi)

Year	Foreign Assets	Domestic Credit (Net) Total	Loans	Govt. Borrowing	Others	Annual Changes (Percent) Foreign Assets	Domestic Credit (Net) Total	Loans	Govt. Borrowing	Others
IMF Estimates										
1978	0.54	185.00	185.00							
1980	(2.78)	169.89	241.43	0.82	(72.36)		26.39%	18.37%		13.61%
1981	2.67	195.10	276.47	(2.48)	(78.89)		14.84%	14.51%		9.02%
1982	16.14	210.43	305.23	(0.56)	(94.24)		7.86%	10.40%		19.46%
1983	23.95	247.33	343.11	0.59	(96.37)	48.39%	17.54%	12.41%		2.26%
1984	27.03	339.35	441.96	9.49	(112.10)	12.86%	37.21%	28.81%		16.32%
1985	23.45	497.83	629.54	(9.33)	(122.38)	−13.24%	46.70%	42.44%		9.17%
Chinese Estimates										
1985	20.83	499.88	627.19	(9.33)	(117.98)					
1986	38.90	670.88	811.65	5.86	(146.63)	86.75%	34.21%	29.41%		24.28%
1987	26.13	812.82	976.63	20.80	(184.61)	−32.83%	21.16%	20.33%	254.95%	25.90%
1988	30.25	987.29	1,142.50	30.56	(185.77)	15.77%	21.46%	16.98%	46.92%	0.63%
1989	37.14	1,164.73	1,346.95	24.66	(206.88)	22.78%	17.97%	17.89%	−19.31%	11.36%
1990	92.67	1,445.90	1,654.13	42.06	(250.29)	149.52%	24.14%	22.81%	70.56%	20.98%
r*		24.39%	20.66%							
r**	34.79%	23.67%	21.40%							

Source: The IMF estimates are taken from IMF, *International Financial Statistics* (1988): 290–291. The Chinese estimates are taken from China Finance and Banking Association (1991: 37).

r* = annual growth rate over 1979-85 based on IMF estimates.
r** = annual growth rate over 198590 based on the Chinese estimates.

rates vary by the types of loans (working capital loans, loans for fixed assets, and equipment loans), the maturity structures of loans, and the borrowers. An examination of the data reveals some preferential treatment for selected enterprises and industry sectors at least up to September 1988. Construction and foreign trade enterprises received lower cost funding to enhance economic reconstruction. Additionally, the industrial and agricultural sectors tended to have lower rates than the commercial sector. However, by the end of the decade, the published rates tended to move closer together. Unofficially, political pressures were exerted to lend to state-owned enterprises at 2 to 3 percent below deposit rates.

The demand for loans increased at an annual rate of about 21 percent over 1979–1990, which led to a rapid expansion in domestic credit: an annual growth rate of about 24 percent (Table 2.6). Loan demand was mainly for economic reconstruction and the operation of business enterprises, as consumer loans and residential mortgages were limited (or nonexistent) during the period under review. Again, the growth in domestic credit was in line with most of the other economic indicators: it significantly exceeded the growth in national income and GNP. The state has been able to use the domestic financial institutions to draw funds from the economy and abroad in order to finance economic reconstruction. As an economic lever, the interest rate policy had a beneficial effect on attracting deposits,

Table 2.7
Lending and Deposit Rates of People's Bank of China (Annual percent)

	1985 Jan. 1	1986 Aug. 1	1987 Sep. 1	1987 Dec. 21	1988 Sep. 1	1989 Feb. 1	1990 Mar. 21	1990 Aug. 21
Deposits by Financial Institutions								
Required reserves	4.32	4.32	4.32	5.04	5.04	7.20	7.92	6.84
Excess reserves	4.32	5.76	5.76	5.76	6.48	8.64	7.92	6.84
Loans to Financial Institutions								
Annual loans	4.68	4.68	7.20	7.20	8.20	10.44	9.00	7.92
Seasonal loans	5.04	6.84	7.20	6.84	7.56	9.72	9.00	7.92
Overnight loans	5.04	6.48	7.20	6.48	6.84	9.00	9.00	7.92
Base loans[1]	4.68	4.68	7.20	7.20	8.28	10.44	9.00	7.92
Rediscount		2	3	3	4	4	4	4

Source: Chen and Zhao (1990: 160); and China Finance and Banking Association (1991: 83).

[1]Loans within the range of the annual credit plan set by PBOC.
[2]Minus 0.3 percent on the basis of loan rates for the same period.
[3]Five to 10 percent reduction of rates on same-period loans.
[4]Five to 10 percent margin on rates of same-period loans.

which was quite important, at least in the closing years of the 1980s. Inflation (which will be discussed shortly) had increased substantially by 1988, and there was a run on savings and an ensuing spending spree on consumer goods. Deposit rates were raised in 1988/89 to dissuade such inflationary behavior with some degree of success (Kaye, 1991: 60). As an economic lever, the interest rate policy was probably not effective in the allocation of credit. (This issue is addressed later in the chapter.)

Lender of Last Resort

PBOC lends to other domestic banks to meet emergencies or other temporary shortages of funds. Its lending rates are shown in the lower half of Table 2.7. As a matter of policy, PBOC lends at rates that are higher than the deposit rates paid by banks; this is intended to minimize borrowing from the central bank. Domestic banks are intended to attract deposits in the economy and not depend on the central bank, and there is an interbank market that may be tapped for temporary funds. Finally, PBOC has a rediscounting facility for acceptable trade bills and other approved securities, but again, the rediscount rate may be higher than that available in established rediscounting centers. Consequently, it is to a bank's advantage to discount bills at the latter.

Reserve Requirement

The reserve ratio on deposits was instituted in 1984: it was 20 percent on enterprise deposits, 25 percent on agricultural deposits, and 40 percent on

Table 2.8
Annual Growth Rates for Selected Economic Activities (Percent)

Year	Retail Price Index	GNP	Social Value of Output	Money Supply		National Income	Investments in Fixed Assets	Retail Sales: Consumer Goods	Salaries and Wages
				Mo	M1				
1980	5.99	11.80	11.69	29.32	24.80	10.09	11.43	21.54	19.44
1981	2.30	6.78	6.33	14.47	16.44	6.86	28.84	11.62	6.16
1982	1.93	8.80	9.82	10.80	8.09	8.04	24.91	8.94	7.45
1983	1.50	11.86	11.69	20.66	18.45	11.23	14.05	11.21	6.07
1984	2.83	19.85	18.33	49.51	15.12	19.34	33.88	19.50	21.27
1985	8.81	22.92	25.90	24.71	16.81	24.20	38.75	31.12	22.02
1986	5.97	13.31	14.85	23.34	26.68	11.95	18.73	15.06	20.04
1987	7.32	16.55	20.95	19.38	16.93	18.50	20.58	16.94	13.31
1988	18.48	23.74	29.40	46.72	20.96	26.04	23.50	27.75	23.13
1989	17.82	23.74	29.40	46.72	20.96	26.04	23.50	27.75	23.13
1990	2.10	12.02	10.07	12.82	19.22	9.51	7.57	2.50	12.70
r* (1979–90)				24.31	23.17				
r* (1979–85)				21.77	17.89				
r* (1979–90)	6.68	14.47	15.70			14.20	18.80	15.57	14.80

savings deposits.[4] These relatively high ratios were subsequently unified and reduced to 10 percent in 1985 and 1986, 12 percent in 1987, and 13 percent in 1988–1990. The required reserve ratio is applied to some negotiated level of deposits that are needed by the banks to meet their credit or loan limits. (The procedures for setting these loan limits are discussed in chapter 3.) Deposits above the negotiated levels are subject to an additional excess reserve ratio: 11 percent in 1985, 10 percent in 1986, 8 percent in 1987, 6 percent in 1988, and 10 percent in 1989–1990. It is argued that the high reserve ratios are needed to limit credit creation by banks, but it is rather suspected that PBOC uses them to draw funds for state use. As an economic lever, this practice is useless in regulating credit in the economy.

Price Stability and Inflation

Generally, prices were not stable during the reform era.[5] Using the annual changes in the general retail price index as an indicator, the inflation rate averaged 6.68 percent over 1979–1990, but the annual fluctuations were rather significant (Table 2.8). The annual inflation rate started at 5.99 percent in 1980 (due to some pricing reforms in 1979), but had dropped to 1.50 percent by 1983. The threat of higher inflation started in 1984 at 2.83 percent and rose consistently to 18.48 percent by 1988; it then dropped to 2.10 percent by the end of 1990. The general retail price index accounts for retail sales of consumer goods and agricultural production materials sold to the processing sector. If only the annual changes in the retail sales of consumer goods are taken into account, the average price increase was 7.95 percent over 1979–1990. The annual changes in the consumer price index were much more volatile than those for the general retail price index. There were several factors that influenced prices and inflation during the reform era, and while it is difficult to measure their individual impact, it is instructive to review their relative influences.

Pricing Reforms. By the end of 1986, the number of commodities controlled directly by the Ministry of Commerce had dropped from 188 in 1979 to 23. Controlled commodities were subject to a contract quota, to be sold to the state at a set price, while above-quota production could be sold on the open market. In the agricultural sector, 25 agricultural and sideline products were subject to unified prices set by the state in 1986, compared to 113 in 1979. Finally, in the industrial sector, the prices of more than 1,000 small commodities (industrial and consumer goods) were decontrolled (Gao, 1987: 21–22). These pricing reforms should have some influence on price increases up to 1988, when price controls were reinstituted as a weapon against high inflation. No serious attempt at pricing reform was taken until 1991 (Niu, 1991: 12–13).

Devaluation of the Currency. The renminbi was devalued from RMB 1.5550/U.S. $1 in 1979 to RMB 4.0150/U.S. $1 by the end of 1990. Devaluation increases the price of imports and, depending on a country's appetite for the consumption of imported goods, it may result in higher price levels in the domestic economy. Normally, this has not been the case in China, as imports have been subject to controls in terms of product types, quantities, and value and, under such controls there should not be much danger of imported inflation. However, in the boom years of 1984–1985 and 1987–1988, some import controls were lifted or violated. As a result, imported consumer goods found their way into the Chinese market and had some adverse impact on price stability. However, considering pricing reforms and devaluation, it is generally agreed that their joint impact on inflation was not significant.

Excessive Money Supply. Whether measured as Mo or M1, the growth rate in the money supply outstripped economic growth, as measured by GNP. China had the classic environment for inflation: "too much money chasing too few goods."

Overheated Economic Development. The national income grew at an annual rate of 14.20 percent, but the demand pressures from investments in fixed assets (at 18.80 percent per annum) and consumption (at 15.57 percent per annum) were enormous. The economy moved from a "buyers' market" at the start of the 1980s to a "sellers' market" in the mid-1980s. Industrial targets and budgets were routinely exceeded, and the rush for super-performance created shortages. The basic industries (energy, transport, and raw and semifinished materials) could not meet the voracious appetites of the processing or industrial industries. Agriculture and sideline production suffered due to poor harvests in the mid-1980s and lower (controlled) pricing. Pricing reforms were in their infancy and gave distorting signals. For example, agricultural production materials for the processing sector had lower prices and discouraged production, while the production of household appliances increased because of (decontrolled) higher pricing. Unfortunately, a lot of the products in the processing sector are becoming antiques in warehouses: supply has not matched the changing demand in the marketplace.

With respect to consumption, the annual growth in retail sales averaged 15.57 percent over 1979–1990 (Table 2.8). Consumers were able to boost demand through attractive salary and wage increases which averaged 14.80 percent per year over 1979–1990.

THE SCORECARD FOR CENTRAL BANKING

PBOC did not assume central bank functions in a reformed financial system. In fact, the central bank had to gain experience on the job, while it was assisting in the financial reform process. The institutional reforms (Figure 2.2) that PBOC assisted in implementing are commendable for the time span and environment in which they were achieved. They are a focus of this book. However, the operations of the reformed financial system leaves much to be desired and have received mixed reviews, mostly negative. The following is a summary of the negative opinions and comments that should be addressed in future financial reforms to promote a stronger PBOC (or its equivalent).[6]

Political Interference Hampers PBOC

The central bank is subject to the supervision and authority of the State Council and lacks autonomy in operations and decision making. Monetary policy is the "prerogative" of the State Council and the State Planning Commission, and state ministries and provinces have a voice in shaping monetary targets. Credit control and associated lending are largely administrative rather than economic decisions. PBOC is viewed as a "printing press" or the "state cashier," and much of its perceived inaction or ineptness may be due to "lack of power to operate an independent monetary policy, free of interference from politically powerful cadres insisting on special consideration for pet projects" (Cheng, 1988: 74).

Specialized Banks are Over-Controlled

The specialized or state banks do not behave as independent entities, despite statements to that effect. The State Planning Commission influences their loan decisions and ensures that funding is available for the state-owned enterprises, despite the fact that about a third of them are loss-making units. PBOC has to go along with the decisions of the state. An estimated 30 percent of loans to state-owned enterprises may be commercially viable and pass reasonable credit screens, but the remaining 70 percent are usually "policy-based," with little commercial merit for credit allocation and flow for projects that are included in the unified credit plan. Once the (inefficient) state sector is looked after, specialized banks may lend to the_more productive economic units in the economy. In times of austerity, the productive sectors of the economy suffer from the credit squeeze, while credit is readily available to the state sector. There are other contradictions. Very often, lending rates to state-owned enterprises are below deposit rates and loans may exceed deposits at a given bank. In true socialist style, the state will intercede with additional funding and interest rate subsidies to save its loss-making enterprises.

Specialized Banks Ignore PBOC

The reform of the financial system was in progress by January 1, 1984, and banks and other financial institutions had some autonomy over their respective operations. Without either the "carrot" or the "big stick" from the State Council, PBOC's directives are routinely ignored by these institutions: "While the head office of the People's Bank issues circulars warning of the dangers of excess credit, they are routinely ignored by everyone from Premier Li Peng to local branches of the central bank itself" (Sender, 1993: 40).

Specialized Banks Circumvent Restrictions and Constraints

The specialized banks (and others) are involved in establishing nonbank financial institutions to circumvent state restrictions and constraints in the banking industry. These newly established nonbanks contribute to credit expansion, and much lending is for investments in nonproductive assets. Many of the institutions are involved in high-risk activities, including speculation in real estate and securities. The pyramiding currently in effect in the banking sector can have damaging consequences when the economy turns down.

Economic/Financial Targets and Budgets Are Ignored

In their quest to measure performance in quantitative terms, economic units follow one basic principle: "construction and more construction, production and more production." In the process, planning targets and budgets are exceeded without notice. Nobody appears to take targets and budgets seriously, as enterprises and politicians delight in announcing super-achievements (Chen, 1992: 4). These attitudes and actions have put a severe strain on macroeconomic management: there is really no sensible monetary policy, domestic credit far exceeds economic growth, and inflation is kept in check through severe austerity measures imposed by the State Council on certain sectors of the economy.

PBOC Is Not Superman

The central bank is asked to do a herculean duty: macroeconomic management plus the supervision and control of banks, nonbank financial institutions, and the financial market. This unified financial management is almost impossible. Moreover, it presents conflicts of interest, and creates inefficiencies. For these reasons, unified financial management should not be applied to a reformed financial system in China. PBOC lacks the resources, including manpower, to carry out even the traditional central bank functions. In October 1992, the Deputy Governor of PBOC made the following optimistic statement at a meeting of fellow bankers: "Through the use of tools as bank reserve requirements, interest rates and foreign exchange rates, China's central bank will shift to a system of indirect control over the nation's money supply and budget" (Ren, 1992: 5).

With all due respect, the deputy governor is not totally correct: those tools are necessary, but they are not nearly sufficient for the job in China.

NOTES

1. During the Cultural Revolution (July 1969), the head office of PBOC was incorporated with the Ministry of Finance. The branches and sub-branches were operated by rules set by the various provinces, municipalities, and autonomous regions. On January 1, 1978, by State Council resolution ("Several Decisions on Consolidating and Strengthening Banking Work," November, 1977), PBOC functioned independently of the Ministry of Finance. By the end of 1978, PBOC had regained its branches and sub-branches and continued normal operations (Chen and Zhao, 1990: 28–29).

2. Langstron (1985a: 58) claimed that CITIC's first (private) bond issue abroad was in Tokyo in 1984.

3. A prefecture is a level of government between that for the county and municipality levels. The prefecture administers two or more counties which, by themselves, are too small to have independent county governments.

4. This discussion draws on Liu (1991) and Shang, Wu, and Luo (1992).

5. The discussion draws on material from Delfs (1983), do Rosario (1987: 76–78), Zhang (1989: 27–28), and Li (1990: 28–32).

6. The discussion draws on material from Lee (1985: 72, 1986: 94, 99), 1987: 102–103), Salem (1987b: 58–59), Cheng (1988: 74, 1989: 50, 52), Tai (1990: 54–55), Han (1991: 35–36), Kaye (1991: 60), and Sender (1993: 40–43).

REFERENCES

Bonavia, David. 1980a. "No Big Loans Yet But Soon China Must Act on Options." *Far Eastern Economic Review,* April 4, 85.
———. 1980b. "The Red Ink on China's Ledger." *Far Eastern Economic Review,* September 9, 69.
Chen Xiao, "Economists Find Inflation Risk in Heating Up Trend." *China Daily* November 21, 4.

Chen Yuan and Zhao Haikuan. 1990. *Almanac of China's Finance and Banking,* Beijing: China's Financial Publishing House.

Cheng, Elizabeth. 1988. "Lender of First Resort." *Far Eastern Economic Review,* November 24, 74.

———. 1989. "Problems Dog Attempts to Modernize." *Far Eastern Economic Review,* September 28, 50, 52.

China Finance and Banking Association. 1991. *Almanac of China's Finance and Banking.* Beijing: China's Financial Publishing House.

China State Statistics Bureau. 1989. "The Chinese Economy in 1988." *Beijing Review,* February 6–12, 21–22.

Delfs, Robert. 1983. "The Spectre of Inflation." *Far Eastern Economic Review,* August 4, 83.

do Rosario, Louise. 1985. "Time to Pay the Piper." *Far Eastern Economic Review,* August 22, 100–101.

———. 1987. "China on the Boil." *Far Eastern Economic Review,* October 26, 76–78.

Gao Shangquan. 1987. "Progress in Economic Reform (1979–86)." *Beijing Review,* July 6, 21–22.

Han Baocheng. 1989. "Sino-EC Symposium on Law, Investment." *Beijing Review,* April 10–16, 42.

Han Guojian. 1989. "Strengthening Taxation's Role as an Economic Lever." *Beijing Review,* August 7–13, 21.

———. 1991. "Banker Speaks Out on Financial Situation." *Beijing Review,* July 8–14, 35–36.

Kaye, Lincoln. 1991. "Manning the Pumps." *Far Eastern Economic Review,* October 17, 60.

Langstron, Nancy. 1985a. "Fame Is the Spur." *Far Eastern Economic Review,* June 6, 58.

———. 1985b. "Waiting—and Wishing—for Some Action." *Far Eastern Economic Review,* April 25, 70–71.

Lee, Mary. 1985. "Change from the Top." *Far Eastern Economic Review,* May 9, 72.

———. 1986. "Coming of Age amid a Flurry of Setbacks." *Far Eastern Economic Review,* March 20, 94, 99.

———. 1987. "Future Directions of Reform Uncertain." *Far Eastern Economic Review,* March 19, 102–103.

Li Ping. 1990. "China's Inflation—Its Causes and Plans for Control." *Beijing Review,* February 19–25, 28–32.

Liu Guoguang. 1989a. "Economic Reform Faces New Challenges." *Beijing Review,* March 27–April 2, 20.

———. 1989b. "A Sweet and Sour Decade." *Beijing Review,* January 2–8, 22–28.

Liu Hongru, ed. 1991. *On Financial Macro-Control and Adjustment.* Beijing: China Financial Press.

"New Bank 'a Major Step' in Shanghai." 1993. *China Daily,* January 9, 2.

Niu Genying. 1991. "Progress in China's Economic Reform." *Beijing Review,* November 11–17, 12–13.

Ren Kan. 1992. "Banks May be Free to Set Their Own Rates." *China Daily,* October 14, 5.

Salem, Ellen. 1983. "Slow Boat to China." *Far Eastern Economic Review,* April 23, 51–53.

————. 1987a. "Cooling off the Economy." *Far Eastern Economic Review*, March 26, 80.

————. 1987b. "A Long Road Full of Obstacles, But It Works." *Far Eastern Economic Review*, May 7, 58–59.

————. 1987c. "Major Hurdles to Revitalization." *Far Eastern Economic Review*, March 19, 62.

SBC Research. 1992. *China Stock Market Overview*, July.

Sender, Henny. 1993. "Out of the Wilderness." Far Eastern Economic Review, January 14, 41.

Shang Ming, Wu Xiaoling, and Luo Lanbo. 1992. *Bank Credit Management and Money Supply*, Beijing: People's University Press.

Shang Ming, ed. 1988. *China Today: Money and Banking*, Beijing: China Social Science Press.

Shrodes, James. 1980. "Rockefeller Meets Rong." *Far Eastern Economic Review*, June 13, 108–110.

Tai Ming Cheung. 1990. "Losers Take All." *Far Eastern Economic Review*, March 1, 54–55.

Zhang Zhenbin. 1989. "Cutting Back Consumption." *Beijing Review*, February 6–12, 27–28.

3

Specialized Banks

Specialized banks operate with permission from the State Council and the central bank (PBOC) in designated or specialized business activities or industrial sectors in China. These business activities or sectors are usually referred to as administrative regions. Traditionally, Chinese banks were not allowed to cross administrative regions to solicit business, but this barrier is gradually being relaxed. Currently, there are six specialized banks: the Industrial and Commercial Bank of China (ICBC), the Agricultural Bank of China (ABC), the Bank of China (BOC), the People's Construction Bank of China (PCBC), China Investment Bank (CIB), and the Housing Savings Bank (HSB). In preparation for a discussion on these specialized banks, it is instructive to review some relationships between the central bank and the specialized (and other Chinese) banks to avoid duplication later and to gain a better understanding of the Chinese banking environment. The details are lengthy and complicated, and the immediate review is merely a summary of relevant points. The role of the central bank is reviewed in chapter 2, while that of the comprehensive banks in China is reviewed in chapter 4.

ADMINISTRATION OF SPECIALIZED BANKS

Specialized banks are state owned, and their general responsibilities and duties are to:

1. Operate as viable business institutions in line with the fundamental regulations of financial business;
2. Grant loans to enterprises in conformity with the state's policies and plans;
3. Borrow and lend funds at interest rates prescribed by the central bank, subject to approved variations;
4. Administer the systematic transfer of funds in the economy;
5. Facilitate credit and settlement transactions;
6. Supervise cash management of enterprises that have account relationships at the bank;

7. Supervise the wage funds of enterprises that have account relationships at the bank;

8. Control the working capital of state-owned enterprises, with the authorization of the central bank;

9. Be responsible for profits and losses; and

10. Handle international financial business with the approval of the State Council or the central bank.

Establishment and Cancellation of Banks

Consistent with the "Provisional Regulations on Management of Banks of the PRC" and other relevant laws, there are preconditions that must be met to establish new banks, branches, and sub-branches in China.

1. The institution must be economically viable. When the existing banks cannot satisfy the actual demand of economic development and social life in number, scale, and types of business and, furthermore, when the demand for financial service can provide sufficient business, a new bank may be beneficial for commodity production and capital circulation.

2. The new bank must have certain minimums in paid-up capital, as follows: (a) nationwide banks with branches and sub-branches: RMB 2 billion; (b) nationwide banks without branches and sub-branches: RMB 1 billion; (c) regional banks: RMB 800 million; and (d) cooperative banks: RMB 500 million. If the bank is expected to handle foreign exchange business, 30 percent of the paid-up capital should be in foreign exchange.

3. There must be qualified personnel to manage the financial business of the institution.

4. As a legal enterprise that is independently operated, the bank should carry out independent accounting, take sole responsibility for profit and loss, and bear all risks.

5. New banks, branches, or sub-branches should be established according to economic regions in order to promote more comprehensive banking. So far, specialized banks are established according to administrative regions, which has, to a great extent, cut off the horizontal relationship of commodity and capital and proven unfavorable to the development of a commodity economy. With this provision, the state is encouraging banks to solicit business across administrative regions in order to encourage some degree of competition.

Once the preconditions have been met, there are prescribed procedures to follow in seeking an operating license. The central bank is authorized by the State Council to approve new banks, branches and sub-branches.

Central Bank Administration of Specialized Banks

All specialized banks are under the leadership, coordination, guidance, supervision, and scrutiny of the central bank. They are supposed to execute all decisions made by the central bank; otherwise, they will be penalized economically or administratively. Four general areas are administratively enforced: credit planning management, management of deposits, management of loans, and management of interest rates on deposits and loans.

Credit Management. The management of the nation's credit follows a basic principle: "Centralized planning, distributing fund, lending and borrowing, and mutual accommodation."

1. Under centralized planning, all RMB credit funds of specialized banks are to be incorporated into the overall credit plan of the state (as discussed in chapter 1). The central bank prepares this credit plan based on the requirements of the physical plan and makes allocations to the specialized banks.

2. *Distributing fund* refers to the self-owned and other credit funds that are used as working capital by specialized banks with approval from the central bank.

3. *Lending and depositing* refers to the transmission of funds from the central bank to specialized banks: the central bank will lend to the banks, but specialized banks must deposit their funds with the central bank.

4. Mutual accommodation permits capital to move horizontally in a region via interbank lending and borrowing.

Since 1989, credit-planning management has been carried out at three levels: credit planning for the whole society, credit planning for the state-owned banks and credit planning for nonbank financial institutions. Credit planning for the state-owned banks, includes credit planning for the central bank and for all specialized and comprehensive banks (chapter 4). The credit plan is prepared by the central bank and approved by the State Council (see chapter 1). Loan limits are set for each specialized bank and are controlled in one of two ways: head offices of all specialized banks are responsible for monitoring and controlling their respective limits, while the regional branches of the central bank monitor and control the limits in their respective administrative regions.

The loan limits for specialized banks are managed by the principle of fixing them once for the whole year, controlling them quarterly, checking them monthly, and adjusting them in a timely fashion. "Fixing them once for the whole year" means that the state sets annual loan limits for all specialized banks by regions in the country at the beginning of a year. Annual loan limits for branches and sub-branches of specialized banks must be approved by the respective head offices. "Controlling quarterly" means that within the annual limits, quarterly quotas or limits are set, which are monitored and controlled by the specialized banks and the regional branches of the central bank. If the quarterly limits are likely to be breached due to special conditions, then permission must be obtained from the central bank to do so. "Checking monthly" refers to the practice whereby the use of funds is monitored to ensure that quarterly limits are maintained. A monthly plan or budget is used as a reference to look for variances from projected quarterly limits and the results must be reported to the regional branch of the central bank. "Adjusting in a timely fashion" means that the central bank may adjust the loan limits of specialized banks and regions, if required.

Management of Deposits. Deposits of specialized banks normally include fiscal deposits, such as the fiscal treasury deposits, the local fiscal extrabudgetary deposits, army units deposits, capital construction deposits, public organ and group deposits, and so on. These types of deposits are the credit funds of the central bank and the specialized banks are not supposed to use them for lending activities. Other deposits taken in by specialized banks such as enterprise deposits, savings deposits, and rural deposits, are credit funds of specialized banks and may be used for lending to clients. These deposits attract reserves which must be deposited with the central bank (discussed in chapter 2). There are prescribed rules governing the transfer of the credit funds of the central bank and reserves to PBOC.

Management of Loans. The central bank manages the level of loans under the principle of quota management and fixing loans according to deposits. Once the loan limits have been set, there is a need to monitor them to protect against abuse or overlending. The deposit plan is fixed by the specialized bank and reported to the central bank; it will be based on the bank's expectations of its ability to attract such funds. Other factors being constant, the level of deposits will influence lending activities. However, if the loan limit for a bank is below the deposit plan, there will be an excess deposit with that bank, since it cannot breach its loan limit without approval. The reverse happens if the loan limit is above the deposit level and in such cases banks have two options: borrow from the central bank or borrow in the interbank market.

Management of Interest Rate on Deposits and Loans. The highest interest rate for deposits and the lowest interest rate for loans are set by the central bank with the approval of the State Council. After this approval, the central bank can make further adjustments to interest rates, depending on the country's economic policies and prevailing economic conditions. The interest rate for interbank lending and borrowing is normally determined by reference to the interest rate on temporary loans from the central bank to specialized banks. Specialized banks must follow the interest rate guidelines unless they receive permission to do otherwise.

Supervision and Examination System

The central bank requires detailed and timely reports from banks to enable it to monitor and control the banking system. Normally, the regional branches of PBOC have the authority to monitor and supervise the specialized banks in their respective jurisdictions (as outlined in chapter 2). Relevant information and reports are requested and received by these regional offices for onward dispatch to the head office in Beijing. Additionally, these regional offices have the powers to audit the books of the specialized banks.

THE INDUSTRIAL AND COMMERCIAL BANK OF CHINA (ICBC)

Establishment and Corporate Organization

The Industrial and Commercial Bank of China was established on January 1, 1984, with the approval of the State Council. ICBC emerged from the Management Bureau of Industrial and Commercial Credit, which handled urban industrial and commercial credit, savings, and settlement within the People's Bank of China. After the establishment of the central bank, the mandate of ICBC was to continue this role of handling urban financial business in China. According to the "Statutes of ICBC," its fundamental tasks are:

in line with the state's policies, laws, rules and important financial resolutions, to strengthen the management of loans and funds, to raise vigorously funds from society, to support development of industrial production and enlargement of commodity circulation, to promote technical innovation and progress and to render service to the modernization of China's socialist construction (ICBC, 1984).

The head office is located in Beijing, and overall management responsibility is entrusted to a president under the supervision of a board of directors, whose members are appointed by the State Council. The functions of the Board of Directors are to: (1) determine and evaluate the bank's business policy and plan; (2) review the working report of the president; (3) check and approve the annual final report and arrangement plan for the distribution of profits; (4) appoint or dismiss the bank's senior executives; (5) examine and approve the establishment and dissolution of domestic and overseas branches; and (6) discuss other important matters concerning the bank. The Board of Directors meets annually.

The Board of Directors is assisted by a Board of Supervisors, consisting of one chief supervisor and a number of other supervisors appointed by the State Council. The functions of the Board of Supervisors are to: (1) supervise the bank's execution of the country's policies, laws, and business guidelines; (2) examine the annual final budget report; and (3) investigate serious cases of mismanagement and suggest remedial action. The Board of Supervisors meets annually. The meetings of the Board of Directors and the Board of Supervisors, as well as their joint meetings, should be attended by over two-thirds of the their respective membership. A decision becomes effective only if it receives a majority vote of those attending.

Branches are located in provinces, municipalities, autonomous regions, and specially listed cities. Central sub-branches are located in prefectural regions and cities of each province, sub-branches in counties, and business offices in districts under which there are sub-offices and savings offices, if necessary. In 1984, the number of affiliated institutions, branches, and sub-branches was 19,199, while in 1989, the total was 31,353, an increase of 63 percent. The total staff in 1984 was 366,248, and in 1989, 480,476; an increase of 31 percent. In addition, the bank had about 20,112 savings

Figure 3.1
Organizational Chart for Industrial and Commercial Bank of China (ICBC)

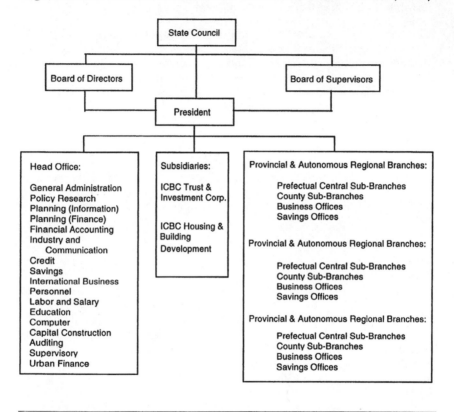

offices, 719,000 agent offices for savings, and 8,200 savings offices jointly established by the bank and business enterprises. Figure 3.1 is an organizational chart for ICBC, whose type of structure is typical for specialized banks.

Business Activities

ICBC engages in and handles the following major kinds of domestic business:

1. Deposits of industrial and commercial enterprises, public undertakings, and individual enterprises;
2. Savings deposits of residents in cities and towns;

3. Loans for working capital, fixed assets, and scientific and technical development to state-owned, collective, or individval enterprises and units for scientific research;

4. Consumer loans to residents in cities and towns;

5. Transfer settlement, cash settlement, commercial paper acceptance, and bill discounting;

6. Entrusting, acting, leasing, investing, advisory business, and so forth;

7. Issue of financial bonds and other securities;

8. Other business entrusted by the central bank and other specialized banks; and

9. Other banking business in line with the policies and laws of the state.

At the end of 1989, the head office and 56 branches were authorized to operate various types of international financial business, including:

1. Deposits in foreign currencies;

2. Loans in foreign currencies;

3. Remittances in foreign currencies;

4. Settlements for trade and nontrade transactions;

5. Exchanges of foreign currencies or bills;

6. Foreign exchange guarantees;

7. Borrowing in foreign currencies;

8. Discounting of foreign currency bills;

9. Issuing, or issuing as agent, securities in foreign currencies;

10. Trading in foreign exchange;

11. Credit advisory and consulting service;

12. On-lending from international financial institutions and foreign governments.

Investments. In 1990, ICBC had total assets of RMB 938.3 billion, an increase of 123 percent from 1986. Revenue was RMB 65.3 billion, up by 173 percent and net income was RMB 13.25 billion, up by 56 percent (Table 3.1). Revenue came exclusively as interest income from the loan portfolio which accounted for over 70 percent of assets over the years. Industrial loans predominate, followed by loans to commercial entities and miscellaneous borrowers. ICBC has become the major source for working capital for China's large and medium-sized industrial and communications enterprises. The bank encourages the development of these enterprises by means of favorable policies such as preferential loans, priority processing of settlement, and as agent in the issue of stocks and bonds. By the end of 1988, ICBC had established credit relationships with more than 100,000 state-owned and collective enterprises, which had a total annual output of

RMB 283.4 billion and shared more than 90 percent of the country's total working capital loans granted to industrial and communications enterprises.

Through its commercial loans, the bank supports commodity circulation and the stabilization of commodity markets and prices. By the end of 1988, commercial loans granted by ICBC had amounted to RMB 2,134.1 billion, with an outstanding value of RMB 497 billion, which reflected an increase of 78 percent over 1984. State-owned enterprises, collective enterprises, and individual commercial enterprises make use of these loans. Loans for technical innovation and scientific and technological exploration facilitate enterprises making use of new techniques and technology, new materials, and new equipment in the production of new products and putting science and technology into the productive forces. The bank supported nearly 40,000 technical innovation projects in more than 40 lines of businesses, and 15,284 scientific and technological projects throughout the country.

The bank takes a serious view of loan management given the importance of these investments. In 1984, ICBC published some important banking regulations and guidelines, including: "ICBC Provisional Measures of Working Capital Management of State-owned Industrial and Commercial Enterprises," "Measures of Loans Granted to Township Individual Economies," "Provisional Regulations of Loans for Exploration, Science, Research, and New Products," "Provisional Measures of Loans for Technical Innovation." In June 1988, ICBC again published a number of regulations and guidelines, including "ICBC Provisional Measures of Loans for Working Capital of State-owned Industrial and Communication Enterprises" and "Provisional Responsibility System of ICBC Working Capital Loans." These declarations have been codified to outline the operational procedures that all credit officers must follow in managing a loan portfolio.

Sources of Funds. At the end of 1990, deposits financed 55.1 percent of assets (Table 3.1), loans from the central bank, 21.6 percent, and other sources, 14.4 percent. Deposits by urban residents and enterprises are important, and the bank has started to improve its service and explore new types of savings instruments. So far, it has offered nearly 20 new types of savings instruments such as bonus bearing certificate, travelers' checks of savings, savings either at fixed time or on demand, and housing savings. Moreover, it has started to transfer payroll moneys for industrial and commercial enterprises as well as government organs and units.

Domestic Trade and Nontrade Settlements. Since ICBC's business offices at various levels have spread throughout the country, the bank provides efficient and timely nationwide services for settlements, cash collection, and payments to industrial and commercial enterprises. At the end of 1988, settlement transactions handled by ICBC involved more than RMB 90,000 billion, covering about 74 percent of the total volume of settlement transactions handled by China's banks. The bank continues to improve settlement procedures by creating new types of settlement operations, including, for example, direct telegraphic transfer of funds, bills of exchange (banker's drafts), travelers' checks, intercity savings deposits and

Table 3.1
Summary Financial Statements for Industrial and Commercial Bank of China (Value in Billions of Renminbi)

	1985	1986	1987	1988	1989	1990	1990 (Indexed to 1986)	Percent Distribution 1986	Percent Distribution 1990
BALANCE SHEET									
Assets									
RMB Loans	296.27	378.64	437.78	496.98	575.19	687.15	181.48%	90.27%	73.23%
Working-capital loans	264.82	335.20	384.65	435.64	507.78	608.74	181.61%	79.91%	64.87%
Fixed-investment loans	31.11	41.88	50.19	57.53	63.69	75.00	179.08%	9.98%	7.99%
Special loans	0.34	1.56	2.94	3.81	3.72	3.41	218.59%	0.37%	0.36%
International business				5.35	13.43	21.75		0.00%	2.32%
Trust & investment business				35.08	32.00	33.60		0.00%	3.58%
Agency business				44.69	51.03	59.03		0.00%	6.29%
Cash	2.38	2.83	2.85	4.01	4.71	5.24	185.16%	0.67%	0.56%
Deposits with the PBC	11.61	13.71	9.82	9.76	17.42	35.77	260.90%	3.27%	3.81%
Reserved requirement	18.48	24.29	36.37	44.19	52.48	66.14	272.29%	5.79%	7.05%
Other assets				27.34	26.27	29.65		0.00%	3.16%
Total assets	328.74	419.47	486.82	667.40	772.53	938.33	223.69%	100.00%	100.00%
Liabilities									
RMB Deposits	193.53	253.72	314.46	356.17	413.11	517.35	203.91%	60.49%	55.14%
Deposits by enterprises	103.97	134.05	158.91	175.43	183.11	223.04	166.39%	31.96%	23.77%
Savings deposits	89.56	119.67	155.55	180.74	230.00	294.31	245.93%	28.53%	31.37%
International business				5.26	13.12	21.20		0.00%	2.26%
Trust & investment business				30.77	52.39	62.13		0.00%	6.62%
Agency business				44.85	52.39	62.13		0.00%	6.62%
Funds borrowed from PBC	94.68	112.69	115.77	140.78	173.65	202.44	179.64%	26.86%	21.57%
Deposits due to other banks	0.35	1.66	2.78	3.59	3.17	3.79		0.00%	0.40%
Financial bonds				3.09	2.46	3.24	195.18%	0.40%	0.35%
Other liabilities	0.00	26.11	24.95	40.17	11.69	10.77	41.25%	6.22%	1.15%
	306.18	394.18	457.96	624.68	721.98	883.05	224.02%	93.97%	94.11%
Capital	22.56	25.30	28.86	32.15	35.34	42.07	166.28%	6.03%	4.48%
Credit funds	18.45	18.45	18.45	18.45	18.45	18.45	100.00%	4.40%	1.97%
Retained earnings	4.11	6.85	10.41	13.70	16.89	23.62	344.82%	1.63%	2.52%
Total Liabilities and Capital	328.74	419.47	486.82	667.40	772.54	938.37	223.70%	100.00%	100.00%
PROFIT AND LOSS									
Total revenues	18.80	23.90	30.40	38.50	62.20	65.30	273.22%	100.00%	100.00%
Interest revenue	18.20	23.40	29.60	37.40	60.40	63.50	271.37%	97.91%	97.24%
Net profit	7.11	8.45	10.87	10.57	15.24	13.25	156.80%	35.36%	20.29%

Source: China Finance and Banking Association (1991).

withdrawals within ten large cities.   Moreover, ICBC offers checking privileges and in 1989, the Peony Credit Card was issued.

International Business. By the end of 1988, ICBC had absorbed foreign exchange deposits valuing U.S. $643 million, granted foreign exchange loans amounting to U.S. $438 million, handled more than 60,000 international settlement transactions, and borrowed funds from abroad totaling U.S. $30 million. Additionally, the bank established correspondent relationships with more than 500 offices of 110 overseas banks in over 30 countries and regions, as well as account relationships with 15 overseas banks involving 13 types of convertible currencies. Since its establishment, the bank has sent more than 60 groups of representatives to observe banking operations outside China.

BANK OF CHINA (BOC)

Establishment and Corporate Organization

The Bank of China was first established in February 1912 and was operated jointly by the Chinese government and merchants from a head office in Shanghai. Its predecessor was the Bank of Great Qing, a government bank of the Qing dynasty, which was overthrown in October 1911. The bank operated as a state bank until 1928, when the Kuomintang government authorized the Bank of China to specialize in international banking activities. In May 1949, when Shanghai was liberated, the People's Government took over the bank, confiscated its assets, and restructured the management team. In November 1949, the head office was moved to Beijing, and in October 1953, the Government Administrative Council designated the Bank of China as a specialized bank to deal with foreign exchange under the leadership of the People's Bank of China. In 1979, the State Council took the bank under its leadership and confirmed its role as a foreign exchange and foreign trade bank.

The bank is managed by a president who is supervised by a Board of Directors consisting of one honorary chairman, one chairman, and a number of vice-chairmen, managing directors, and directors, all appointed by the State Council. There is also a Board of Supervisors, as is the case for ICBC. The functions for the Board of Directors and the Board of Supervisors are similar to those described previously for ICBC.

Bank of China establishes branches in China and abroad. By the end of 1989, the bank's domestic network totaled 3,613 branches, located mainly in the country's large or medium-sized cities, major ports, special economic zones (SEZs), and overseas Chinese settlements, and the domestic staff totaled about 62,000. In addition, Bank of China has branches in London, New York, Hong Kong, and other overseas centers. Together with the Bank of China Group in Hong Kong and Macao and its wholly owned subsidiaries, the number of overseas offices reached 442, with a staff of 13,577 by the end of 1989.

Business Activities

The overall task of BOC is to accumulate, control, and utilize foreign exchange; to deal with all types of foreign exchange business; to take part in international financial activities; and to serve China's modernization construction. In line with these tasks, Bank of China is authorized or entrusted to handle the following businesses:

1. Foreign trade and nontrade settlements;

2. International interbank deposits and loans;

3. Overseas Chinese and other international remittances;

4. Foreign currency deposits and loans, as well as domestic currency deposits and loans in regard to foreign exchange business, as approved by PBOC;

5. Foreign exchange transactions;

6. International gold transactions;

7. Syndicated loans;

8. Investment in Hong Kong, Macao, and foreign countries or jointly running banks, financial companies, or other enterprises;

9. Issuing foreign currency bonds and other securities authorized by the state;

10. Trust business and consultancy; and

11. Other banking services approved or entrusted by the state.

Investments. In 1990, total assets reached RMB 859 billion, an increase of 149 percent over 1986; revenue was RMB 49 billion, an increase of 237 percent; and net profit was RMB 6.7 billion, an increase of 116 percent (Table 3.2). Loans accounted for about 39 percent of total assets and were mostly in the form of foreign currency loans. The bank is actively involved in the international financial markets to raise funds for key projects in China and has made use of instruments such as bilateral bank loans, government mixed loans, import credits, international syndicated loans, Japanese yen and deutsche mark bond issues, and Japanese energy loans. Any of these funds are for on-lending to domestic projects such as the Daya Bay Nuclear Power Station in Guangdong Province (HK $1.6 billion) and the expansion of the Yangtze and Qilu ethylene project (U.S. $200 million). By the end of 1988, the total amount of foreign exchange loans approved by the bank had reached U.S. $9.783 billion, with U.S. $5.69 billion drawn down, U.S. $2.370 billion repaid, and U.S. $3.320 billion outstanding.

In implementing the economic strategy for the coastal areas, the bank supports new enterprises with foreign investment. In 1988, the total foreign exchange loans to about 3,000 such enterprises reached U.S. $59 million. In addition, the number of foreign investment enterprises involved in business relationships with the bank exceeded 10,000. By the end of 1988, the outstanding foreign exchange and RMB loans granted to foreign investment enterprises had amounted to U.S. $2.246 billion and RMB 6.531 billion,

Table 3.2
Summary Financial Statements for the Bank of China (Value in Billions of Renminbi)

	1985	1986	1987	1988	1989	1990	1990 (Indexed to 1986)	Percent Distribution 1986	1990
BALANCE SHEET									
Assets									
Loans and overdrafts	94.70	133.60	162.80	183.70	247.50	332.50	248.88%	38.72%	38.70%
LCs and guarantees	60.50	85.00	95.60	103.00	132.80	127.20	149.65%	24.64%	14.81%
Due from banks	49.00	57.20	91.30	118.00	150.00	210.60	368.18%	16.58%	24.51%
Securities and investments	16.30	19.70	23.80	29.30	27.40	43.50	220.81%	5.71%	5.06%
Forward contract receivables	13.30	12.20	17.20	21.60	39.60	47.00	385.25%	3.54%	5.47%
Receivalbes for customers	14.90	20.90	30.80	80.70	43.70	53.50	255.98%	6.06%	6.23%
Trust assets	3.60	8.40	12.40	11.80	13.20	16.70	198.81%	2.43%	1.94%
Other assets	8.20	8.00	8.10	11.60	23.10	28.10	351.25%	2.32%	3.27%
Total assets	260.50	345.00	442.00	559.70	677.30	859.10	249.01%	100.00%	100.00%
Liabilities									
Deposits	116.20	151.50	196.00	214.40	276.30	390.50	257.76%	43.91%	45.45%
Due to banks	35.00	39.00	51.30	72.30	102.10	140.20	359.49%	11.30%	16.32%
Payable under forward contracts	15.70	12.00	17.80	22.20	37.00	51.10	425.83%	3.48%	5.95%
Collections for customers	14.90	20.00	30.80	80.70	43.70	53.50	267.50%	5.80%	6.23%
LCs and guarantees	60.70	85.00	95.60	103.00	132.80	127.20	149.65%	24.64%	14.81%
Trust liabilities	3.50	8.40	12.40	11.80	13.20	16.70	198.81%	2.43%	1.94%
Bonds	0.00	4.80	7.90	9.50	11.70	13.60	283.33%	1.39%	1.58%
Other liabilities	5.20	8.70	13.20	21.10	24.30	23.50	270.11%	2.52%	2.74%
	251.20	329.40	425.00	535.00	641.10	816.30	247.81%	95.48%	95.02%
Capital	3.00	5.00	5.00	10.00	10.00	15.00	300.00%	1.45%	1.75%
Surplus and reserves	4.50	6.70	8.10	10.00	16.10	21.60	322.39%	1.94%	2.51%
Net profit	1.80	3.10	3.90	4.30	5.20	6.20	200.00%	0.90%	0.72%
Total liabilities and capital	260.50	345.00	442.00	559.70	677.30	859.10	249.01%	100.00%	100.00%
PROFIT AND LOSS									
Revenue	13.66	14.69	18.32	24.58	41.67	49.55	337.30%	100.00%	100.00%
Net profit	1.84	3.10	3.90	4.30	5.70	6.70	216.13%	21.10%	13.52%

Source: China Finance and Banking Association (1991).

respectively. The bank emphasizes export-oriented projects that are potentially viable as earners of foreign exchange.

The bank has over 24 percent of its assets in cash and advances to other banks (Table 3.2). Traditionally, the bank monopolized the foreign exchange business in China and other Chinese banks looked to it for foreign exchange. However, this privileged position is being eroded as other banks are accorded similar status. Moreover, the bank has account relationships worldwide with financial claims against foreign banks. In order to enhance the management and efficiency of international settlements and ensure the timely and accurate collection of the state's foreign exchange, the bank has computerized its system for international settlements. In May 1985, the bank formally joined the telecommunications network of the Worldwide Banking and Finance Telecommunication Institute. By the end of 1988, the bank had installed telecomputers in hundreds of branch offices across the country to facilitate the quick transfer of deposits and withdrawals among banks. Finally, the bank facilitates foreign trade, and about 15 percent of its assets are classified as line of credit guarantees (Table 3.2).

Sources of Funds. RMB and foreign currency deposits provide about 45 percent of funds, and loans from other banks, 16 percent (Table 3.2). In addition, about 27 percent of funding is trade related: forward contracts, 6 percent; payable to customers, 6 percent; and letter of credit guarantees, 15 percent (Table 3.2). Bank of China has taken a series of measures to enhance its deposit base, including opening branches in strategic locations, issuing new types of savings instruments, offering attractive interest rates on deposits (especially foreign currency deposits), and improving the quality of service. In 1981, the bank began to handle foreign credit cards as an agent, and by the end of 1988, more than 2,000 commercial units in China had accepted credit cards, including MasterCard, Visa, American Express, Dalai, JCB, and Fada. In 1986, the bank began to issue the Great Wall Credit Card, and by the end of 1988, more than 60,000 RMB and foreign currency credit cards had been issued. These credit cards, including Great Wall MasterCard, are widely accepted in about 170 countries and regions around the world.

Management of Foreign Exchange Loans

As stated, the bank plays a key role in raising foreign exchange for on-lending in China to finance imports, with some special lending procedures for foreign loans.

Permitted Activities. Bank of China extends foreign exchange loans to support export-oriented production and imports for key economic construction projects. It grants short-term foreign exchange loans to those enterprises that are deemed as creditworthy and whose products may, directly or indirectly, earn foreign exchange for China. Applications may be made for loans to support the following: (a) importing advanced technology, equipment, and materials to expand export capability, raise product quality, diversify products, and improve packaging and decoration;

(b) importing raw materials to assist in product processing; (c) developing communications and transportation, tourism, and overseas contract projects; (d) supporting external export processing and assembling as well as compensation trade; and (e) supporting short-term working capital needs for items that can, directly or indirectly, earn foreign exchange.

Supporting Documentation. Applications for foreign exchange loans must be accompanied with supporting documentation such as import documents, project approvals from the appropriate authorities, and plans for loan repayment. In cases where enterprises expect to repay loans from export earnings, they should present sales and reimbursement contracts or agreements with the foreign firms or institutions. The borrower is required to maintain an account with the bank, and the use of funds is monitored. Many of the procedures are geared to limit the "leakage" of foreign exchange from China.

Lending Limits. Lending or credit limits are set by the head office of the bank. Usually, the administration of loans to ministries of the State Council is handled by the head office, while other loans are handled by branches throughout the country.

Term and Interest Rates. The term of the loan begins from the drawdown date and ends when all the interest and principal are paid. Loans for importing raw materials to process goods for export usually have maturities of about one year, while loans for importing equipment cannot exceed three years. Most other loans are not longer than three years, and loans for seller's credit are not longer than five years. Interest rates on foreign exchange loans are calculated as the cost of raising funds in the international markets plus a premium for the bank's management fees.

Reimbursement. The borrower should repay the loan and pay interest on schedule, in line with the borrowing contract. However, if the borrower cannot make repayment at maturity, the guarantor is responsible to repay the loan. Normally, the guarantor is a government department or ministry. If necessary, BOC or the PBOC can retain foreign exchange from the accounts of the borrower and its guarantor to settle the debt. Borrowers who earn foreign exchange repay their loans with such proceeds, while those who do not earn foreign exchange directly repay the loan with renminbi, subject to prior approval by the bank.

Loans for Foreign Funded Enterprises. In line with the country's policies, BOC grants loans for construction projects and production operations of Sino-foreign joint ventures, cooperative ventures and foreign-owned enterprises employing high economic efficiency and advanced technology. Loans granted to foreign-funded enterprises include fixed-assets loans, buyer's credit, consortium loans, project loans, and working-capital loans. Loans are usually collateralized by security devices including foreign currencies, real estate, machinery and equipment, inventories, and foreign exchange securities and bills. The bank is entitled to monitor the use of loans by enterprises and to request progress reports on their projects. Breaches in the borrowing contract are not taken lightly by BOC, and several remedial and drastic measures may be taken including an order that the borrower correct its default, a decision to stop further loans, a request for repayment before maturity, a request that the guarantor repay the loan, or a decision to sell the collateral.

Bank of China Group in Hong Kong and Macao

The Bank of China Group in Hong Kong and Macao is an important component of BOC as well as the mainstay of financial institutions with China's capital in Hong Kong. It is composed of 13 banks in Hong Kong and one bank in Macao. The group is led by the Hong Kong–Macao division of Bank of China, which has overall management control over the banks. However, all banks in the Group are independent enterprises and are responsible for their profits or losses. At the third session of its Managing Directors Meeting, held by the Fifth Convention of the Board of Directors on March 22, 1989, it was resolved, with the approval of the central bank, that a portion of the paid-up capital of seven banks (Sin Hua Trust, Savings & Commercial Bank Ltd.; Kincheng Banking Corporation; China & South Sea Bank Ltd.; China State Bank Ltd.; National Commercial Bank Ltd.; Yien Yieh Commercial Bank Ltd.; and Kwangtung Provincial Bank) should be allocated to the Bank of China. This decision effectively made six of the banks subsidiaries of BOC.

THE PEOPLE'S CONSTRUCTION BANK OF CHINA (PCBC)

Establishment and Corporate Organization

The People's Construction Bank of China (PCBC) was established during China's first Five-Year-Plan (1953–57). Shortly after the foundation of the People's Republic of China in 1949, there was a need to restructure the economy and to efficiently utilize scarce funds for capital investment. In February, 1951, the People's Bank of China authorized the Bank of Communications to manage the budget appropriations for capital construction. However, as the first Five-Year-Plan was being implemented, the volume of capital construction expanded and the Bank of Communications proved unable to handle the managerial work load. Thus on September 9, 1954, the Government Administrative Council decided to establish PCBC within the Ministry of Finance to handle budget appropriations for capital construction. The assigned tasks were to supervise the distribution of funds to designated projects, grant working-capital loans to units in charge of construction, and deal with the settlement business for capital construction activities. On October 1, 1954, PCBC was officially established, and the bank quickly became a center for appropriations, loans and settlements for the country's capital construction.

During the Great Leap, which started in 1958, PCBC was turned into the Capital Construction Financial Division of the Finance Ministry, and almost all its branches throughout the country were closed. This action resulted in serious disruptions in capital construction activities. Several attempts were made to revive the bank but it was not until 1972 that a successful revival was achieved. On August 28, 1979, the State Council took PCBC under its ownership, with management responsibilities assigned to the State Construction Committee and the Finance Ministry on behalf of the State Council. On April 20, 1983, PCBC was approved by the State Council to carry out significant systematic reforms and assist in the country's economic development. The bank has independence of operation; it is under the leadership of the Ministry of Finance with regard to its fiscal business and is subject to the central bank for its credit policies.

The head office of PCBC is located in Beijing and is under the management of a president. The bank has branches in all provinces, autonomous regions, municipalities, and specially listed cities, and has central sub-branches in regional and urban areas, and sub-branches or offices in the counties. It also has specialized branches or sub-branches at locations of key projects. By the end of 1989, the bank had 17,352 subsidiary offices across the country, with a staff of 195,804.

Business Activities

PCBC is a specialized bank with both fiscal and banking functions. In its role as a fiscal agent, the bank has handled most of the budget allocations for capital construction since the founding of the PRC. Before 1979, government investment was made in the form of budget appropriations through the national credit plan. After 1979, the State Council transformed budget appropriations into loans and in 1988, the state decided to set up a capital construction fund and to transfer government investment into fund management under PCBC.

As a fiscal agent, the main duties of the bank include:

1. Management of the capital construction fund, including the distribution of funds, supervision of projects implemented, settlements, and auditing;

2. Management of financial accounts for capital construction, including the examination and approval of annual financial plans and budget reports, the supervision of financial affairs, the control of financial outputs, and the drafting of financial management regulations for the state, local administrative departments, state-owned specialized investment companies, and construction units;

3. Management of financial accounts of construction and installation enterprises, which involves the examination and approval of annual financial plans and reports of the enterprises, the checking of contract plans, the supervision of financial affairs, and the drafting of financial management regulations;

4. Management of budgetary estimates, budgets, and settlements of construction projects, including examining the budgetary estimates of construction enterprises, project budgets, and settlements of project accounts; and

Table 3.3
Summary Financial Statements for PCBC (Value in Billions of Renminbi)

	1985	1986	1987	1988	1989	1990	1990 (Indexed to 1986)	Percent Distribution 1986	Percent Distribution 1990
BALANCE SHEET									
Assets									
Loans	132.20	187.70	241.60	294.70	343.10	413.80	220.46%	81.72%	79.92%
Gov't. Investment	62.20	86.80	109.10	119.30	128.00	139.90	161.18%	37.79%	27.02%
Entrusted	14.80	23.50	33.20	54.10	65.20	81.10	345.11%	10.23%	15.66%
Others	55.20	77.40	99.30	121.30	149.90	192.80	249.10%	33.70%	37.23%
Deposits with PBC	31.60	34.30	23.10	20.90	29.40	45.20	131.78%	14.93%	8.73%
Other assets	5.00	7.70	13.10	23.80	35.00	58.80	763.64%	3.35%	11.36%
Total Assets	168.80	229.70	277.80	339.40	407.50	517.80	225.42%	100.00%	100.00%
Liabilities									
Deposits	57.60	69.50	82.30	96.70	115.20	158.00	227.34%	30.26%	30.51%
Gov't. investment funds	64.00	85.80	105.50	114.30	128.20	140.00	163.17%	37.35%	27.04%
Entrusted funds	16.70	24.40	34.70	55.40	67.40	83.80	343.44%	10.62%	16.18%
Due to other banks		0.80	4.50	9.20	13.70	22.30	2787.50%	0.35%	4.31%
Due to PBC	5.80	13.00	6.00	10.50	25.30	44.00	338.46%	5.66%	8.50%
Other liabilities	6.30	15.20	18.10	25.20	27.80	37.30	245.39%	6.62%	7.20%
Total Liabilities	150.40	208.70	251.10	311.30	377.60	485.40	232.58%	90.86%	93.74%
Capital funds	17.10	19.70	24.90	26.30	27.90	30.20	153.30%	8.58%	5.83%
Provision for bad debts				0.20	0.20	0.20		0.00%	0.04%
Retained earnings	1.30	1.30	1.60	1.60	1.80	2.00	153.85%	0.57%	0.39%
Total liabilities and capital	168.80	229.70	277.80	339.40	407.50	517.80	225.42%	100.00%	100.00%
PROFIT AND LOSS									
Revenue	3.90	5.30	7.00	9.90	15.70	17.90	337.74%	100.00%	100.00%
Net profit	1.30	1.30	1.60	1.60	1.80	2.00	153.85%	24.53%	11.17%

Source: China Finance and Banking Association (1991).

5. Management of the financial accounts of geological-prospecting activities, including the payment budget and supervision of the state-appropriated fund for these activities.

The banking function developed slowly in the early 1980s and was prompted by at least two causes. First, budget allocations were declining relative to the demand for capital construction, meaning that more funds were needed and alternative sources of financing had to be exploited. Second, the bank was placed in the credit business after appropriations were changed to loans and banking expertise became desirable. As a specialized bank, PCBC's scope of business is similar to that of ICBC or BOC within their respective administrative regions.

Investments. The total assets of the bank were RMB 518 billion in 1990, reflecting an increase of 125 percent over 1986. Revenue was RMB 17.9 billion, reflecting an increase of 137 percent, and net profit was RMB 2 billion, reflecting an increase of 53 percent (Table 3.3). During the first 24 years of its existence, the bank focused almost exclusively on government-sponsored projects. For example, in 1954, the bank's total assets were RMB 11.8 billion, with government investment accounting for 93.7 percent, while in 1978, with total assets of RMB 59 billion, government investment accounted for 72.94 percent. In its banking role, and apart from government investments (which it handles as a fiscal agent), the bank makes loans to various sectors of industry (Table 3.3). Loans fall into various categories including fixed-asset loans, working-capital loans, equipment and reserve loans, trust and entrusted loans, and foreign exchange loans. By the end of 1990, the outstanding loans amounted to nearly RMB 270 billion, with more than 200,000 customers.

International Financial Business. The bank's international financial business commenced in 1986 at three branches located in the special economic zones in Shengzhen, Xiamen, and Zhuhai. Since then it has expanded to involve 42 branches employing more than 1,700 employees. The bank's international financial business falls into three categories: raising funds abroad, foreign exchange loans and international banking services, including foreign currency deposits, foreign currency loans, and foreign currency remittances. By the end of 1989, the outstanding foreign currency deposits totaled U.S. $560 million, an 80.6 percent increase (of U.S. $250 million) over 1988, and the foreign currency loans amounted to U.S. $770 million, 108.1 percent increase (of U.S. $400 million) over the same year. The volume of international settlement transactions, such as letters of credit, collections, and remittances was also several times over the levels for 1988.

PCBC has actively developed international linkages by setting up correspondent relationships with over 100 foreign banks and signing business cooperation agreements with over 30 banks in more than ten countries and regions. In 1989, PCBC became a formal member of the International Master Card Group. In the same year, the bank cooperated with Nomura Securities Co. and other institutions in establishing China's largest joint-venture leasing company (Union International Leasing Company Ltd.) and also purchased the shares of China North International Leasing Company Ltd., another joint venture in China, to become one of that company's largest shareholders.

Sources of Funds. Loans to government-approved projects are financed mainly from budget allocations, which was the main source of funding unto 1979. For example, in 1979, budget allocations accounted for 90 percent of the bank's funding. Thereafter, as the bank assumed a commercial banking role, deposits became increasingly important and, by 1990, deposits accounted for about 30 percent of total assets. Enterprise deposits account for about two-thirds of total deposits and, by the end of 1990, more than 360,000 enterprises and public organizations had accounts with the bank. Deposits by residents have been on the increase since 1986, and the number of savings accounts has increased from 66,300 in that year to over 2,600,000 by the end of 1990. The major types of savings accounts are demand and term deposits, progressive interest deposits, bonus savings, agent business savings, special-item savings, across-bank remittance deposits, individual units settlement savings, and similar instruments.

In an effort to increase its deposits, the bank started to handle trust deposits in 1980, and by September 1989, PCBC had set up 186 trust and investment companies across the country with RMB 2.677 billion in capital, taking in deposits valuing RMB 10.328 billion. In addition, since 1985, the bank has issued bonds and, by the end of 1989, the outstanding amount of bonds was more than RMB 17 billion.

AGRICULTURAL BANK OF CHINA (ABC)

Establishment and Corporate Organization

Agricultural Bank of China (ABC) was first established in March 1955 but was closed after 21 months and merged with the operations of the People's Bank of China. In November 1963, ABC was revived, caused to operate independently of PBOC for 22 months, but then, in 1964, the bank was again merged with PBOC and discontinued business. In December 1978, the Third Plenary Session of the 11th Central Party Committee approved a draft decision to hasten agricultural development, and it was felt that a special bank should be responsible to finance related projects. This event led to the reestablishment of ABC when the State Council issued the "Notice to Restructure ABC" in February 1979. ABC was owned by the State Council but was administered by PBOC on behalf of the State Council. In September 1983, when PBOC commenced its role as a central bank, ABC became an independent economic unit.

The head office of ABC is located in Beijing, and branches are located in all provinces, autonomous regions, and municipalities, and are directly controlled by the central government. Furthermore, the bank has prefectural and municipal branches as well as subcentral branches in provincial cities and regions using representative offices, banking offices, and savings offices. By the end of 1989, the bank had 53,611 branches and associated offices with 453,622 staff members.

Business Activities

The main business activities of ABC are:

1. Handling deposits from rural government institutions, groups, army units, enterprises, cooperative organizations, collective and private industrial and commercial house-holds, and individual savings;

2. Providing loans to state-owned agricultural, industrial, and commercial enterprises, township enterprises, collective organizations, supply-and-marketing cooperatives, farm households, and private industrial and commercial households;

3. Handling deposits and loans of the rural credit cooperatives;

4. Handling transfer and cash setttlements and bill discounting;

5. Providing services of trust, agency, lease, and consultation;

6. Handling foreign exchange transactions similar to those of ICBC;

7. Issuing financial bonds and trading in securities; and

Table 3.4

Summary Financial Statements for ABC (Value in Billions of Renminbi)

	1985	1986	1987	1988	1989	1990	1990 (Indexed to 1986)	Percent Distribution 1986	Percent Distribution 1990
BALANCE SHEET									
Assets									
Total Loans	168.77	199.60	231.90	263.20	305.80	377.40	189.08%	84.25%	79.69%
Working-capital	140.53	162.90	187.20	213.10	248.30	307.10	188.52%	68.76%	64.84%
Agriculture	22.17	28.00	33.90	39.70	46.40	56.30			
Fixed assets	2.20	3.80	5.80	5.80	6.60	7.60	200.00%	1.60%	1.60%
Others	3.87	4.90	5.00	4.50	4.50	6.40	130.61%	2.07%	1.35%
Required Reserves	7.77	10.90	16.10	20.20	25.90	34.00	311.93%	4.60%	7.18%
Deposits with PBC	16.51	17.70	14.10	13.30	25.00	38.80	219.21%	7.47%	8.19%
Due from Banks	1.31	4.00	7.20	12.70	10.50	16.80	420.00%	1.69%	3.55%
Cash	4.74	4.70	4.30	4.90	6.00	6.60	140.43%	1.98%	1.39%
Total assets	199.10	236.90	273.60	314.30	373.20	473.60	199.92%	100.00%	100.00%
Liabilities									
Total Deposits	91.20	121.20	148.70	171.40	205.50	264.00	217.82%	51.16%	55.74%
Enterprises	20.20	26.30	30.50	35.10		43.50	165.40%	11.10%	9.18%
Agricultural sector	47.50	58.80	65.70	67.20	72.20	85.70	145.75%	24.82%	18.10%
Savings	15.50	25.80	42.60	59.40	84.80	121.20	469.77%	10.89%	25.59%
Others	8.00	10.30	9.90	9.70	11.60	13.60			
Borrowing from PBC	75.20	77.50	83.40	99.40	118.30	143.90	185.68%	32.71%	30.38%
Due to Banks	1.90	1.50	5.50	8.80	16.00	27.60			
Others	9.40	13.10	11.20	8.80	6.60	10.10	77.10%	5.53%	2.13%
Total liabilities	177.70	213.30	248.80	288.40	346.40	445.60	208.91%	90.04%	94.09%
Capital								0.00%	0.00%
Credit funds	20.40	22.50	23.40	24.50	25.70	26.80	119.11%	9.50%	5.66%
Net Profit	1.00	1.10	1.40	1.50	1.20	1.20	109.09%	0.46%	0.25%
Total liabilities and equity	199.10	236.90	273.60	314.30	373.20	473.60	199.92%	100.00%	100.00%
PROFIT AND LOSS									
Revenue	19.00	22.50	33.40	50.10	76.30	74.90	332.89%	100.00%	100.00%
Net profit	1.00	1.10	1.40	1.50	1.20	1.20	109.09%	4.89%	1.60%

Source: China Finance and Banking Association (1991).

8. Handling any business stipulated by the state or entrusted to it by PBOC or other financial institutions.

Investments. In 1990, total assets of the bank reached RMB 473.6 billion, an increase of 99 percent over 1986; revenue was RMB 74.9 billion, an increase of 233 percent; and net profit was RMB 1.2 billion, an increase of 9 percent (Table 3.4). About 80 percent of the bank's assets are in loans, mainly to support commodity production and expand commodity circulation. Traditionally, the bank supported the agricultural sector, but recently, loans have been granted to other primary industries (such as forestry and fisheries), communications, commerce, and service trades. In the past, the bank targeted the collective enterprises in the communes but now focuses as well on the millions of farm households. Loans are available for rural state-owned industry, for rural commerce (including loans for grain production, supplying and selling cooperatives, buying sideline agricultural products, commodity circulation, collectives, or individuals), technical innovation, state-owned and collective agriculture, exploration, farm households, and credit cooperatives. By the end of 1989, the total outstanding value of loans granted by the bank reached RMB 305.8 billion. Rural commercial loans accounted for 61 percent of total loans in 1989.

Loans were made to promote the production and sale of such important products as chemical fertilizers, pesticides, and plastic films. In addition, the bank supported 550 projects in the "Spark Program," which applied the results from scientific and technological research to production processes in township industries.

One of the primary responsibility of the bank is to manage the working capital of state-owned agricultural enterprises. This duty involves the following: (a) prepare a working-capital agreement with an enterprise; (b) hold state-appropriated funds in safe custody; (c) examine the working-capital plan and final report, as submitted by a state-owned agricultural enterprise; (d) advance loans when needed; (e) supervise the application of working capital by the enterprise; and (f) recover the loan, as per agreement. The bank provides loans for working capital on the principle of "different treatment and support of the better" and "lending on the basis of sale," and in line with the country's policies and credit plan. Rural industrial loans are usually made for working capital and the acquisition of fixed assets, borrowers are evaluated in terms of their ability to repay, and terms are set based on these evaluations.

Sources of Funds. ABC obtains funds mainly from deposits, loans from the central bank and the interbank market, and the agricultural credit fund of the state. In 1990, deposits accounted for 55 percent of investments in assets (Table 3.4). ABC places high priority on deposits from enterprises and rural residents, and the bank has expanded its savings network, launched savings advertisements, and trained personnel in expanding its customer base. The bank has introduced new savings instruments, including index-linked savings, bonus-bearing certificate, and savings for housing. In addition, it has special savings accounts for consumer durables and pensions. By the end of 1990, all deposits totaled RMB 264 billion, with enterprises accounting for about 40 percent; individuals, 35 percent, and rural credit cooperatives, 25 percent. In addition to deposits, the bank borrows heavily from the central bank. For example, in 1990, the outstanding balance with the central bank was RMB 144 billion (Table 3.4).

International Business. In the autumn of 1981, ABC began to exchange information on China's agricultural resources and investment with the World Bank and the International Agricultural Development Fund. Subsequently, in November 1981, the World Bank sent a delegation to Beijing to investigate the bank's operations. In 1982, the bank was authorized by the state to act as an intermediary with international financial organizations dealing with rural credit, and by the end of 1988, 26 branches of ABC had started international financial businesses. The year-end outstanding value of deposits in foreign exchange was U.S. $190 million and in foreign exchange loans, U.S. $180 million. In December 1988, the Foreign Exchange Clearance Operation Center and International Operation Department were set up at the head office. By the end of the same year, ABC had established cooperative relationships with the World Bank, the Asian

Development Bank, and 62 foreign banks, and had raised foreign capital amounting to U.S. $405 million. These funds assisted more than ten provinces and regions in China to explore and exploit rural natural resources; develop plantation, breeding, agricultural, and sideline products, and make up for the shortage of long-term credit funds for agriculture.

By the end of 1989, branches dealing with international business had increased to 48 and the outstanding value of foreign exchange deposits and loans had doubled since the previous year. In addition to loans from international financial institutions and foreign governments, ABC raised commercial loans of U.S. $41 million in the international financial market. In 1989, ABC established correspondent relationships with an additional 42 foreign banks and began to use 11 major currencies in financial centers such as Hong Kong, Tokyo, New York, Frankfort, Sydney, and San Francisco.

Contract Responsibility System

ABC was the first bank to experiment with the contract responsibility system, under which the bank must deliver to the state a fixed (or base) profit in each given year. If there is a loss, the bank is still obliged to deliver the base profit. Any excess profit (above the base) is split; one-tenth goes to the state, and the balance is kept for the bank. Since adopting the system in 1988, the bank has met the contract terms.

CHINA INVESTMENT BANK (CIB)

Establishment and Corporate Organization

China regained its legal position in the World Bank in 1980 and subsequently decided to establish a financial institution to manage World Bank loans and loans from other international lending agencies that were expected for industrial projects in China. On December 23, 1981, with approval of the State Council, CIB was officially established as the financial intermediary that would perform this task. The bank is headquartered in Beijing and is managed by a president under the supervision of a Board of Directors. By the end of 1988, CIB had set up nearly 60 branches in major cities across China and had a staff of 1,338.

Business Activities

The main business activities include:

1. Raising medium- to long-term funds in foreign exchange abroad;
2. Granting foreign exchange and RMB loans and providing capital to small- and medium-sized Chinese enterprises for capital construction or technological renovations;

Table 3.5
Summary Financial Statements for China Investment Bank
(Value in Billions of Renminbi)

	1985	1986	1987	1988	1989	1990	1990 (Indexed to 1986)	Percent Distribution 1986	1990
BALANCE SHEET									
Assets									
Cash and due from banks	0.401	0.779	0.741	1.135	0.936	1.802	231.32%	30.30%	13.23%
Loans and investment	0.709	1.715	2.800	4.467	7.657	9.124	532.01%	66.71%	66.97%
Other assets	0.148	0.077	0.289	1.102	1.416	2.698	3503.90%	2.99%	19.80%
Total Assets	1.258	2.571	3.830	6.704	10.009	13.624	529.91%	100.00%	100.00%
Liabilities									
Deposits	0.014	0.020	0.066	0.854	1.359	1.866	9330.00%	0.78%	13.70%
Borrowing	0.635	1.319	1.869	3.116	4.917	7.101	538.36%	51.30%	52.12%
Other liabilities	0.178	0.226	0.534	1.221	2.019	2.727	1206.64%	8.79%	20.02%
	0.827	1.565	2.469	5.191	8.295	11.694	747.22%	60.87%	85.83%
Net worth	0.431	1.006	1.361	1.513	1.714	1.930	191.85%	39.13%	14.17%
Total liabilities and capital	1.258	2.571	3.830	6.704	10.009	13.624	529.91%	100.00%	100.00%
PROFIT AND LOSS									
Revenue	0.430	1.380	2.250	3.970	6.300	8.560	620.29%	100.00%	100.00%
Net profit	0.180	0.590	0.940	1.500	1.600	1.190	201.69%	42.75%	13.90%

Source: China Finance and Banking Association (1991).

3. Providing consultancy and advisory service to borrowers;

4. Issuing securities abroad; and

5. Handling other foreign exchange business, as approved by the central bank.

In 1990, total assets were RMB 13.624 billion, an increase of 429 percent over 1986; revenue was RMB 0.856 billion, an increase of 520 percent; and net profit was RMB 0.119 billion, an increase of 101 percent (Table 3.5).

Up to 1989, the bank actively negotiated with the World Bank on four occasions and raised U.S. $945.6 million in hard and soft loans. Other loans were secured from the Asian Development Bank (U.S. $100 million in 1987) and from banks in the international financial markets. In addition to these foreign currency funds, the Ministry of Finance supplies the bank with RMB capital. By the end of 1990, the bank had approved over 1,200 projects for funding valued at RMB 9.1 billion (Table 3.5). Priority is given to export-oriented projects or projects that will save foreign exchange, and in 1989, the composition of loans was: 30.23 percent for the textile industry; 23.99 percent for light industry; 4.02 percent for the metallurgical industry; 4.42 percent for service; 8.59 percent for the machinery industry; 9.19 percent for the electronics industry; 9.23 percent for the oil and chemical industry; and 10.33 percent for others. Borrowers use foreign exchange to import advanced technology and equipment, carry out equipment renovation and technical innovation, expand production capability, improve production techniques, and raise economic efficiency.

Other Services. By the end of 1989, the bank had been authorized to handle foreign exchange business, as previously discussed for the other specialized banks. The bank had correspondent relationships with more than 100 foreign banks by the end of 1989, and 16 branches were involved in international settlements. Some branches have started to handle deposit business both in RMB and in foreign exchange and to trade in the financial markets.

Sources of Funding. The foreign currency loans, referred to earlier, provide about 50 percent of the bank's financing. Deposits and miscellaneous liabilities provide about 33 percent, and capital from the Ministry of Finance provides the balance (Table 3.5). The extent to which the bank can continue to attract foreign currency loans will influence its future growth.

HOUSING SAVINGS BANKS

China has established two regional specialized banks to commercialize its stock of housing: Yantai Housing and Savings Bank and Bengbu Housing and Savings Bank. In typical Chinese style, this banking strategy is another experiment in the reform of the banking system.

Yantai Housing and Savings Bank

Yantai Housing was established on October 29, 1987, with the approval of the central bank and opened for business on December 1, 1987. The shares are owned by the local government of Yantai, the specialized banks, and People's Insurance Company of China (PICC). The head office in Yantai is managed by a President under the supervision of the Board of Directors, and the bank had a staff of 134 at the end of 1988. Total assets at the end of 1988 were RMB 145.3 million.

Bengbu Housing and Savings Bank

Bengbu Housing and Savings Bank was established on December 8, 1987, with the approval of the central bank. The shares are owned by the local government of Bengbu City, the specialized banks, and the PICC. The head office is in Bengbu City under the direction of a President who is supervised by a Board of Directors. Total staff at the end of 1988 was 34 and total assets at the end of 1990 were RMB 107 million.

REFERENCES

Chen Yuan and Zhao Haikuan. 1990. *Almanac of China's Finance and Banking.*
    Beijing: China's Financial Publishing House.
China Finance and Banking Association. 1991. *Almanac of China's Finance and
    Banking.* Beijing: China's Financial Publishing House.
China Handbook Editorial Committee. 1990. *Economy.* Beijing: Foreign Languages
    Press.

Donnithorne, Audrey. 1967. *China's Economic System*. London: George Allen and Unwin.

Huang Dang, Liu Hong Yu, and Zhang Xiao, eds. 1990. *The Encyclopaedia of Finance and Banking in China*. Beijing: Economic Management Press.

King, Frank H. H. 1968. *A Concise Economic History of Modern China (1849–1961)*. New York: Praeger.

Li Mao-sheng. 1987. *Study on the Chinese Financial Structure*. Shanxi: Shanxi People's Publication House.

Liu Hongru, ed. 1991. *On Financial Macro-Control and Adjustment*. Beijing: China Financial Press.

Liu Suinian and Wu Qungan. 1986. *China's Socialist Economy: An Outline History (1949–1984)*. Beijing: Beijing Review.

SBC Research. 1992. *China Stock Market Overview*. July.

Shang Ming, ed. 1988. *China Today: Money and Banking*. Beijing: China Social Science Press.

Shang Ming, Wu Xialing, and Luo Lanbo. 1992. *Banking Credit Management and Money Supply*. Beijing: People's University.

Xinhua. 1983. *A History of Chinese Currency*. Hong Kong: Xinhua Publishing House.

Young, Arthur N. 1965. China's Wartime Finance and Inflation, 1937–1945. Cambridge, Mass.: Harvard University Press.

4

Comprehensive Banks

Since 1949, China's financial system has been developing in a piecemeal manner. The institutions that had evolved by 1990 were shown in Figure 2.2. The monobanking system (Figure 1.2) dominated until 1979, when the country started significant reforms in its economic and financial systems. The specialized banks were established (as discussed in chapter 3), and by 1983, the People's Bank of China had been established as the central bank. Up to 1983, there was no comprehensive bank in China and very little competition among the specialized banks. To develop its economy further, China permitted the development of comprehensive banks to operate on a national basis or to serve the economic and financial needs of specific regions. Two well-known comprehensive banks, the Bank of Communications and CITIC Industrial Bank (CITICIB), operate on a national basis, while some regional comprehensive banks conduct business in specific provinces or economic regions in China. In the following discussion, more emphasis is placed on the operations of the Bank of Communications since it the largest comprehensive bank and serves as a model for other comprehensive banks. The regional comprehensive banks are relatively new; their operations are provided here in summary format.

BANK OF COMMUNICATIONS (BOCOM)

Establishment

The Bank of Communications, established on March 4, 1908, is one of the few banks that has a long history in China, and it is relatively influential at home and abroad. In an attempt to raise funds to redeem the Jin Han Railways and make it easier to regulate the flow of funds among the departments of shipping, railway, telecommunications, and the postal service, the Post and Transportation Ministry at that time presented a proposal to the government of the Qing dynasty to raise funds through a new bank: the Bank of Communications. BOCOM has a history of more than 80 years, including four periods of operation under the Qing dynasty,

Beiyang Warlord government, Kuomintang government, and People's Republic of China. Before 1949, it played an active role in financing projects in transportation, telecommunications, and the postal services, as well as in the financing of industry and commerce. In the course of its earlier evolution, it adopted banking operations and management practices prevailing in foreign (capitalist) countries. It was the first bank in China to establish branches in Hong Kong and Singapore, as well as a correspondent office in Vietnam. In its business, it dealt with financial mortgage credit; was engaged in negotiating, accepting and discounting bills; and developed some subsidiary business in storage, transportation, and insurance. In short, it established a good foundation in comprehensive banking in its operations up to 1949.

After 1949, BOCOM was taken over and consolidated by the People's Government and reformed with respect to its ownership, operation, and management. In its new role, the bank provided loans to publicly owned enterprises in several industries, especially mining, transportation, and shipping. As China's socialist state developed, the bank was designated as a specialized bank to supervise the financial affairs of joint state-privately owned enterprises and to make final disposal of the state ownership in joint state-privately owned enterprises. Afterwards, it was designated as the long-term credit bank to manage financial business relating to industry, especially mining and transportation, and undertook to allocate and administer funds under State budget guidelines.

In 1951, the head office of BOCOM was moved from Shanghai to Beijing. After 1958, the head office and the Hong Kong branch continued to operate international business, while domestic business was amalgamated with the People's Bank of China and the People's Construction Bank of China. As the reform of China's economic system progressed after 1979, the horizontal economic interrelationships among government departments was improved rapidly in order to promote the planned commodity economy in China. This event required horizontal capital circulation, and China's specialized banks could not satisfactorily meet the needs of cross-region, cross-profession capital circulation, due to their centralized ways of allocating funds under planned credit administration. With a view to enhance financial support for the commodity economy and make full use of the function of a bank in the national economy, the State Council enacted the "Notice of Restructuring the Bank of Communications" on July 25, 1986. Consistent with this Notice and after a series of preparations, BOCOM officially started (or restarted) business on April 1, 1987, when the head office was relocated in Shanghai.

Ownership

BOCOM is a joint stock company and the People's Bank of China, on behalf of the State, holds 50 percent of the total shares outstanding. The remaining shares are held by various investors, including provincial and municipal governments, government departments, enterprises, other public institutions and individuals. There is a limit on individual share ownership in that an individual can subscribe for at most 20 shares (RMB 500 per share) and the total individual share ownership cannot exceed 10 percent of outstanding shares.

Corporate Organization and Management

BOCOM is managed by a president who is subject to supervision by a Board of Directors with broad management powers over the entire organization and composed of 25 members appointed by the state or elected from shareholders' representatives. The chairman and vice-chairmen are appointed by the State Council upon the recommendations of the board, which is to meet at least once a year. There is a Standing Board (usually with nine members from the board) which may hold meetings in emergency situations or else holds a meeting every two months. Board members are elected or appointed for a four-year term and may be reappointed or reelected at the end of their respective terms. The functions of the board are similar to those for the specialized banks (discussed in chapter 3).

The Board of Directors is assisted by a Supervisory Board which is composed of three supervisors appointed by the central bank or chosen from the representatives of the shareholders. The principal supervisor is elected by the supervisors and presides over annual meetings; the term of the principal supervisor and supervisors is four years. The Supervisory Board functions as an internal auditor and its duties are to: (a) investigate the bank's business operations and financial standing; (b) request the Board of Directors to investigate and report on matters of importance to the bank's operations; and (c) provide independent advice on the bank's operations at the annual meeting of shareholders.

At the head office, there is the president and several executive vice-presidents, who are appointed by the State Council upon recommendations of the Board of Directors. The president executes the decisions made by the board, implements those tasks which are authorized by the board and manages and leads the bank's daily operations. The president is the legal representative of the bank and is assisted by the executive vice-presidents. In addition, BOCOM has an Advisory Committee at the head office and hires specialists and scholars to advise on important matters with regard to business development by the bank. The head office is subdivided into several functional departments, as shown in Figure 4.1.

The domestic branches of BOCOM are generally located in central cities according to economic regions approved by the central bank. In practice, the head office evaluates a potential location for a branch based on local economic and financial business conditions. Then, an application is made to the local branch of the People's Bank of China, which has the authority to approve subject to orders from its head office in Beijing. A summary of the branches and sub-branches, as of December, 1989, is shown in Figure 4.1. The domestic branches of BOCOM are classified as first-rate, second-rate, and third-rate according to the relative importance of their business operations. The head office has control over five aspects of the operations of

Figure 4.1
Organizational Chart for the Bank of Communications (BOCOM)

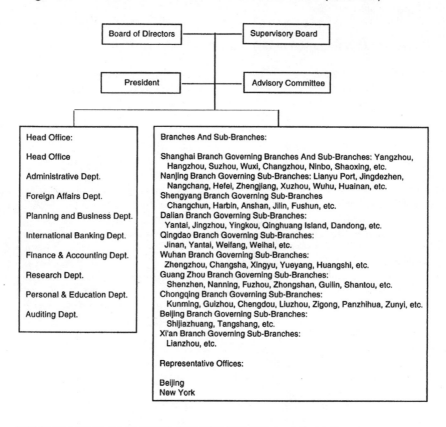

a branch: the appointment or dismissal of important personnel, business policy, overall planning for the organization, basic regulations and principles, and foreign affairs. Except for these five aspects, every domestic branch is granted autonomy over its operations and holds responsibility for its profits and losses. The domestic branches have to pay taxes as required by law and undertake civil legal responsibilities. With respect to the distribution of dividends, every domestic branch is authorized to determine the distribution according to the profits it has made.

A branch is managed by a branch president under the supervision of an Administrative Committee, which has functions that are similar to those of the board at the head office. BOCOM, with the approval of the People's Bank of China, can establish branches or subsidiaries abroad or establish cooperative or joint financial institutions or correspondent relationships with foreign financial groups. Meanwhile, as a member of the Bank of China Group in Hong Kong, the daily operation and administration of the Hong Kong Branch is entrusted to the Hong Kong-Macao Administration Office of the Bank of China. By the end of 1989, apart from the Hong Kong branch and the New York representative office, BOCOM had established correspondent relationships with 354 offices of 226 leading banks worldwide, with 41 of them having account relationships.

By the end of 1989, the bank had set up branches in 60 large- and medium-sized municipalities at home. The head office had 151 staff members; there were 2 provincial, municipal, and autonomous regional branches with 1,132 staff; 10 branches in specially listed cities, with 3,247 staff; and 45 prefectural branches, city branches, and central sub-branches, with 5,204 staff. On December 20, 1989, the bank established a representative office in New York and started business in the United States.

Business Activities

The major business activities of BOCOM are to:

1. Handle RMB and foreign currency deposits;

2. Provide loans, overdrafts, and other credit in RMB and foreign currency for working capital and investments in fixed assets;

3. Handle domestic and international settlements, remittances, and exchanges of currency;

4. Issue RMB and foreign bonds and other securities;

5. Handle domestic and international interbank lending, borrowing, deposits, and discounts;

6. Handle transactions of foreign exchange, stocks and securities in foreign currency;

7. Invest in Hong Kong, Macao, and foreign countries or jointly operate banks, financial companies, or other enterprises with partners;

8. Lead or take part in international syndicated loans;

9. Offer domestic and international trust, consignment, insurance, investment, lease, consultation, guarantees, custody, correspondent activities, and similar functions;

10. Set up subsidiaries to conduct approved business activities;

11. Handle housing business;

12. Issue various kinds of stocks and bonds and handle the assignment, buying, and selling of securities;

13. Operate other businesses as entrusted, required, or authorized by the central bank; and

14. Take part in other international financial activities authorized by the State Council and the central bank.

Investments. At the end of 1990, total assets had reached RMB 78 billion, up by 78 percent from 1987; revenues were RMB 6.26 billion, up by 611 percent; and profits were RMB 1.62 billion, up by about 2,000 percent (Table 4.1). Lending to industry and commerce grew at a phenomenal rate: 488 percent over the 1987–1990 period. In 1990, loans accounted for 50 percent of total assets compared to 15.1 percent in 1987. Financial assistance was extended to enterprises producing and acquiring export-oriented, renowned, extraordinary, or high-quality products, and to those producing types of energy and raw materials that are in great demand. In addition, loans were granted to support the purchase of agricultural and associated products to boost the agro-industry. In 1990, loans in the above categories accounted for 74 percent of the bank's total working-capital loans and more than 90 percent of the new loans granted in that year. The loans strategy of BOCOM is to allocate funds for China's development in a rational and efficient manner.

Cash and due from banks (32 percent of total assets in 1990) and letter of credit advances to customers (6 percent of total assets in 1990) reflect the bank's involvement in trade and nontrade settlements. As indicated, the bank has extensive correspondent relationships with foreign banks and has also made agreements with seven foreign financial institutions to sell traveler's checks as an agent and to cash credit cards. The business with credit cards include the travelers' check and credit card (Express Card) of American Express Inc., the travelers' check of Bank of America, the travelers' check of the Fuji Bank Ltd., the BOT travelers' check in Japanese yen and U.S. dollars of the Bank of Tokyo, Ltd., and the Visa travelers' check in U.S. dollars of Barclays Bank, Ltd.

The bank participates in the domestic capital market and handles interbank lending and borrowing, security issues and over-the-counter trading of securities involving the use of collateral loans, financial bonds, and other new types of credit instruments. Many branches have commenced trading in government bonds, financial bonds, and enterprise bonds and shares. The capital market in Shanghai, led by the Shanghai Branch of BOCOM, had 47 participants by the end of 1987, and the value of interbank lending and borrowing amounted to RMB 4.13 billion. In addition, the bank has established the Haitong Securities Company, which specializes in the trading of securities.

In 1988, BOCOM entered the domestic and overseas insurance business with the approval of the central bank, and the major branches have established insurance departments, with business expanding yearly. In addition, the bank has a reinsurance relationship with the central bank intended to strengthen its ability to undertake risks. Meanwhile, the bank has also increased its contacts with international insurance circles and by the end of 1988, the total value insured had reached RMB 8 billion and correspondent relationships had been established with more than 70 institutions in over 50 countries and regions. At present, the major domestic insurance handled by the bank includes corporate property insurance, insurance of contents, cargo insurance, automobile insurance, hull

Table 4.1

Summary Financial Statements for BOCOM (Value in Billions of Renminbi)

	1987	1988	1989	1990	1990 (Indexed to 1986)	Percent Distribution 1986	Percent Distribution 1990
BALANCE SHEET							
Assets							
Loans	8.74	12.39	17.11	25.56	292.45%	19.81%	32.56%
Gov't. Investment	6.68	18.55	27.73	39.32	588.62%	15.14%	50.08%
Entrusted	25.19	2.44	1.36	1.36	5.40%	57.11%	1.73%
Others	2.08	3.34	3.75	5.01	240.87%	4.72%	6.38%
Deposits with PBC	1.42	5.50	3.05	7.26	511.27%	3.22%	9.25%
Total assets	44.11	42.22	53.00	78.51	177.99%	100.00%	100.00%
Liabilities							
Due to banks	4.08	9.38	13.41	15.57	381.62%	9.25%	19.83%
Deposits	9.35	19.63	26.13	44.43	475.19%	21.20%	56.59%
Letters of credit and guarantees	2.08	3.34	3.75	5.01	240.87%	4.72%	6.38%
Other liabilities	26.00	6.61	4.74	6.87	26.42%	58.94%	8.75%
	41.51	38.96	48.03	71.88	173.16%	94.11%	91.56%
Capital funds	2.00	2.50	3.04	4.00	200.00%	4.53%	5.09%
Provision for bad debts	0.52	0.54	0.79	1.01	194.23%	1.18%	1.29%
Retained earnings	0.08	0.22	1.14	1.62	2025.00%	0.18%	2.06%
Total liabilities and capital	44.11	42.22	53.00	78.51	177.99%	100.00%	100.00%
PROFIT AND LOSS							
Revenue	0.88	2.00	4.44	6.26	711.36%	100.00%	100.00%
Net profit	0.08	0.22	1.15	1.62	2025.00%	9.09%	25.88%

Source: China Finance and Banking Association (1991).

insurance, and automobile insurance against third-person responsibility. The overseas insurance business includes property insurance, import-export marine cargo insurance, building project and installation project insurance, insurance against damage to machinery, insurance against public or employer's responsibility, personal accident insurance, and personal insurance for those going abroad.

Sources of Financing. The bank has to attract funds by way of deposits and loans in order to finance its operations. In 1990, RMB and foreign currency deposits accounted for 50 percent of total financing compared with 19 percent in 1987 (Table 4.1). BOCOM attaches priority to its RMB deposit business, and continuously innovates and implements new methods to attract deposits so as to increase financial resources. The bank has offered "out-door" service and made use of various credit instruments to attract deposits such as the "Large Face Value Deposit Certificate for Enterprises." On the other hand, it has improved its internal management system by adopting the contract responsibility system among branches, sub-branches, and offices in order to attract deposits. Under this system, bonuses for employees are based on the volume of deposits obtained by the respective branches, sub-branches, and offices.

Foreign currency deposits and loans are important sources of funding, and the bank has extensive and full foreign exchange operations. As a window to attract foreign capital, BOCOM is striving to be creative and has made great progress in its foreign exchange operations. In 1988, the bank took in foreign currency deposits amounting to U.S. $139.55 million, offered bank; and

14. Take part in other international financial activities authorized by the State Council and the central bank.

Normally, the central bank does not provide credit funds to BOCOM, which forces the bank to attract deposits, raise loans, or use equity to provide credit. BOCOM has no obligation to grant funds to any enterprise, but it has the right to make loans with reference to the integrity, solvency, and economic performance of the enterprise, as well as its own financial position. Whenever there is a deficit, the bank may obtain funds by rediscounting or mortgaging commercial bills or other securities with the central bank. The loans of working funds and fixed funds granted by the bank are not subject to the state's centralized credit plan or the administrative target for loans but rather are managed in accordance with the bank's capital position. Therefore, the bank has adopted an inside management mechanism of self-adjusted assets and liabilities to manage its loan portfolio. This management mechanism is a self-controlled system composed of a series of targets and measures which fall into three categories of operating guidelines.

Self-Controlled System of Proportional Management. To promote the efficient and rational allocation of funds, the bank uses eight targets:

1. The ratio for fixed-asset loans, (outstanding volume of fixed assets loans at year-end)/ (capital + accumulation + total deposits), should be less than 20 percent.

2. The ratio for agricultural loans, (agricultural loans) / (capital + accumulation + total deposits), should be less than 10 percent.

3. The ratio of fixed assets loans offered to township enterprises, (fixed assets loans offered to township enterprises) / (appvoved volume of agricultural loans), should be less than 30 percent.

4. As a target for management vitality, the ratio of (total outstanding loans) / (capital + accumulation + total outstanding deposits) should be less than 85 percent.

5. As a target for the limit of medium- and long-term loans, the ratio of (medium- and long-term loans) / total fixed assets loans) should be less than one-third.

6. The maximum amount of loans granted to one enterprise—(loans granted to one enterprise / total loans)—should be less than 8 percent.

7. The ratio for collateral and discounting loans—(outstanding collateral and discounting loans / outstanding loans for working capital)—should be more than one-third.

8. The ratio for approved investments in RMB, (total volume of investment in RMB / (funds received the same year + accumulation), should be less than 10 percent for the first year, 20 percent for the second year, 30 percent for the third year, and then continuously lessened as time goes on.

The above eight targets are made from different points of view and with different requirements to control the movement of funds. The first three targets are usually associated with the state's macroeconomic policy and reflect policy targets relating to the use of funds. The last five targets reflect some administrative controls that are placed on management to prevent abuse of loan granting privileges.

Targets for Analyzing and Supervising. To assess managerial performance, the bank has a set of targets for management activities, including targets for funds, costs, and profits. In addition, there are some targets for the management of assets and liabilities, such as the ratio of long-term debts to total liabilities, the ratio of long-term assets to total assets, and other similar measures.

Regulation System of Organization and Procedure Management. Apart from these targets, BOCOM adopted a series of measures to promote a balanced management of assets and liabilities. For example, it has strengthened the function, power, and responsibility of the planning department to regulate and control overall planning and statistical supervision as well as to adjust and supervise the earning power and safety of funds. Again, for example, in the management of loans, the bank has established committees to examine loans at the branches and promote democratic decision-making procedures for loans for important programs. Every loan application must first be checked by the loans officer, then rechecked by the department manager, and finally verified by the president.

BOCOM has made some modifications in the management of personnel and the treatment of wages and employee welfare. To speak more exactly, the bank has adopted a hiring cadres system which has broken the life-time cadres system in its personnel management. In the area of wages and employee welfare, the bank has certain powers to make decisions similar to those of a capitalist entity. Based on the principle of combining authority, duties, and benefits, the bank has taken measures to reward employee performance with bonuses to motivate employees and circumvent egalitarianism in the allocation of benefits.

CITIC INDUSTRIAL BANK (CITICIB)

Establishment and Ownership

CITIC Industrial Bank emerged from the former Banking Department of China International Trust and Investment Corporation (CITIC) which is a ministerial corporation under the State Council (see chapter 5). CITIC was established on October 4, 1979, with a registered capital of RMB 1.2 billion, and its main tasks are to use foreign capital to invest in projects and introduce foreign technology, equipment, and management skills. Its business includes some banking operations involving foreign exchange, international settlements, and external guarantees. CITIC is a holding corporation, and its constituent enterprises combine production, technology transfer and development, finance, trade, and service.

The Banking Department was set up in December 1985, and quickly accumulated valuable experience in the operations of deposits and loans, external guarantees, foreign currency transactions, international trade settlements, syndicated loans, international bond issues, leasing, and the trading of foreign currencies and securities. With this banking experience and its expert personnel, the Banking Department was established as the CITIC Industrial Bank (CITICIB) in May 1987, with the approval of the central bank and the State Council. The registered capital of CITICIB is RMB 800 million, and paid-up capital is RMB 300 million (including U.S. $50 million). As a comprehensive bank under its parent, CITIC Industrial Bank is a socialist state-owned enterprise that deals with domestic and international financial business.

Corporate Organization and Management

The management of CITICIB is common in many respects with China's specialized banks (discussed in chapter 3). In line with the "Articles of Association of CITIC Industrial Bank" approved by the People's Bank of China and the State Council, and in order to keep power and responsibility separate, the bank is managed according to international business practice. That is, a president assumes full responsibility for the bank's daily operations under the supervision of a Board of Directors. The Board of Directors is made up of 15 persons who are selected from CITIC (Holdings) and other relevant institutions, including the People's Bank of China and other specialized banks. The board holds a meeting once a year presided over by the chairman, and the functions of the Board of Directors are similar to those outlined in chapter 3 for the specialized banks.

Under the Board of Directors, there is the president, who is in charge of the overall business, and several vice-presidents. The head office is located in Beijing, and corporate activities are departmentalized into such traditional categories as executive office, coordination and planning department, capital department, credit department, and leasing department. Each department has a manager and several deputy managers who are in charge of daily business. The bank can establish branches or subsidiaries in China and abroad in specified lines of business, subject to the approval of the People's Bank of China. At the end of 1989, CITICIB had three branches: Shanghai Branch, Shenzhen Branch, and Dalian Branch. In addition, the Shenzhen Branch has sub-branches in Shangbu, Docheng, and Hongling. Additional branches have been established in Hong Kong and Macao.

With the experienced personnel from the Banking Department as a base, CITICIB quickly upgraded its staff to include employees with varying levels of financial skills and has raised the management skills of the whole bank through specially designed training programs. Thus a team of well qualified, highly specialized and motivated people is involved in the bank operations. At the end of 1988, the bank had 224 staff members, with 151 at head-quarters. Among the staff, about 78 percent is less than 35 years old, about 72 percent have at least secondary school education, and about 24 percent are in the middle or advanced professional ranks in the bank. The well-qualified staff paves the way for the development of CITICIB in the future.

With regard to internal management, CITICIB has established, and is still perfecting, a set of working procedures to promote scientific management and motivate its staff. For example, in order to ensure the maximum economic performance and social influence of lending programs, an inside evaluation system has been established. Under this system, there is a set of comparatively objective standards for selecting, evaluating, approving, and monitoring borrowers. It is hoped that approaches like these will improve the bank's efficiency and management techniques.

Business Activities

The authorized business activities for the bank are similar to those outlined earlier for the Bank of Communications. CITICIB is a foreign-oriented bank whose major business involves foreign exchange transactions. Therefore, as a window to the outside world, the bank operates to support the development of a foreign-oriented economy. Furthermore, as a member of the CITIC Group, the bank is effectively integrated with the Group's business activities: production, technology transfer and development, finance, trade, and service. The bank is like a "captive" financial institution for the CITIC Group, despite the fact that it has significant business with enterprises and other economic units that are not associated with the group. It conducts wholesale and retail banking business at home and abroad without regional or industrial restrictions. By competing with specialized banks in a fair way, the bank injects fresh vitality into China's financial system.

The bank is administered and supervised by the People's Bank of China, but as a subsidiary of CITIC, it is also under the leadership of the parent corporation. In line with its business and distinctive features, the bank has been authorized to bear risks, balance its accounts, and develop its business since its establishment in accordance with the provisions made by the People's Bank of China. The branches or subsidiaries of CITIC Industrial Bank located in Hong Kong, Macao and abroad can operate all banking business authorized by the host country laws and regulations. Since its establishment and under the leadership of the People's Bank of China and CITIC (Holdings), CITICIB has made a great contribution to China's economic construction by upholding and executing state policies and guiding principles and by continuously expanding, developing, and creating its business during the reform era.

Investments. In 1990, total assets reached RMB 21.43 billion, up 144 percent from 1987; revenue was RMB 1.474 billion, up 288 percent; and after-tax profits were RMB 121 million, up 142 percent (Table 4.2). Lending is one of the major operations of the bank, and in 1990, loans accounted for 57 percent of the bank's assets, up 221 percent from 1987. The bank gives priority to businesses connected with technological innovation and development, key projects, as determined by the state, and exports. In line with the nation's industrial policy, the bank also emphasizes the industries of energy, transportation, and raw materials involving large or mid-size key enterprises as well as export-oriented, foreign-currency–earning enterprises. In addition to the normal line of credit loans, the bank offers collateral

Table 4.2
Summary Financial Statements for CITICIB (Value in Millions of Renminbi)

	1987	1988	1989	1990	1990 (Indexed to 1987)	Percent Distribution 1986	1990
BALANCE SHEET							
Assets							
Due from domestic banks	0.310	0.542	0.686	1.638	528.39%	3.54%	7.64%
Due from overseas banks	2.860	3.395	1.878	3.724	130.21%	32.65%	17.37%
Loans	3.834	6.886	10.396	12.321	321.36%	43.77%	57.48%
Lease receivable	0.634	0.549	0.553	0.572	90.22%	7.24%	2.67%
Accounts receivable	0.082	0.527	0.260	0.673	820.73%	0.94%	3.14%
Investment securities	0.848	1.212	1.548	2.250	265.33%	9.68%	10.50%
Leased assets	0.136	0.161	0.169	0.143	105.15%	1.55%	0.67%
Other assets	0.055	0.054	0.289	0.113	205.45%	0.63%	0.53%
Total assets	8.759	13.326	15.779	21.434	244.71%	100.00%	100.00%
Liabilities							
Deposits	4.926	5.787	7.318	10.745	218.13%	56.24%	50.13%
Debts	3.031	4.242	7.331	9.150	301.88%	34.60%	42.69%
Lease payable	0.146	0.119	0.069	0.004	2.74%	1.67%	0.02%
Accounts payable	0.194	0.462	0.402	0.457	235.57%	2.21%	2.13%
Guaranty deposits	0.112	0.148	0.175	0.245		1.28%	1.14%
Financial bonds		2.114	0.006			0.00%	0.00%
Other liabilities			0.001	0.204		0.00%	0.95%
	8.409	12.872	15.302	20.805	247.41%	96.00%	97.07%
Total equity	0.350	0.454	0.477	0.629	179.71%	4.00%	2.93%
Total liabilities and capital	8.759	13.326	15.779	21.434	244.71%	100.00%	100.00%
PROFIT AND LOSS							
Revenue	0.379	0.917	1.181	1.474	388.92%	100.00%	100.00%
Net Profit	0.050	0.096	0.074	0.121	242.00%	13.19%	8.21%

Source: China Finance and Banking Association (1991).

loans, export credits, on-lending, guaranteed lending, and syndicated loans in RMB and foreign currencies including the U.S. dollar, deutsche mark, French franc, and Japanese yen. While most of the bank's loans are domestic, some funds are invested overseas. For example, the bank is a member of syndicates providing loans for the sea-floor tunnel between England and France, a second sea-floor tunnel in Hong Kong, and projects in Turkey and Pakistan.

In 1990, the bank had 25 percent of its assets (compared to 36 percent in 1987) in balances owed by domestic and foreign banks; most of these funds were committed to trade and nontrade settlements. The bank is involved with foreign trade, and letters of credit are issued for the CITIC Group of enterprises, as well as for other Chinese enterprises in Beijing and other parts of the country. In order to facilitate the letter of credit business, the bank has developed correspondent relationships with foreign banks. By the end of 1989, the bank had established correspondent relationships with 311 foreign banks in 46 countries and regions in the world. In addition, nontrade settlements are developing on a rather large scale. In addition to the foreign exchange business and the selling of travelers' checks on an agency basis, the bank has signed agreements to handle the credit card business with American Express, Inc., and NanYang Commercial Bank, Ltd.

With respect to leasing, the bank is one of the first institutions in China to play an important role in introducing leasing operations in the financial markets. The bank is widely recognized by enterprises and enjoys a leading position in the leasing business in China. Moreover, its business is extending throughout the country as new types of leasing business have been continuously introduced. In 1987, the bank concluded 46 leasing contracts with a total value of RMB 63.44 million, mainly in textiles and other light, export-oriented industries. Also in 1987, the bank and Paine Webber Inc. of U.S.A. arranged a leverage lease for one Lockheed 100–30 cargo plane for the Civil Aviation Administration of China. This was the first time a Chinese financial institution had participated in the business of international plane leasing using a leverage lease. The year 1988 did not look promising for the leasing business, causing the bank to respond quickly. On one hand, the bank promptly adjusted its operations to strengthen the management of its traditional (nonairplane) leasing business. On the other hand, the bank focused on the business of plane leasing and concluded 44 leasing contracts valued at U.S. $31 million, including the leasing of two large-size Boeing passenger planes for Guangzhou People's Airlines and Xiamen Airlines. In addition, the bank successfully arranged another financial lease of a Boeing 747–400 passenger plane for China International Airlines.

The bank is an active participant in the domestic and foreign securities markets as a dealer/broker, and about 10 percent of its assets are invested in these activities. The bank has daily trading relationships in foreign exchange with more than 60 foreign banks, and by 1989, a dealing room had been installed with the Reuters Monitor System, Reuters Dealing System, and CCM System to handle international settlements. CITICIB trades in precious metals in the spot and forward markets, currency and interest rate options and swaps, and bond futures and options. Furthermore, with the installment of advanced telecommunications systems and prompt access to information from international financial markets, the management of capital and the planning of investments for customers can be conducted on an efficient basis.

Sources of Financing. Debt financing comes mainly from RMB and foreign currency deposits plus RMB and foreign currency loans. It is important that CITICIB obtain foreign exchange funds, mainly to finance the operations of the CITIC Group. In the international financial markets, where the U.S. dollar fluctuates against other major currencies, the bank is relatively successful in obtaining funds at comparatively low cost. For instance, under the unfavorable circumstances in the international financial markets in 1987, after careful investigation and research, CITIC Industrial Bank seized favorable opportunities to float three issues of Japanese bonds equal to U.S. $400 million. At the same time, the bank had loans of U.S. $450 million in major international currencies at relatively attractive interest rates. The other important source of foreign exchange for the bank is the foreign currency deposit which it attracts by providing quality service and innovative savings accounts for Chinese exporters, residents, and foreign investors. The bank has installed foreign-currency–exchange desks in many international hotels located in Beijing and other cities, increased the number of shops that accept credit cards, and sold a variety of travelers' checks in an effort to capture funds from tourists and other visitors to China.

CITICIB places great emphasis on its RMB business and has been quite innovative in providing service to clients and designing various types of savings instruments in its efforts to increase RMB deposits. Examples of improved services include the training of staff, the provision of some services at the customer's office, and the establishment of a Business Exploitation Division to create closer contacts with customers. Examples of innovative savings instruments include the Convertible Time Deposit Certificate–Large Face Value denominated in RMB, and Contractual Deposit accounts, which offer more flexibility and higher returns than traditional accounts.

Providing access to the outside world, the bank has won worldwide fame in China's financial circle by establishing relationships with international financial institutions. In 1988, the bank sent representative groups to financial centers in Japan, Hong Kong, and West Germany and signed a series of cooperative agreements. In a seminar held by Euro-Currency in Tokyo in February 1988, the bank introduced China's reform and open door policy and investment environment to foreign financial institutions and enterprises and enhanced the cooperation between the foreign and Chinese financial institutions. In May 1989, the bank sent a representative group, headed by the chairman, to attend the 22nd Annual Meeting of the Governing Board of the Asian Development Bank, which was held in Beijing to exchange information with representatives from other countries. In addition to these cooperation relationships and exchange movements, the bank is known for the international financial guarantees that it provides for some large programs at home.

REGIONAL COMPREHENSIVE BANKS

China's economic reforms have prompted the establishment of regional comprehensive banks, and here the focus is to summarize their operations and management of four of these institutions. While these regional banks are not as large as the specialized banks (see chapter 3) or the two national comprehensive banks (discussed earlier in this chapter), they illustrate opportunities for expanding China's financial system as models of banks that may be set up to serve regional interests in the country. The following discussion focuses on the China Merchants Bank (Shekou, Shenzhen), the Guangdong Development Bank (Guangzhou), the Shenzhen Development Bank (Shenzhen), and the Fujian Industrial Bank (Fuzhou).

China Merchants Bank (CMB)

Establishment. China Merchants Bank was established in April 1987 with the approval of the central bank. The bank emerged from the Shekou Finance Co., which was a wholly owned subsidiary of the China Merchants Holdings Co., Ltd. (CMH). The parent company was first established in

1872 as a shipping company called the China Merchants Steam Navigation Co., Ltd. (CMSN) and in 1950, CMSN (Hong Kong branch) became a state-owned enterprise of China operating in Hong Kong. In recent years, CMSN developed into a multifunctional international organization to assist in developing China's planned commodity economy and promote the open door policy. In order to strengthen the centralized leadership and management of all enterprises owned by the China Merchants Group and to coordinate the operations of various businesses, the China Merchants Holdings Co. Ltd. was established with the approval of the State Council in November 1985. CMH is the principal representative of the Ministry of Communications of China in Hong Kong and is authorized to supervise and guide all subordinate units of the Ministry that are based in Hong Kong.

Ownership, Corporate Organization and Management. Consistent with its articles of association, as amended and approved in 1989, China Merchants Bank is a joint stock company with seven shareholders: the China Merchants Holdings Co. Ltd., China Ocean Shipping Company, the Eastern Nanhai Petroleum Corporation of the CNOOC, the Guangzhou Marine Transportation Bureau, the Qinhuangdao Harbor Bureau, the Highway Administration Bureau of the Communications Department of Guangdong Province, and Industrial Material Supplies Corporation of the Communication Department of Shandong Province. At the end of 1990, the registered capital of China Merchants Bank was RMB 1.2 billion, and the paid-up capital was RMB 400 million (including some foreign exchange).

A Board of Directors has the highest managerial authority, and its directors are recommended or appointed by the shareholders. The Board may elect one chairman and several vice-chairmen to serve four years, and the term of office for directors, chairman and vice-chairmen may be renewed at the end of every four years. The responsibilities of the Board of Directors are similar to those outlined for the Bank of Communications. At the head office, the board is assisted by a Supervisory Board, which is composed of officials recommended by the shareholders. The Supervisory Board chooses a chief supervisor and can function for a term of four years. The chief supervisor is responsible for presiding over the supervisory meetings.

The head office is located in Shekou, Shenzhen, and is headed by a general manager under the supervision of the Board of Directors. The general manager is appointed by the Board of Directors subject to the approval of the central bank and is the bank's legal representative. The head office has the typical departmental structure, including Credit, Planning and Statistics, International Business, Off-Shore Banking, Accounting, Personnel, and General Affairs.

Branches are established with the approval of the central bank in accordance with the needs of business expansion. At the end of 1989, there were four branches, in Shekou, Louhu, Shangbu, and Dongmen, and representative offices in Beijing and Liaoning. Branches in Beijing, Shanghai, and Guangzhou will be discussed here.

Business Activities. China Merchants Bank is subject to the leadership, administration, coordination, supervision, and auditing of the central bank.

Like other banks, CMB must establish a separate financial management and accounting system, keep reserves for bad accounts, and maintain reserves at the central bank. Furthermore, it must determine the interest rates of deposits and loans in accordance with the relevant provisions made by the central bank, submit its work plan and annual report to the central bank, and execute the state's credit plan. However, as a joint stock enterprise, the bank is responsible to its shareholders, must raise its own funds, has responsibility for gains and losses, and bears business risks. The bank pays taxes, and the Board of Directors decides on profit sharing and dividends.

Investments. Business activities extend across industry sectors and are conducted in RMB and foreign currencies as with the Bank of Communications. Since its establishment, the bank has provided credible, flexible, and innovative services to its customers. The bank exploited new business opportunities and expanded its base of financial resources in a variety of innovative ways consistent with the country's economic and financial policies and guidelines. In 1989, assets were RMB 3.33 billion, revenues were RMB 137 million, and profits were RMB 42 million, while in 1990, the values were RMB 4.08 billion, RMB 283 million, and RMB 64 million, respectively.

In 1989 and 1990, loans accounted for about 84 percent of the bank's assets, up from 72 percent in 1987. Loans are provided in RMB and foreign currencies, and the bank attaches importance to the safety and earnings capability of its lending business. Applicants are evaluated and assigned a credit rating based on an internal rating scheme on which the terms of a loan are set. In general, the bank attempts to diversify its loan portfolio in working-capital loans, project loans, and loans for workers' housing. The bank is authorized to vary the interest rate within a margin of 0.20 percent of that set by the central bank, depending on the terms and types of loans and the demand and supply of funds. It is standard policy for the bank to finance large projects in the communications sector, including for example, the highways between Shenyang and Dalian, between Xian and Lingtong, and between Guangzhou and Fushan. By the end of 1989, the bank had administered loans from the Communications Ministry valuing RMB 750 million and had granted financial assistance to the building of 18 highways and three bridges in 13 provinces and municipalities.

With respect to trade and nontrade settlements, the bank provides prompt service in the same city or across different regions in China. In addition, it has access to major countries in the world to deal with international settlements, an activity that is enhanced given the bank's location in the Shenzhen Special Economic Zone and its proximity to Hong Kong. By the end of 1989, the bank had established correspondent relationships with 34 banks in 15 countries and regions such as the U.S., Great Britain, Japan, West Germany, Switzerland, Australia, Italy, Singapore and Hong Kong.

The bank started offshore financial business with the approval of the State Administration of Exchange Control in May, 1988. In October of the same year, a group of specialized staff members, led by the General Manager, traveled to Europe to make investigation on offshore banking business. This visit laid a good foundation for China's financial circle to enter the offshore banking business.

Sources of Financing. In 1989 and 1990, deposits provided 66 percent of funding; loans (mostly interbank), 15 percent; and other liabilities, 12 percent. The deposit business is important, and the bank places a priority on high-quality service for its customers. In addition to demand and time deposits for enterprises, the bank has created new businesses including notifying of deposits, payment of salaries as agent for enterprises, and a long-distance communications service. Meanwhile, it also increased deposit sources by providing services seven days a week and on-site services for major customers.

Shenzhen Development Bank (SDB)

Establishment and Ownership. Shenzhen Development Bank (SDB) was established as a joint stock company in December 1987, with the approval of the central bank. Initially, share capital was provided by six credit cooperatives located in the Shenzhen Special Economic Zone. In May 1987, SDB issued 500,000 common shares to the public (the nominal value of each share being RMB 20); 111 enterprises and institutions (such as Shenzhen Investment Management Co. and Shenzhen International Trust and Investment Co.) and 7,276 individuals participated in this initial public offering. Thereafter, SDB had three more equity issues, and by March 1990, there were 4.85 million common shares outstanding. Individuals as a group accounted for 39 percent of outstanding common shares. In addition to common equity, the bank sold preferred shares in Hong Kong (HK $10.36 million), of which individuals purchased 40 percent.

Corporate Organization and Management. The corporate structure of the bank is similar to that of the China Merchants Bank. The Board of Directors is nominated or elected by the shareholders and has the highest managerial influence. The head office in Shenzhen has a general manager who is responsible to the board, and activities are departmentalized (there were 14 departments in 1989). At the end of 1989, there were 9 branches and 54 sub-branch offices located throughout the Shenzhen Special Economic Zone. Branches and sub-branches keep independent accounts, have sole responsibility for gains and losses and are evaluated on specific targets set by the head office. The total staff was 500 at the end of 1989.

The common and preferred stocks of the bank are publicly traded, and the public owns a relatively large percentage (39 percent) of outstanding shares. It is therefore crucial that the bank keep its shareholders reasonably well informed on its operations. To fulfill this requirement, there is an annual shareholders' conference (or meeting) at which management is required to account for its stewardship. Meetings may also be called on an emergency basis.

The shareholders' conference is entitled to:

1. Listen to and examine the work report, the bank's development plan, business policies, yearly business plan, operating results, financial budget, and final report for the year, as presented by the Board of Directors;

2. Examine and approve the yearly profit distribution plan or loss-compensation methods recommended by the board;

3. Amend the articles of association and elect or dismiss directors;

4. Approve decisions on the bank's increase or decrease of capital, issue of bonds, amalgamation or transference, dismissal of employees, clearance, and other important matters.

Business Activities. SDB was established to provide financing in the Shenzhen Special Economic Zone in particular, and for the development of the economy in general. The bank is responsible for its gains and losses, and has independence of operation in various business activities consistent with the demands of the planned commodity economy and China's relevant laws and financial policies. As a comprehensive bank, SDB has handled deposits and loans for collectives and industrial or commercial enterprises or units, as well as savings deposits of residents, in both urban and rural areas. Furthermore, the bank is authorized to conduct business in foreign currencies. In line with its Articles of Association, the major business activities are very similar to those of the other comprehensive banks.

Investments. In 1989, the total assets of the bank reached RMB 1.653 billion with loans accounting for 67.4 percent of these funds; the comparable values for 1990 were RMB 2.929 billion and 67.7 percent, respectively. Loans increased every year under a controlled management system as in the case of the Bank of Communications. The bank has self-control targets for its credit business and grants loans to support enterprises and projects with good economic efficiency. For example, the bank is one of the financial supporters of the Modern Advancement (Shenzhen) Co., Ltd., which is the biggest color kinescope factory in China. Another project that received the bank's support is the tunnel through Wutong Mountain, an important local traffic project linking Shatoujao with Wutong. With the approval of the State Administration of Exchange Control, the bank conducts business in foreign currencies and has developed relationships with overseas financial institutions.

Sources of Financing. The bank started operations on a trial basis in June 1987, and then, in December 1987, it started to deal with the general public. The deposit business was crucial for survival, and SDB braved a disinflation policy when it began business. Faced with intense competition among the specialized banks and a restricted branch system, the bank had to be innovative. It began to provide service at the doors of its customers' place of business and expanded banking hours to attract and build customer relationships. Meanwhile, SDB has a policy whereby an employee bonus is tied to the ability to attract deposits. By means of various savings slogans and methods, SDB has become known to the public as a business with the aim of "Being enthusiastic, considerate, flexible, and efficient." In 1990, deposits from individuals and enterprises provided about 81 percent of asset financing.

Fujian Industrial Bank (FIB)

Establishment and Ownership. Fujian Industrial Bank (FIB) was established in Fuzhou, Fujian Province, on August 26, 1988, with the approval of the central bank. The bank emerged from the Fujian Fuxing Financial Affairs Co., which was established in 1981. At the time when it was converted into a bank, the finance company had assets of about RMB 1.55 billion and investments in 667 projects. An initial offering of common and preferred shares netted the firm RMB 500 million. The common stocks were sold to finance departments of the various levels of government in Fujian Province, domestic financial institutions, local residents, local enterprises, China-owned enterprises in Hong Kong and Macao, and overseas Chinese and "compatriots" in Hong Kong, Macao, and Taiwan. The preferred stocks were sold only to local residents and overseas Chinese and "compatriots" in Hong Kong, Macao, and Taiwan.

Corporate Organization and Management. The bank is a joint stock company and has responsibility for its profits and losses. A Board of Directors is elected by the shareholders and has broad management responsibility for the bank. The board elects a chairman and several vice-chairmen to undertake the duties that are required of directors. The Board of Directors is assisted by a Board of Supervisors which performs an internal audit function of the bank's operations. A president is in charge of daily operations, assisted by three vice-presidents. Management reports to shareholders at an annual meeting or, in case of emergencies, at special meetings. The head office in Fuzhou is departmentalized (nine departments in 1989) to handle the varied activities of the bank. In addition, there are representative offices through Fujian Province (Xiamen, Sanming, Zhangzhou, Longyan, and Quanzhou), which solicit business.

Business Activities. Like other banks, FIB is subject to the leadership, administration, coordination, supervision, and auditing of the central bank. In addition, its operations are similar to those of the comprehensive banks. By the end of 1989, its total assets had reached RMB 1,915 million, an increase of 18.19 percent over those at the end of 1988, while profits reached RMB 30.5 million. Loans accounted for 89.7 percent of the assets and interest income, for 78.2 percent of sales. Financing has been provided to many infrastructural projects to boost the attractiveness of Fujian as a location for joint ventures. For example, in order to accelerate development in the Xiamen Special Economic Zone, the bank provided a loan of RMB 25 million for the construction of a bridge between Gao Qi and Ji Mei in Xiamen.

Deposits provide about 47 percent for investments, and interbank loans, about 27 percent. The bank has a restricted branch system, which hinders its ability to attract deposits from residents and enterprises. While FIB is actively exploring business in RMB, it also makes full use of its location in the coastal region to develop its foreign exchange business. Since 1989, the bank has started accepting deposits, granting loans, and offering guarantees in and trading in foreign currencies. The bank has established correspondent relationships with 17 foreign banks in the United States, Japan, Singapore, Switzerland, Luxembourg, Hong Kong, and Macao, and has furthermore signed business cooperation agreements with some of the banks. This strategy has laid a good foundation for the bank to enter the international financial market.

Guangdong Development Bank (GDB)

Establishment, Corporate Organization, and Management. Guangdong Development Bank was established on September 8, 1988, with the approval of the central bank. It is a joint stock company with registered capital of RMB 1.5 billion and paid-up capital of RMB 100 million (including some denominated in foreign currencies). It issued equity shares for sale to the general public, which holds a majority of the shares.

The bank is an independent operation with independent accounting and has sole responsibility for its gains and losses. The Board of Directors has broad managerial responsibility over the affairs of the bank; it elects a chairman and several vice-chairmen every four years. The term of office for directors, chairman, and vice-chairmen is renewed if they are reelected. A president is in charge of daily operations under the supervision of the Board of Directors.

Branches are established on the basis of economic potential, and in 1989, there were seven branches and five representative offices in Guangdong Province with a total of 853 employees. Branches keep independent accounts and have sole responsibility for gains and losses under the leadership of the head office. The manager of every branch is nominated by the president and appointed by the Board of Directors, while vice-managers are nominated by the managers of the branches and appointed by the president.

Business Activities. The bank's activities are similar to those of the other comprehensive banks. By the end of 1989, total assets had reached RMB 3.53 billion, reflecting an increase of 130.87 percent over 1988. Loans dominated the investment of funds. In 1989, the bank granted RMB loans with a gross value of RMB 3.393 billion (with working capital loans covering 97 percent) and foreign currency loans with a gross value of U.S. $112 million. In addition, the bank's domestic interbank borrowing totaled RMB 1.459 billion and external interbank borrowing in foreign exchange totaled U.S. $46.65 million. The bank has established correspondent relationships with 50 foreign banks in 14 countries and regions abroad.

Guangdong Development Bank uses its base in Guangdong to open China's doors to Hong Kong and Macao, to spread business to inner regions of the country, and to create favorable conditions for expansion abroad. Since its establishment, it has been making progress in various respects, including the use of operation and management systems of a joint stock enterprise with majority public ownership, adapting to the needs of the development of a commodity economy, supporting the development of the regional economy, and exploring new fields of business.

REFERENCES

Chen Yuan and Zhao Haikuan. 1990. *Almanac of China's Finance and Banking.* Beijing: China's Financial Publishing House.
China Finance and Banking Association. 1991. *Almanac of China's Finance and Banking.* Beijing: China's Financial Publishing House.
China Handbook Editorial Committee. 1990. *Economy.* Beijing: Foreign Languages Press.
Donnithorne, Audrey. 1967. *China's Economic System.* London: George Allen and Unwin.
Huang Dang, Liu Hong Yu, and Zhang Xiao, eds. 1990. *The Encyclopaedia of Finance and Banking in China.* Beijing: Economic Management Press.
King, Frank H. H. 1968. *A Concise Economic History of Modern China (1849–1961).* New York: Praeger.
Li Mao-sheng. 1987. *Study on the Chinese Financial Structure.* Shanxi: Shanxi People's Publication House.
Liu Hongru, ed. 1991. *On Financial Macro-Control and Adjustment.* Beijing: China Financial Press.
Liu Suinian and Wu Qungan. 1986. *China's Socialist Economy: An Outline History (1949–1984).* Beijing: Beijing Review.
SBC Research. 1992. *China Stock Market Overview.* July.
Shang Ming, ed. 1988. *China Today: Money and Banking.* Beijing: China Social Science Press.
Shang Ming, Wu Xialing, and Luo Lanbo. 1992. *Banking Credit Management and Money Supply.* Beijing: People's University.
Xinhua. 1983. *A History of Chinese Currency.* Hong Kong: Xinhua Publishing House.
Young, Arthur N. 1965. *China's Wartime Finance and Inflation, 1937–1945.* Cambridge, Mass.: Harvard University Press.

5

Nonbank Financial Institutions

Reforms in the banking sector proceeded side-by-side with some reforms and developments in the nonbanking financial sector. The latter include rural credit cooperatives (RCCs), Urban credit cooperatives (UCCs), trust and investment companies (TICs), leasing companies, finance companies, and insurance companies. As discussed in chapter 1, RCCs emerged with some importance after liberation but then suffered some setbacks over 1958–1980. However, they were reformed and played an important role after 1979; moreover, their philosophy and business practices were emulated in the urban centers with the establishment of UCCs in the reform era. Concurrent with these events, the trust business reemerged and the reform era witnessed the rapid (and turbulent) growth of TICs. Furthermore, Chinese enterprises realized that they could acquire assets through leasing, and some developments have occurred in this financial activity. Finally, finance and insurance companies emerged to play an important role in the accumulation of savings and the financing of China's economic reconstruction.

RURAL CREDIT COOPERATIVES (RCCs)

Rural credit cooperatives are financial collective organizations that have developed as an important part of the Chinese financial system. RCCs are legal entities with independent operation, separate accounting, democratic management, and sole responsibility for profits or losses. The collective is owned by its members and operates as a shareholding enterprise. Rural households (mostly peasants) buy the shares voluntarily and can withdraw their funds freely. The assets of the RCC belong to the collective, which holds them on behalf of all the shareholders.[1]

While RCCs existed prior to liberation in 1949, it was in the Communist era that they catapulted into importance and, perhaps, chaos (Donnithorne, 1967: 208–209). In the preliberation years, wealthy landlords, other rich farmers, and merchants were the main sources of financing for farmers, but these sources dried up after the confiscation of bureaucratic capital in the early 1950s. With the founding of the People's Republic of China in 1949 and the subsequent land reform (see chapter 1), three forms of rural cooperatives developed rapidly for agricultural activities: the mutual aid cooperative for production, the rural supply-and-marketing cooperative for distribution of products, and the rural credit cooperative (Chen and Zhao, 1990: 80–81). The functions of the RCCs were (and continue to be) to:

1. Collect idle funds in the rural areas, take in deposits, and provide loans for rural (mainly agricultural) development;

2. Handle the settlement of accounts and control cash in the rural areas;

3. Train and guide the bookkeepers in the other collectives in proper cash management;

4. Assist rural businesses and residents with financial problems to minimize usury (China Handbook Editorial Committee, 1990: 367).

After liberation in 1949, the need for rural development was urgent, and in February 1954, PBOC held the first meeting on RCCs with the theme of "active lending and steady development." Initial plans called for the establishment of 34,000 to 40,000 RCCs in 1954, but this was revised in July 1954 to 100,000 by the local managers of PBOC. In fact, the number of RCCs was estimated at more than 130,000 at the start of 1955, with 1 RCC in most villages throughout China (Donnithorne, 1967: 409). Considering that there were less than 3,000 at the start of 1953, the growth in RCCs was staggering. The abnormally rapid development of RCCs brought about many problems, including too many institutions, not enough business, weak financial strength of the RCCs, and poor-quality staff and management. Accordingly, PBOC took swift action to adjust the growth policy and streamline the operations of RCCs, and the result was a downsizing of the movement to about 103,000 RCCs by the end of 1956.

The Great Leap (1958–60) dealt another blow to the RCCs when they were relegated to the status of commune credit departments. They were regarded as merely collectors of cash, and most of their "banking" functions were taken away. The communes transferred the deposit-taking and loan-granting functions to the local branches of PBOC. Apparently, the conservative elements of the CCP viewed RCCs with suspicion, and regarded them as a disguise for another capitalist institution. Mismanagement and the misappropriation of funds were rampant, and by the end of 1962, deposits had dropped to RMB 970 million, from RMB 2 billion in 1958. Again, PBOC came to the rescue, and with "Regulations on Rural Credit Cooperatives" (October 1962), it defined the nature and position of RCCs, and explained that they were complementary to the national banking system and this position was important in the Chinese socialist financial system. The implementation of the "Regulation" helped the recovery and development of the RCCs, and by the end of 1965, deposits of all types increased to RMB 4.8 billion, and loans, to RMB 1.5 billion.

Just as the recovery and development were gaining momentum, the Cultural Revolution (1966–76) began, and RCCs suffered again. Because of the ultra-leftist trend of thought at this time, RCCs were transferred to the charge of "poor and lower-middle class peasants," but there was really no one in charge, and the operations of the RCCs were left in limbo. In 1970, in order to offset the negative effects of transferring the RCCs to the people's communes, and to avoid a stalemate situation, PBOC began to treat RCCs as its grass-roots units in the countryside; they now operated like branches of PBOC. This shift in policy meant that the RCCs lost their collective status. However, in 1977, PBOC restored the collective status, and declared that RCCs were financial collective organizations with national status; this action set the stage for reform in the RCC movement for the 1980s.

Reforming the RCCs for the 1980s

The general objectives of the reform of RCCs were to regain the organizational image in the agricultural sector, restore democracy in management, encourage flexibility in operation to regulate rural funds, and adapt to the quick development of the rural economy. In October 1980, the Agricultural Bank of China held a national meeting on RCCs, studied the reform of credit cooperatives, and suggested three steps for the reform of rural credit cooperatives. These reforms were as follows:

1. Reactivate and expand the credit cooperatives over 1980–1982, and liberalize and reform the management of RCCs through output-related performance criteria and the contract responsibility system. This strategy eased tensions between collective management and the Agricultural Bank of China, under whose supervision RCCs were placed.

2. Regain the organizational image, restore democracy in management, and encourage flexibility in operation over 1983–1984 through the following actions:

   a. RCCs were to operate independently and have sole responsibility for profits and losses.

   b. RCCs and ABC were to mutually agree on a division of operational activities.

   c. RCCs should have the option to decide its loan and interest rate policies without interference from ABC.

   d. The relationships between ABC and the RCCs should be governed by economic factors.

3. Further reforms should be undertaken after 1985, following implementation of the previous steps.

Organization of RCCs

Figure 5.1 shows the organizational relationships among the various units

Figure 5.1
Organizational Relationships among Units Involved with a Typical RCC

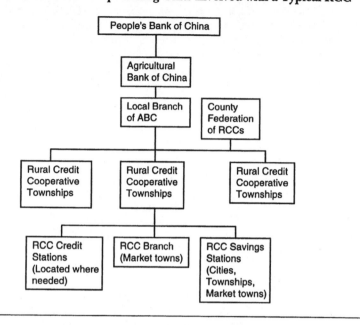

which are involved with a typical RCC.[2] The majority of RCCs are located in townships with concentrated economic activities and are under the supervision of ABC, which itself is supervised by PBOC. Usually, there are county federations of RCCs under the leadership of the local branches of ABC, which provide financial and consultancy services. RCC branches are located in market towns which have a lower economic status than the townships, or in other locations where buying and selling activities require their services. RCC credit stations are located wherever they are needed to serve the rural industries and are staffed by part-time employees, while RCC savings stations are normally located in the towns, market towns, and cities, where they handle deposits and withdrawals. At the end of 1988, the RCCs had about 400,000 institutions and service units (including 60,800 RCCs) throughout rural China, employing about 767,000 people full time.

The management structure is typical of that for a shareholding enterprise. The organ of power in the RCC is the annual Peasants' Representative Conference, where the management team reports on stewardship to the shareholders. Daily management is with a general manager under the supervision of an elected Board of Directors and Board of Supervisors. The Board of Directors is elected by the shareholders, and its principal functions are similar to those for specialized banks (as discussed for ICBC in chapter 3). The peasants, as shareholders, are entitled to dividends after the distribution of the profits along mandatory guidelines.

Nature of Business

Rural credit cooperatives can deal with the following types of business.

1. Accept deposits associated with rural personal savings and the cash flow from rural collectives.

2. Grant loans and conduct settlement transactions for rural households, rural cooperative economic organizations, and enterprises.

3. Deal with deposits, loans, security exchanges, and other cash-collecting and paying business on behalf of national banks and other institutions.

4. RCCs in larger townships can take part in bill clearance within the township, with the approval of PBOC.

5. Conduct other business, as authorized by PBOC.

In conducting their business, RCCs have to be mindful of the following operating guidelines:

1. Loans should not exceed 75 percent of total deposit plus capital. The general principle is that the volume of loans should be determined by the ability to attract deposits. The state has indirect control, since the loan limits of the RCCs should be included in the unified credit plan.

2. Capital plus specified categories of self-owned funds should not be less than 10 percent of total loans. Further, a single loan should not exceed 50 percent of the capital of an RCC. These loan/equity requirements are supposed to guard against insolvency.

3. Fixed-asset loans outstanding should not exceed 20 percent of total loans outstanding, and total fixed assets of the RCC should not exceed 30 percent of capital plus the accumulated fund. These provisions channel increased funds for the procurement and sale of commodities, which are important activities in rural communities.

4. RCCs must provide for reserves against deposits, and the proportion is determined by PBOC. In addition, RCCs must have free reserves to meet daily payments. The proportion of free reserves to various types of deposits are determined through discussions with the county branch of ABC, and all reserves must be deposited with ABC.

5. The deposit and lending rates of RCCs can float within an approved range of the rates set by PBOC. The interest rate on required reserves is determined by PBOC, and that for free reserves, by ABC.

6. With regard to financial management, the following general principles should be observed:

   a. RCCs must practice financial discipline, obey financial rules, and accept the supervision of local finance, auditing, and tax authorities.

   b. RCCs must pay taxes according to the law, at least 50 percent of after-tax profits must be accumulated, and dividends should not exceed 20 percent of profits after taxes. Accumulated profits are allocated to shareholders by issuing new shares.

Table 5.1
Summary Balance Sheets for Rural Credit Cooperatives
(Value in Billions of Renminbi)

	1985	1986	1987	1988	1989	1990	1990 (Indexed to 1986)	Percent Distribution 1986	Percent Distribution 1990
Assets									
Cash					3.32	3.46		0.00%	1.15%
Deposit with banks	40.14	49.32	55.19	57.97	65.61	77.25	156.63%	40.26%	25.75%
Deposit with PBOC			4.75	4.91	3.69	5.26		0.00%	1.75%
Total Loans	40.00	56.85	77.13	90.86	109.07	141.30	248.55%	46.41%	47.11%
Loans to collective farming	4.13	4.46	6.45	8.01	10.64	14.31	320.85%	3.64%	4.77%
Loans to township ent'prises	16.44	26.58	35.93	44.02	54.09	70.07	263.62%	21.70%	23.36%
Loans to households	19.42	25.80	34.00	37.24	41.40	51.82	200.85%	21.06%	17.28%
Other loans			0.75	1.60	3.00	6.00		0.00%	2.00%
Other credit assets	15.43	10.78	14.33	19.99	9.64	12.09	112.15%	8.80%	4.03%
Other assets		5.54	10.45	17.40	39.66	60.59	1093.68%	4.52%	20.20%
Total assets	95.57	122.49	161.85	191.13	230.99	299.95	244.88%	100.00%	100.00%
Liabilities									
Deposits	72.49	96.23	122.52	139.98	166.34	214.49	222.89%	78.56%	71.51%
Collectives	16.01	19.62	21.95	25.75	25.66	30.33	154.59%	16.02%	10.11%
Farm households	56.48	76.61	100.57	114.23	140.68	184.16	240.39%	62.54%	61.40%
Due to banks	3.28	4.15	3.77	3.60	3.76	4.20	101.20%	3.39%	1.40%
Other liabilities	15.40	12.82	21.80	29.46	46.09	64.21	500.86%	10.47%	21.41%
Total liabilities	91.17	113.20	148.09	173.04	216.19	282.90	249.91%	92.42%	94.32%
Capital									
Shares		1.61	2.34	3.66	6.27	7.94	493.17%	1.31%	2.65%
Self-owned	3.15	6.36	10.05	13.32	7.66	8.23	129.40%	5.19%	2.74%
Profit	1.25	1.32	1.37	1.11	0.87	0.88	66.67%	1.08%	0.29%
Total liabilities and capital	95.57	122.49	161.85	191.13	230.99	299.95	244.88%	100.00%	100.00%

Source: China Finance and Banking Association (1991).

    c. Reserves for bad debts must be maintained.

    d. Salary levels must be approved by ABC.

This list of rules and regulations is not complete, but it serves to illustrate the state's concern for the solvency of RCCs, the protection of rural savings, and the promotion of rural development. A viable financial institution for rural development eluded the state since liberation, and every effort has been made to ensure that RCCs succeed. The assets of RCCs more than tripled, from RMB 95.57 billion in 1985 to RMB 299.95 billion in 1990, as shown in Table 5.1. Loans to the rural collectives and households accounted for nearly 50 percent of assets. RCCs have emphasized loans to businesses for grain production, technological improvements to enhance agricultural production, and the development of infrastructure for most rural industries. Loans to rural households have also been given priority. The deposits with banks are mainly reserves, which are mandatory and are held by ABC

Deposits from households and collectives accounted for over 70 percent of funding for RCCs, which is evidence of how well they have been able to mobilize rural funds. In addition, RCCs have the authority to borrow from banks and other lenders, and miscellaneous liabilities accounted for about 20 percent of funding.

Reforming the RCCs for the 1990s

Since the reforms in the 1980s, the RCCs have done reasonably well, and there are suggestions for further reforms in the near future. The suggested reforms are as follows (Li, 1991; Zhen and Wu, 1993):

1. RCCs in economically developed areas (e.g., larger cities and associated suburbs) along the coastal zone should be upgraded to cooperative shareholding banks in order to serve a larger array of clients.

2. RCCs in the "middle" economically developed areas (e.g., smaller cities and larger towns) should be upgraded to cooperative shareholding banks to service mainly collective and individual enterprises.

3. RCCs in less developed areas (e.g., the farming areas and smaller towns) should remain as credit cooperatives to serve the peasants. Moreover, it is suggested that there should be some consolidations or mergers of RCCs that are not operating on a sound economic basis.

RCCs have succeeded to date, and they have operated well under ABC since they were reformed in the early 1980s. Their success has been envied in the cities, where there is a movement to set up urban credit cooperatives. The following section is a summary description of the UCCs and some of their main differences compared to RCCs. The nature of operation and the rules and regulations of RCCs and UCCs are quite similar, and will not be reiterated.

URBAN CREDIT COOPERATIVES (UCCs)

When the reforms started in 1979, the collective and individual economies in cities and towns developed quickly, and the number of collective enterprises and associated employment multiplied. The banking system in existence had difficulty in providing the various and flexible services required by the collective and individual enterprises. In some places, it was very difficult for collective enterprises and individuals to open bank accounts, deposit money, borrow from the banks, or settle accounts. UCCs emerged to partially fill these needs. In 1979, the first UCC in China was established in Luohe County, Hebei Province, and after 1979, UCCs developed very quickly. Enabling legislation was passed by PBOC in 1986: "The Provisional Regulations for the Administration of the UCC" (July 1986). By the end of 1989, there were 3,409 urban credit cooperatives around the country, with 60,308 employees. The UCCs helped to absorb idle capital in the urban society and to support the development of the collective and individual economy in cities and towns.

The UCCs are under the supervision of PBOC and, like the RCCs, are independent legal entities with separate accounting, independence of operation, and sole responsibility for profits or losses and for democratic management. The stockholders include collective enterprises, private industrial and commercial households, and citizens in cities and towns. The

Table 5.2
Summary Balance Sheets for Urban Credit Cooperatives
(Value in Billions of Renminbi)

	1987	1988	1989	1990	1990 (Indexed to 1986)	Percent Distribution 1986	Percent Distribution 1990
Assets							
Cash and bank deposits	1.11	2.24	3.40	5.97	537.84%	34.80%	21.01%
Required reserves	0.13	0.46	1.43	2.28	1753.85%	4.08%	8.02%
Total loans	1.95	6.34	13.39	19.63	1006.67%	61.13%	69.07%
Collectives in industry	0.72	2.39	4.47	7.02	975.00%	22.57%	24.70%
Collectives in commerce	0.61	1.77	4.02	7.77	1273.77%	19.12%	27.34%
Individual proprietor	0.23	0.68	1.22	1.74	756.52%	7.21%	6.12%
Others	0.39	1.50	3.68	5.10	1307.69%	12.23%	17.95%
Other assets			0.28	0.54		0.00%	1.90%
Total assets	3.19	9.04	18.50	28.42	890.91%	100.00%	100.00%
Liabilities							
Total deposits	2.95	7.56	15.71	22.08	748.47%	92.48%	77.69%
Collectives in industry	0.81	1.66	2.64	3.28	404.94%	25.39%	11.54%
Collectives in commerce	0.94	1.78	3.78	44.60	4744.68%	29.47%	156.93%
Individual proprietor	0.35	0.62	0.95	1.14	325.71%	10.97%	4.01%
Savings: time	0.05	0.50	1.18	3.33	6660.00%	1.57%	11.72%
Savings: demand	0.04	0.31	0.89	1.62	4050.00%	1.25%	5.70%
Capital funds	0.76	2.69	6.27	8.26	1086.84%	23.82%	29.06%
Provision for bad debts	0.18	0.80	1.34	2.72	1511.11%	5.64%	9.57%
Other liabilities	−0.16	0.23	0.32	0.76		−5.02%	2.67%
Capital							
Self-owned funds	0.14	0.28	0.71	1.88	1342.86%	4.39%	6.62%
Net profit	0.08	0.17	0.42	0.98	1225.00%	2.51%	3.45%
Total liabilities and capital	3.19	9.04	18.50	28.42	890.91%	100.00%	100.00%

Source: Chen and Zhao (1990).

management style is similar to that for RCCs: the general manager reports to the Board of Directors and Board of Supervisors, which, in turn, report to shareholders at either general or special meetings.

There are two main types of UCCs: urban credit cooperatives and urban credit cooperative affiliates. Normally, the urban credit cooperatives are located in large- and middle-sized cities, and have no branches. Their main business is to take deposits, grant loans, and undertake settlement and remittance transactions for collective enterprises and private industrial and commercial households. On the other hand, the urban credit cooperative affiliate is usually a financial organization owned by urban credit cooperatives. The affiliate is a legal entity with separate accounting, independent operation, sole responsibility for profits or losses, and an independent obligation to pay taxes. While transactions between a UCC and its affiliate should be on an arm's-length basis, in reality, the affiliate is like a "paid servant" in a location where the UCC may not be otherwise represented.

The total assets of UCCs increased eightfold from RMB 3.19 billion in 1986 to RMB 28.42 billion in 1989 (Table 5.2). Loans accounted for about 69 percent of assets, and these loans were granted to businesses and individuals as is the case for RCCs. Funding comes mainly from deposits from businesses and individuals. Considering only aggregate assets, RCCs are about ten times the size of UCCs, which is not surprising. RCCs have a longer history, and they dominate in rural China, where over 80 percent of the country's population resides. In addition, the UCCs compete against China's monolitic (and oligopolistic) banks in the urban areas and it is quite commendable to observe their considerable progress in their short history.

Reforming the UCCs for the 1990s

UCCs are relatively new institutions and operate in market areas that are somewhat different from those for RCCs. During their brief history, UCCs have encountered some growing pains in the areas of ownership, administration, and operations, including the following (Qi, 1992; Jia, 1992):

1. UCCs are supposed to be collective organizations, but in some cases, a few individuals own the majority of shares and the UCCs operate like private financial institutions. In addition, there are cases where state-owned enterprises, foreign companies and government institutions are allowed to own shares, a practice that runs counter to the philosophy of collective organizations.

2. UCCs are supposed to provide services for collective and private enterprises. However, there are cases where UCCs attract deposits from state-owned enterprises, government institutions, and the army, a practice that results in conflicts with the specialzed banks.

3. There are cases of lax management and poor financial management. Operating regulations are normally set by the various branches of PBOC and tend to vary across administrative regions. Therefore, there is no unified set of permissible business activities across UCCs as there is with RCCs.

Given the above and other problems in the UCC movement, suggested reforms include the following:

1. Establish the ground rules for operations on a national basis and strengthen the capital requirements to protect against insolvency.

2. UCCs should restrict their clientele to the collective and private enterprises, as there is a reasonable level of business in these sectors.

3. Larger UCCs should be converted into cooperative shareholding banks to service specific regions in the country.

TRUST AND INVESTMENT COMPANIES IN CHINA

The trust industry in China began in the 1920s as a humble activity involving the safekeeping of property. In 1917, the head office of Shanghai Commercial Savings Bank established a "Storage Department" to hold property in trust for customers. Four years later, the storage department became a "Trust Department." Similar cases occurred over this period. In

1918, Zhejiang Xinye Bank began to rent lockers or safety deposit boxes, and in 1919, the Shanghai Branch of Juxing Bank established a trust department. Then in 1921, the first specialized trust and investment company was established in China: the Chinese Commercial Trust Company was founded in Shanghai.

After liberation in 1949, the People's Government tried to establish socialist oriented financial institutions and several new trust and investment institutions, emerged in Beijing, Wuhan, Shanghai, Kunming, and other larger cities. The notables included a trust department in the Shanghai branch of PBOC (January 1949), the Tianjin Trust and Investment Company (June 1951) and the Overseas Chinese Investment Company in Guangdong Province (March 1955). However, by the end of the 1950s, China implemented its centralized economic planning system and there was no need for trust and investment institutions. These institutions faded away (as discussed in chapter 1).

Deng Xiaoping's open door policy and its resulting economic reforms since 1979 led to a revival of TICs. Under central planning, funds moved vertically from PBOC through the specialized banks to enterprises. This vertical flow of funds was quite unsuitable for economic reconstruction and development, since surplus funds tended to remain under the control of the units to which they were allocated under the national credit plan. In the meantime, units in need of funds found it difficult to implement worthwhile projects due to lack of funding. The state began to encourage the Chinese banks to promote the horizontal flow of capital across banks and industrial sectors. In August 1980, at a meeting of the presidents of the branches of PBOC, a decision was taken to encourage enterprises to deposit (or trust) their surplus capital with banks for loans or investment in order to spur economic growth. This decision prompted banks to set up trust departments to handle this function. Regulations for trust and investment operations were contained in a release by PBOC: "The Notification on Activating Trust Industry" (September 1980). This release was followed by a forum involving PBOC and 13 provinces and cities, in July 1981. At the meeting it was decided that the trust and investment operations must be expanded to promote horizontal capital movements and economic reform. A subsequent meeting, in August 1981, came to the same conclusion, and by the end of 1981, there were more than 600 TICs in China.

A Rocky Start

In early 1982, many TICs competed for business and funds, causing disruptions in the national credit plan and its associated planned distribution of funds. The rapid growth in the money supply and domestic credit that occurred at that time had serious implications for the state's macroeconomic policies. It was suspected that many TICs engaged in unauthorized borrowing for their respective sponsors. For example, a local government would use its "captive" TIC to raise funds that were not authorized under the national credit plan. Even if these unauthorized activities did not occur, sponsors of TICs viewed them as supplementary sources of funds to enhance investments. Local governments and enterprises would be tempted to make bold forecasts of investments for the national physical plan based on the feeling that their TICs would secure funding to cover shortfalls from the national credit plan. In order to control credit and strengthen regulation, the state Council released "Notification on Rectification of the Trust and Investment Business and Strengthening of the Regulation of Rebuilding Funds" in April 1982. Under this directive, trust and investment business could only be conducted by specialized banks or TICs authorized by the state Council and PBOC. Effectively, enterprises were prevented from establishing TICs, and only "favored" local governments could do so, provided they obtained permission. However, the situation did not improve; if anything, it worsened (Appendix). Investments and the growth in domestic credit continually exceeded targets set by the state, so in early 1983, PBOC stopped, temporarily, the trust and investment business.

By 1984, the Chinese economy had expanded rapidly, the demand for credit was great, and the growth in the money supply was deemed excessive. Austerity measures were taken to cool the economy and minimize the outflow of foreign exchange to pay for (unauthorized) imports (Appendix). In early 1985, the State Council ordered banks to stop their trust loan and investment business and reduce existing operations in an attempt to reduce the growth in domestic credit. There was a suspicion that banks were mixing trust funds with bank capital to take advantage of lending opportunities. With this in mind, the PBOC released "Provisional Regulations on Financial Trust and Investment Institutions" in April 1986. The objective of this directive was to make TICs independent legal entities and consolidate the authority of PBOC over the establishment and supervision of TICs.

After 1986, a large number of TICs were established, in spite of regulations aimed at controlling the trust and investment business. It is quite easy to understand how this increase in TICs occurred. For example, before the regulation, a bank would conduct trust activities through provincial and county branches, there would be no TICs count. However, after regulation, a bank would, in its efforts to retain its trust business, establish TICs in every major branch across the country. Even if a bank established only 1 TIC in every province, the TIC count would be 30, compared to 0 before the regulations. Toward the end of 1988, there were 745 trust and investment institutions in China, with total assets of RMB 73.55 billion (Table 5.4). There were also many problems, including a surfeit of institutions, given their level of business and poor management. The austerity measures taken during 1984–1985 were relaxed in 1986–1987, and the Chinese economy again began to heat up. As a result, the State Council had no choice but to reimpose even stricter austerity measures in late 1987 and 1988 (Appendix). With respect to TICs, in October 1988, the State Council took action to clean up the industry. After the cleanup, about 300 TICs remained, and these were owned only by banks and governments.

In summary, TICs are encouraged to mobilize surplus cash from enterprises, governments, institutes, and similar sources, and to hold these funds in trust for the respective depositors. During the holding period, the funds are invested in approved projects. Of course, TICs have been used to finance projects outside the national physical plan, actions that disrupted the national credit plan and adversely affected the state's macroeconomic policies. The development of TICs has been rather cyclical: contractions occurred in 1982, 1986, and 1988. The contractions in the trust and investment business tended to occur when the economy was overheating. Whenever the state applied austerity measures to control the growth in domestic credit, TICs suffered declines, and the reverse also held true.

Relevant Regulations

The following discussion is based on the State Council's "Provisional Regulations on Financial Trust and Investment Institutions" (April 1986), as amended for the 1988 cleanup. PBOC has the authority to approve the establishment of TICs and to supervise their operations. The following is a summary of the operating guidelines that were set to regulate the actions of TICs after 1988.

Minimum Legal Capital. A national TIC must have at least RMB 80 million, while a TIC at the provincial level must have at least RMB 50 million. Where TICs are engaged in foreign exchange business, the national TIC must have at least U.S. $5 million, and the provincial TIC, U.S. $2 million.

Location. TICs are allowed in large and mid-sized cities in China. By 1988, the state had decided that financial markets should operate only in cities where business volume was adequate to ensure profitable operations.

Ownership. TICs are owned (or sponsored) by Chinese banks and governments. The State Council controls one TIC (China International Trust and Investment Corporation, discussed later in this chapter). Moreover, the state has equity interests in other TICs, including China Agribusiness Trust and Investment Corp. and China Venturetech Investment Corp. Provincial and municipal TICs cannot establish branches in China or abroad, and TICs are barred from dealing with nonfinancial enterprises without the approval of PBOC.

Types of Business and Management. The nature of the operations of TICs is summarized in Table 5.3. While there are common rules and regulations (Part 3, Table 5.3), there are also special rules and regulations for TICs that conduct RMB business (Part 1) and for TICs that conduct foreign exchange business (Part 2).

Business Activities

The total assets of TICs increased threefold, from RMB 23.89 billion in 1986 to RMB 77.44 billion in 1989, as shown in Table 5.4. The largest TIC is China International Trust and Investment Corporation (CITIC), and the financial statistics for this TIC are shown separately, in Table 5.5. Next in size to CITIC are the national TICs owned by banks and certain state

Table 5.3
Permitted Business Activities and Managerial Requirements for TICs

1. TICs Engaged in RMB Business

Scope of business

The following activities are within the scope of business for TICs.

A. Trust investment and trust loans to projects designated by consignors (category A).
B. Ordinary trust investment and trust loans (category B).
C. Financial leasing.
D. Property storage and the issuing of securities on behalf of third parties.
E. RMB debts guarantee and testimony.
F. Economic consultation.
G. Security issuing authorized by PBOC.
H. Other business authorized by PBOC.

Management of deposits

TICs can absorb the following trust deposits with duration equal to or greater than one year.

A. Trust funds for trust investment or trust loans entrusted by the treasury.
B. Trust funds for trust investment or trust loans entrusted by enterprises.
C. Funds entrusted by labor insurance institutions.
D. Funds entrusted by scientific research institutes.
F. Funds entrusted by various societies and foundations.

Management of loans

TICs must follow these guidelines with respect to loans.

A. The proportion of category B deposits used for fixed assets loans and lease must be decided by PBOC.
B. TICs can extend circulation loans to their clientele. Circulating loans extended to other enterprises cannot be longer than 3 months.

2. TICs Engaged in Foreign Exchange Business

Scope of business

The following activities are permissible for TICs engaged in foreign exchange business:

A. On-shore and off-shore foreign exchange trust deposits.
B. Off-shore foreign exchange loans.
C. Issuing foreign exchange securities on behalf of third parties.
D. Foreign exchange trust investment.
E. Foreign exchange loans to their clientele.
F. International financial leasing.
G. Providing guarantee and testimony to foreigners for loans and contract bid and performance.
H. Credit investigation and consultation to promote international economic and trade cooperation.
I. Other business authorized by national foreign exchange administrative bureau.

Management of deposits and loans

The following guidelines apply to deposits and loans.

A. The necessary RMB capital can be obtained by attracting one-year (or longer) trust deposits and issuing RMB securities with the authorization of PBOC.
B. TICs engaged in foreign exchange business cannot deal with RMB loans, lease, or investment unless they have the necessary RMB capital.

3. Management of the Operations of All TICs

Planning management

A. The sources and application of RMB funds must be examined and approved by PBOC, while the sources and application of foreign exchange funds must be examined and approved by the national foreign exchange administrative bureau.

B. The fixed-asset loans, other investments, and leases must be within the national investment plan for fixed assets.

Management of reserves

A. TICs must open accounts with local branches of PBOC and deposit therein a prescribed proportion of its category B deposits. TICs engaged in foreign exchange business must open accounts with local branches of the Bank of China, where they must deposit foreign exchange reserves.

B. TICs must maintain reserves for bad debts.

Management of interest rates

The RMB and foreign exchange deposit and loan interest rates are determined by PBOC.

Financial management

TICs must submit the following documents to PBOC: annual working plan, summary quarterly and monthly performance report of source and application of capital, annual final statements and important business reports. In addition, TICs engaged in foreign exchange business must submit the above-mentioned documents to the national foreign exchange administration bureau.

---

departments, with assets between RMB 1 billion and RMB 5 billion. With few exceptions (e.g., Guangdong International Trust and Investment Corp.), the regional TICs are relatively smaller financial institutions, with most having assets of less than RMB 1 billion.

Deposits are the main source of funding, accounting for about 67 percent of total funding; entrusted and trusted deposits account for most of the deposits (Table 5.4). Deposits flow mainly from enterprises, governments, institutes, and similar sources. Entrusted deposits are funds for designated projects and are held in trust until needed to finance implementation. Trust deposits are surplus funds that are not targeted for any special use. Contrary to expectations, TICs have not been heavy users of the securities market, as long-term debt levels are the least used source for generating funds. Self-owned funds play a key role, accounting for about 30 percent of funding.[3]

The granting of loans is the primary investment of TICs and the loan portfolio has generally accounted for about 90 percent of assets (Table 5.4). Entrusted loans and trust loans accounted for about 74 percent of assets; these are extended to a "patronage-type" clientele, in accordance with the regulations that govern the operations of TICs. Other important activities are investments (mainly in state bonds) and financial leasing.

The Attractiveness of TICs

As noted, the State Council wanted to promote the horizontal flow of capital in the Chinese economy, a function that TICs appear to be fulfilling, to some degree.[4] These institutions provide some competition for the

Table 5.4
Summary Balance Sheets for TICs (Value in Billions of Renminbi)

	1986	1987	1988	1989	1989 (Indexed to 1986)	Percent Distribution 1986	Percent Distribution 1989
Assets							
Loans	21.77	43.90	66.06	69.44	318.97%	91.13%	89.67%
Entrusted loans	6.92	13.80	28.13	32.34	467.34%	28.97%	41.76%
fixed asset loans	3.64	9.37	15.45	16.24	446.15%	15.24%	20.97%
Trust loans	8.45	20.28	28.21	26.28	311.01%	35.37%	33.94%
fixed asset loans	5.52	9.12	10.57	9.66	175.00%	23.11%	12.47%
Investment	3.52	4.95	3.63	4.21	119.60%	14.73%	5.44%
Discount loans	0.09	0.13	0.16	0.11	122.22%	0.38%	0.14%
Mortgage loans	0.02	0.16	0.36	0.51	2550.00%	0.08%	0.66%
Bills discounted		0.13	0.20	0.22		0.00%	0.28%
Financial leasing	2.09	3.37	3.60	3.27	156.46%	8.75%	4.22%
Other loans	0.64	1.14	1.77	2.50	390.63%	2.68%	3.23%
Deposit with PBOC	1.94	3.27	2.63	3.76	193.81%	8.12%	4.86%
Required reserves	0.16	0.93	2.35	1.66	1037.50%	0.67%	2.14%
Bonds purchased			1.03	1.15		0.00%	1.49%
Foreign exchange equivalent	0.02	0.06	1.48	1.43	7150.00%	0.08%	1.85%
Total assets	23.89	48.16	73.55	77.44	324.15%	100.00%	100.00%
Liabilities							
Deposits	12.98	29.91	49.18	52.17	401.93%	54.33%	67.37%
Entrusted deposits	8.13	16.92	32.36	36.70	451.41%	34.03%	47.39%
Trusted deposits	4.01	10.65	13.84	10.47	261.10%	16.79%	13.52%
Guaranty fund deposits	0.32	0.31	0.30	0.27	84.38%	1.34%	0.35%
Other deposits	0.52	2.03	2.68	4.46	857.69%	2.18%	5.76%
Bonds	0.50	1.11	0.70	0.48	96.00%	2.09%	0.62%
Agency marketing	0.33	0.55	0.60	0.61	184.85%	1.38%	0.79%
Transactions with specialized banks	1.53	1.42	−0.81	−2.34	−152.94%	6.40%	−3.02%
Financial institutions transactions	0.54	0.38	0.09	1.05	194.44%	2.26%	1.36%
Reserve for bad debts	0.03	0.12	0.20	0.21	700.00%	0.13%	0.27%
Self-owned funds	7.29	12.53	19.79	21.92	300.69%	30.51%	28.31%
Others	0.01	0.39	1.06	0.88	8800.00%	0.04%	1.14%
Net profit	0.15	0.53	1.29	1.22	813.33%	0.63%	1.58%
Total liabilities and capital	23.89	48.16	73.55	77.44	324.15%	100.00%	100.00%

Source: Chen and Zhao (1990).

Chinese banks in the local government and enterprise sectors where they are allowed to operate.[5] However, a more important role for TICs is to provide a mechanism for local governments to secure funding for approved projects. Over the 1952–1980 period, the state provided 82 percent of the funding for capital construction or investments. However, the state's contribution has been declining for budgetary and other reasons. By 1990, the state was providing only about 38 percent of funding for capital construction (Appendix) and enterprises, provincial and municipal governments and foreigners now play a greater role in financing capital construction. From a Western perspective, a TIC is a hybrid between a trust company and a development bank. It can accept deposits like a trust company in a Western country and finance projects, as approved by the state, like a development bank.

Chinese banks are interested in TICs since they can use these institutions to circumvent some banking regulations. Under present conditions, the credit limits of a bank and its associated branches are fixed annually and cannot be exceeded without PBOC approval. In the best of times, it is a tedious task to get such approval due to bureaucratic delays and political meddling. The "captive" TIC becomes handy when a bank or one or more of its branches reaches its approved credit limits. The typical solution is to refer the potential client to the TIC and charge an agency fee.

In general, the TIC can circumvent interest rate guidelines that are set by PBOC. PBOC interest rates are used as the nominal rates for loans. However, by charging for extra services (e.g., agency fees, legal fees, insurance, consultancy fees, etc.) and other devices (e.g., the method of loan takedown, the method of interest calculation, etc.), the effective interest rates tend to exceed PBOC guidelines. It may surprise the reader to learn that this practice is legal in China.

Provincial and municipal governments tend to use TICs to circumvent the national credit plan and raise funds for approved projects (as discussed earlier). In addition, they hope to use TICs to borrow overseas to obtain foreign currency in order to supplement allocations from SAEC (chapter 6). It is quite common for a local government to have one TIC for domestic operations and another for foreign exchange business. However, the state takes a dim view of this practice, and only a few TICs (e.g., Guangdong International Trust and Investment Corp.) have approval to borrow overseas.

In summary, TICs can be viewed as "extension departments" of their sponsors, established to handle a variety of activities, including project management, the issuing of securities, consultancy, and leasing. The loans and deposit structures indicate that they have relatively few clients and are not retail operations like banks or credit cooperatives. Sponsors of TICs conducting foreign exchange business hope to raise foreign currency loans to supplement foreign currency allocations from the state. The emphasis on (and jealousy of) regional development in China has pressured local governments to take every conceivable measure to procure funds for regional projects. TICs happen to be one available strategy to achieve this objective. Either the local government establishes the TIC or the local government pressures the local branch of a bank to do so.

The largest and most important TIC in China is China International Trust and Investment Corporation; the following is a brief review of the firm. TICs that are sponsored by governments attempt to emulate the developmental initiatives of CITIC in their respective jurisdictions. For those TICs that are involved in the foreign exchange business, CITIC has paved the way by developing goodwill in the international arena.

China International Trust and Investment Corporation (CITIC)

China International Trust and Investment Corporation was established on October 4, 1979. It is state-owned, under the State Council, and head-quartered in Beijing. CITIC has been used by the state for economic and, potentially, political purposes both at home and abroad. This 14-year-old TIC, with assets of RMB 33.78 billion in 1990 (Table 5.5) rivals the 81-year-

Table 5.5
Summary Balance Sheets for CITIC (Value in Billions of Renminbi)

	1986	1987	1988	1989	1990	1990 (Indexed to 1986)	Percent Distribution 1986	Percent Distribution 1989
Total Assets								
Cash and deposits	2.44	3.47	5.29	3.49	6.36	260.66%	30.39%	18.83%
Total loans	3.09	6.53	10.15	13.22	15.45	500.00%	38.48%	45.74%
Investments	0.91	1.28	2.44	2.80	3.08	338.46%	11.33%	9.12%
Overseas investment	0.28	0.33	0.61	1.21	3.02	1078.57%	3.49%	8.94%
Securities	0.30	0.81	1.40	2.99	2.58	860.00%	3.74%	7.64%
Real estate	0.23	0.30	0.63	1.28	1.49	647.83%	2.86%	4.41%
Other assets	0.78	1.50	1.23	1.66	1.80	230.77%	9.71%	5.33%
Total assets	8.03	14.22	21.75	26.65	33.78	420.67%	100.00%	100.00%
Liabilities								
Trust deposits	1.56	2.11	5.30	6.29	10.65	682.69%	19.43%	31.53%
General debts	2.00	5.15	7.42	9.98	11.73	586.50%	24.91%	34.72%
Bonds	2.86	5.12	5.66	6.49	7.34	256.64%	35.62%	21.73%
Other debts	0.79	0.83	1.25	1.17	1.03	130.38%	9.84%	3.05%
Total debts	7.21	13.21	19.63	23.93	30.75	426.49%	89.79%	91.03%
Shareholders' equity	0.82	1.01	2.12	2.72	3.03	369.51%	10.21%	8.97%
Total debt and equity	8.03	14.22	21.75	26.65	33.78	420.67%	100.00%	100.00%

Source: China Finance and Banking Association (1991).

old Bank of China (with assets of RMB 859.10 billion) for international recognition on behalf of China (Langstron, 1985; Friedland, 1990). The operating guidelines for CITIC are similar to those summarized in Table 5.5 but, due to its link with the state, it appears to have a "most favored TIC status" compared to other TICs in China. At the general level, the main tasks of CITIC are:

to guide, absorb and utilize funds of overseas Chinese, Hongkong and Macao compatriots and foreign nationals for long-term investments in China, to organize joint ventures or cooperative production, to undertake leasing business, and to make investments with the foreign funds it has raised. It operates under the Law on Chinese-Foreign Joint Ventures and other relevant laws, decrees and regulations.[6]

CITIC is a holding company with diverse interests in production, technology, finance, trade, and services employing over 20,000 people at its 24 subsidiaries at home and abroad. The assets of CITIC for 1990 were RMB 33.78 billion (Table 5.5). Excluding cash and deposits, the percentage distribution of these assets was as follows: loans to domestic enterprises, 45.74 percent; investments in domestic enterprises, 9.09 percent; overseas investment, 8.91 percent; securities, 7.64 percent; real estate, 4.41 percent; and other assets 3.97 percent. This distribution of assets reflects the diverse nature of the CITIC Group, which is different from the typical TIC discussed earlier. In terms of funding, debt financing accounted for 91 percent comprising trust receipts (31.53 percent), general debts (34.72 percent), corporation debentures (21.73 percent), and other liabilities (3.02 percent). Again, this funding pattern is different from that of the typical TIC.

The following discussion highlights the main activities that have been undertaken by CITIC to propel it to "towering heights."[7]

1. CITIC is China's contact for foreign investors who are interested in investing in China but have no specific cooperating partner. Consequently, CITIC was busy on a person-to-person level with such investors and by 1989, CITIC had invested in 114 Sino-foreign joint equity or contractual ventures.[8]

2. CITIC raises funds abroad to assist in the importation of technology and equipment. In this capacity, CITIC is constantly discussing and organizing domestic joint-equity or contractual ventures. Unto 1989, 189 such deals were concluded, and CITIC is the sole owner of 37 of these projects. While most of the projects were in the light and heavy industrial sectors, others were in mining, petrochemicals, and animal husbandry.

3. CITIC promotes the development of high-technology projects through its subsidary, CITICTECH. This subsidiary combines imported technologies with proficient Chinese research resources and achievements and comercializes them. For example, a U.S. satellite was launched by CITICTECH using China's LM-3 rocket, and a MINI-5H Chinese-and-English word processor was developed with foreign help.

4. CITIC actively follows the international financial market and floats foreign currency bonds. China's first foreign currency bond since liberation was floated by CITIC in Tokyo in 1982. Over 1982–1989, CITIC floated 12 bond issues in foreign currencies for the equivalent of U.S. $1.598 billion. These were some of the funds that CITIC used for its various investments.

5. CITIC is heavily involved in leasing through a group of institutions: China Oriental Leasing Co., Ltd.; China Leasing Company, Ltd.; the Leasing Department of the CITIC Industrial Bank; a CITIC subsidiary; and two leasing companies with CITIC's investment—Shanghai International Leasing Co., Ltd., and China Southwest Leasing Co., Ltd., in Chendu. This group of institutions had participated in over 1,500 leasing projects by the end of 1989.

6. CITIC funded and built the first office complex for foreign business executives in Beijing, a facility that opened in 1985. Then, by 1990, CITIC (either in conjunction with other developers or by itself) funded 19 office and apartment buildings, hotels, and villas in Beijing and ten other locations in China.

7. Due to its international exposure, the CITIC organization provides consultancy services for Chinese firms on the international markets.

8. CITIC is actively involved in investing in foreign countries, as shown in Table 5.6. CITIC has been used by the state to gain access to supplies of raw materials in the United States, Australia, Canada, and Hongkong. In addition, CITIC has built a strong and powerful position in transportation, finance, and utilities in Hongkong, probably in preparation for 1997.

LEASING INSTITUTIONS

Lease financing is a form of debt whereby a lessee (or borrower) acquires the use of an asset under an agreement to compensate a lessor who is the

Table 5.6
Major International Holdings of CITIC, 1990

TRANSPORTATION	MANUFACTURING	TELECOMMUNICATIONS
Hongkong	Hongkong	Hongkong
Cathay Pacific	Concordia Paper	AsiaSat
(airline, 12.5%)	(paper, 65%)	(satellite, 33.3%)
Eastern Harbour Crossing	HK Petrochemical	Hutchison Cablevision
(roadlink, 24.5%)	(plastics, 33.3%)	(cable TV, 10%)
Dragonair	CITIC Walbro	HK Telecom
Plus: 18 Cargo ships	Macao	Macao
	Macao Cement	Companhia
FINANCE	(cement, n.a.)	Telecommunications
	United States	(telephone, 20%)
Hongkong	CITIFOR	Stake in proposed
Ka Wah Bank	(timber, 100%)	HK-Macao electricity
(bank, 71.4%)	CITISteel	
China Investment	(steel mill, 70%)	REAL ESTATE
and Finance	Australia	
(OTC, 100%)	Portland Aluminum	Hongkong
Peregreen International	(smelter, 10%)	Projects at Hutchison
(stockbroking, n.a.)	Canada	Kwai Chung
West Germany	Celgar Pulp	Lam Tin
CITIC Industrial Bank	(pulp and paper, 50%)	United States
(bank, n.a.)		Property in
		Arizona and Oregon

Source: Friedland (1990), p. 35.

owner of the asset (and the lender). Leasing was not used in China during 1949–1979, as the funds for capital construction were provided mainly by the state and the assets acquired were state owned. Enterprises were precluded from acquiring assets that were not authorized under the unified physical plan. This situation continued into the early 1980s for domestic firms. However, the foreign-funded firms that ventured into China after it implemented the open door policy in 1979 saw leasing as an attractive means to secure productive assets in China. For example, in 1979, Goodyear Printing Press (GPP) of Hongkong was able to get the Hongkong branch of Japan Oriental Leasing to lease machinery (costing HK $13 million) for a production facility in Shenzhen (Lee, 1980). This experience, for the lessee (GPP) and the lessor (Japan Oriental Leasing), started a trend in lease financing in China. This section reviews the development of lease financing in China since 1979. The review does not deal with the leasing of state assets, a topic covered elsewhere (Yue, 1987). Under these types of leases, the state is the lessor, and collectives or individuals are the lessees. Usually, the leasing of state assets is done to improve operating and financial efficiency, and leasing conditions are determined in a social, economic and political context.

An operating lease is a short-term agreement to rent an asset such as a car for a weekend or an apartment for a year. This contrasts with a financial (or capital) lease, which is normally for the economic life of the asset. Under the financial lease, the lessee bears the economic risks associated with the asset, and the compensation to the lessor is usually for the purchase price (or its equivalent) of the asset plus a reasonable return on capital.[9] As in all countries worldwide, operating leases are prevalent in China and are not the focus of attention in this discussion. On the other hand, financial leases have gained some degree of prominence in China since 1979, and the institutions involved are widespread and varied.

Development of Leasing since 1979

In January 1980, the first leasing company in China, China Oriental Leasing Co. (COLC), was established as a joint venture involving Japan Oriental Leasing, with 50 percent; CITIC, with 20 percent; and Peking Machine and Electric Equipment Corp., with 30 percent (Lee, 1980; Yue, 1986). This joint-venture leasing company concentrated on financing export-oriented industries to benefit from hard-currency earnings. In the first five years of operations, COLC completed about 480 deals worth U.S. $340 million and involving interests from the United States, Japan, Britain, Germany, Italy, and France.

The state was reducing its investment in the economy and the need for foreign currency was growing, so as a result joint venture leasing was regarded as an attractive way of securing foreign funds and importing technology. By the end of 1985, there were about 32 joint venture leasing companies, doing about U.S. $700 million annually, with COLC accounting for about 23 percent of this figure. The following are some further examples of these joint venture leasing companies:[10]

1. China Universal Leasing Co.: Bank of China Trust and Consultancy Co. (BoCTCC), 24 percent; Sanwa Bank, 23 percent; Dresdner Bank, 23 percent; three State trading corporations under the Ministry of Foreign Economic Relations and Trade, 30 percent.

2. China International Packaging Leasing Co.: BoCTCC, 25 percent; Banca Commerciale Italiana, 20 percent; Banque Paribas, 20 percent; China National Packaging Industry Corp., 35 percent.

3. China International Non-Ferrous Metals Leasing Co.: BoCTCC, 20 perent; Banque Nationale de Paris, 20 percent; First Interstate Bank of California, 20 percent; China National Non-Ferrous Meals Industry Corp., 30 percent; Industrial and Commercial Bank of China, 10 percent.

4. International Far Eastern Leasing (China): involving People's Construction Bank of China, China National Chemicals Import and Export, Nippon Credit Bank (Japan), Crown Leasing (Japan), and Korea Industrial Leasing.

With the establishment of COLC, the Chinese started to see leasing as an alternative means of financing and another way of obtaining foreign exchange. Within a year (August 1981), the first state-owned leasing company (Chinese Lease Co., Ltd.) was established by CITIC and the National Materials Bureau. The stage was set for further growth in the domestic leasing industry. By the end of 1990, there were about 400 "independent" leasing institutions throughout China. In addition, all banks and TICs were, either directly or indirectly, involved in leasing. The independents are mainly local or regional operations, and their activities are limited compared to those of the joint venture leasing companies and those of the financial institutions and their associates.

Establishment and Supervision

PBOC has the authority to approve the establishment of leasing companies and to supervise and monitor their operations. Certain key criteria must be met for the establishment of leasing companies including the following:

1. The operation must be potentially viable, and sponsors of leasing companies are required to conduct the normal feasibility analysis for submission to PBOC.

2. For lease institutions with only Chinese capital, the minimum (cash) paid-in capital must be RMB 30 million. For those firms engaged in export lease, there must be at least U.S. $5 million foreign exchange capital.[11] For lease institutions with Chinese and foreign capital, the minimum (cash) paid-in capital must be equivalent to U.S. $8 million, with a minimum of foreign exchange cash capital of U.S. $5 million.

3. At least half of the members of the Board of Directors must have specialized knowledge in financial leasing, and the general manager must have at least two years' experience.

4. The proposed leasing company must demonstrate that it can raise funds to promote its leasing business, as outlined in its prospectus or feasibility study to PBOC.

In their daily operations, leasing companies are monitored to ensure that they conform to the following operating and financial guidelines:

1. They have to maintain certain maximum financial ratios, as follows:

    a. The lease obligation of a single lessee should not exceed 30 percent of the capital of the leasing company.

    b. The total volume of leasing business should not exceed 10 times the capital of the leasing company.

    c. Investment in fixed assets by the leasing company should not exceed 10 percent of capital.

    d. Where a leasing company offers guarantees for loans, the debt involved should not exceed 20 times the capital of the leasing company.

2. The projects that are financed through leasing must be included within the State physical plan and be taken into account in the associated credit plan. This means that the lessee has to plan ahead to ensure that lease financing will be available when needed.

3. Leasing institutions must open RMB accounts with PBOC or banks designated by PBOC. Financial lease institutions engaged in import and export leasing must open foreign exchange accounts with banks designated by the State Agency for Exchange Control (SAEC), which is an arm of the central bank.

4. Provisions must be made for potential bad debts.

5. Financial-leasing institutions must keep separate accounting records and hold separate responsibility for profits and losses.

Nature of Business

In general, leasing companies may engage in the following types of business:

1. Lease and sublease of equipment to be used in productive activities that are approved by the State.

2. Purchase equipment needed for leasing.

3. Sell and dispose of leased assets at the termination of contracts, subject to prescribed rules.

4. Offer financial and technical consultation on projects where assets will be leased.

5. Conduct foreign exchange business, as authorized by SAEC.

6. Undertake RMB security business, as authorized by PBOC.

7. Offer guarantees on RMB loans that relate to the leasing business.

8. Undertake other business as authorized by PBOC.

There is very little publicly available information about the leasing industry in China. However, the following examples give some idea of the nature of the industry and some of the participants and the types of transactions involved.

CITIC Industrial Bank is a comprehensive bank in China, and in 1990 it reported assets of RMB 21.434 billion (see chapter 4). The bank is one of the earliest institutions to introduce lease financing in China. In 1987, the bank concluded 46 lease contracts with a total value of RMB 63.44 million, mainly in textiles and other light industries; nearly half the contracts involved export-oriented projects. One of the 1987 contracts was done jointly with Paine Webber, USA, and involved a leverage lease of a Lockheed 100–30 cargo plane for China Airlines. This was the first time that a Chinese financial institution had participated in the leasing of an airplane. In 1988, the bank concluded 44 leasing contracts involving airplanes for Guangzhou People's Airlines and Xiamen Airlines, and assisted in arrangements for a lease for a Boeing 747–400 passenger plane for China International Airlines.

CITIC is a large conglomerate organization and is heavily involved in leasing through a set of institutions: China Oriental Leasing Co., Ltd.; China

Leasing Company, Ltd.; the leasing Department of CITIC Industrial Bank; and two subsidiaries, Shanghai International Leasing Co., Ltd., and China Southwest Leasing Co., Ltd., in Chendu. By the end of 1989, this group of institutions had participated in over 1,500 leasing projects involving airplanes, ships, production machinery, commercial and industrial real estate, and similar undertakings.

There are about 300 TICs in China, all of which are involved in leasing. For these TICs, investment in leased assets increased from RMB 2.09 billion in 1986 to RMB 4.46 billion in 1990, reflecting an increase of 113 percent over the period (Chen and Zhao, 1990: 54). For the typical TIC, leasing revenue ranges from 5 to 10 percent of gross revenues.

Over 1988–1991, three joint venture leasing companies were established in Shanghai: International Leasing Co., Ltd. (foreign partner, Mitsui Group); United Leasing Co., Ltd. (foreign partner, Tokyo Trust and Banking Co., Ltd.; and Pacific Leasing Co., Ltd. (foreign partners, Leasing Co. Ltd. of Japan and Long-Term Credit Bank of Japan). While these companies are prepared to do business nationwide, their focus so far has been in the provinces of Hebei, Jiangshu, Zhejiang, and Guangdong. By the end of June 1991, these companies had signed about 316 leasing contracts worth about RMB 2.723 billion (or U.S. $476.82 million at current exchange rates). While the leases involved a wide array of businesses, a high proportion was with the textile and electronics sectors (Wang, 1992).

The smaller independent leasing companies are mainly involved in local and regional business involving such assets as minibuses, trucks, light equipment, and small factories. For example, there are about 300 leasing companies in Henen Province, which are owned by financial institutions and local governments, and in 1991, they had leasing contracts worth RMB 43.57 million, U.S. $1.13 million, and Yen 1.13 billion (Chen, 1992). (Such leasing institutions do not play a significant part at the national level.) Finally, there are about 32 joint venture leasing companies associated with financial institutions, which play a much larger role in the economic reconstruction of China. Their operations are controlled based on the wishes of the state, which determines priority areas for economic development.

Some Problems in the Leasing Industry

The leasing industry in China is in its infancy, and some serious problems face both lessors and lessees.[12] The following is a summary of some of the major difficulties that have been encountered in Henan Province and by the three joint venture leasing companies in Shanghai. It is not clear whether such problems are experienced elsewhere in the country.

1. There is a lack of local personnel (or managers) experienced in the leasing business. As a result, feasibility reports for projects are poorly prepared and leasing contracts are not properly managed. Therefore, leased assets are exposed to relatively high risks.

2. There are foreign exchange controls in China (see chapter 6) and lessees involved in import leases may not have ready access to the foreign currencies needed to meet lease obligations.

3. Lessors tend to prefer short lease periods, ranging from 2 to 5 years, and lease rentals are onerous under such conditions. Lessees tend to have difficulties meeting lease payments given the short duration of the lease contracts. Usually, a relatively high percentage of lease payments are in arrears. For example, in 1991, the percentage of lease rentals in arrears for United Leasing Co., Ltd., was 40 percent; International Leasing Co., Ltd., 20 percent; and Pacific Leasing Co., Ltd., 10 percent. In fact, some of the lessees with United and International went bankrupt.

4. Lease financing involves medium- to long-term capital on the part of lessors. Usually, the foreign partners in a joint venture leasing company have to provide the foreign exchange for import leases. This may not be a problem if the international financial market is receptive, as the foreign partner can borrow in foreign currencies on favorable terms.[13] However, at times when that marketplace contracts or is subject to a pessimistic mood, it is difficult to raise foreign capital at low cost and desired maturities.

5. The flow of information on the leasing business in the domestic market is poor, and lessors have to employ extraordinary and costly promotional approaches to attract business.

Implications for Foreign Banks in China

Since 1979, overseas banks have been allowed entry into China on a gradual basis (see chapter 8). In December 1979, the State Council permitted overseas banks to establish representative offices in Beijing, and later, in 1991, this privilege was extended to allow representative offices in 14 open cities in China. In April 1985, overseas banks were allowed to establish branches in China's special economic zones, including Shenzhen, Xiamen, Zhuhai, Shantou, and Hainan. In 1990, this privilege was extended to include Shanghai. By the end of 1992, there were over 200 representative offices and 49 foreign branches operating in China (see chapter 8). The development of foreign banking coincided with that of joint venture leasing, and the following discussion focuses on some interesting relationships between the two financial sectors.

Some overseas banks that do not have permission to establish branches in China tend to be partners in joint venture leasing companies, which gives them an opportunity to enter China and participate in financial activities in that country. First Interstate Bank of California, a partner in China International Non-Ferrous Metals Leasing Co., is a typical example. Even if an overseas bank has a branch in China, it is a common strategy for it to also be involved in joint venture leasing. Sanwa Bank, a partner in China Universal Leasing Co., is a typical example.

Joint venture leasing companies are subject to a lower minimum capital requirement and are not subject to any deposit reserve requirement.

Foreign Banks are required to have at least a foreign currency equivalent of RMB 40 million and are subject to deposit reserve requirements. For example, the foreign banks in Shenzhen are subject to a 5 percent reserve ratio on deposits. Foreign banks are at a competitive disadvantage compared to joint venture leasing companies.

Leased assets that are imported qualify for lower duties. Equipment for start-up operations has a 100 percent exemption, while other leased assets have an exemption of 50 percent. Duties range from 50 to 200 percent, depending on the imported products, and duty reduction results in significant savings. Imported equipment financed by commercial loans does not normally qualify for duty exemption, and there is a preference for assets leased by Chinese enterprises.

FINANCE CORPORATIONS OF ENTERPRISE GROUPS

In the reform era, some enterprises have either expanded in conglomerate-like fashion or established common and mutual business relationships; it is estimated that there are more than 100 such enterprise groups in China. The appearance of enterprise groups speeds up the pace of adjustment by the industrial structure, promotes the technical progress of enterprises, and provides for the continued employment of management and employees. The year 1987 was particularly bad for funding, and some enterprise groups established finance companies to handle their financial difficulties. In a sense, these are captive finance companies, and they serve only members of the sponsoring enterprise groups, which use them to finance production and other business activities. Between 1987 and 1990, about 20 finance companies were established, with a combined asset base of about RMB 5 billion.

Finance companies must be established with the approval of PBOC, and their main sources of funding are deposits from the members of the enterprise groups and approved borrowing. The firms act like banks for the enterprise groups and have to follow certain financial and other guidelines, including the following:

1. The members of the sponsoring enterprise group must be legal persons and must be engaged in key industries supported by the state.

2. The production or services provided by the sponsor enterprise group must be competitive and profitable in the domestic or foreign market.

3. The aggregate funds for the finance company should not be less than RMB 100 million, and cash capital should not be less than RMB 50 million. Foreign exchange for a finance corporation engaged in foreign exchange business should not be less than U.S. $5 million.

4. The finance corporation must be a legal entity with independent accounting and must be responsible for its profits and losses.

5. The capital and accumulation of the finance corporation should not be less than 10 percent of its total assets; fixed assets loans and investment should

not exceed 50 percent of deposits, debt, and equity capital; and total fixed assets should not exceed 5 percent of deposits plus capital.

6. The amount of guarantees for loans should not exceed 20 times the amount of capital, a single loan should not exceed 40 percent of capital, and loans to or investment in a single enterprise cannot exceed 30 percent of the enterprise's total assets.

7. Fixed-asset loans and leases must be included in the unified credit plan, and interest rates on deposits and loans must confirm to PBOC guidelines.

8. Finance corporations must open accounts with local PBOC branches, deposit reserves against deposits as prescribed by PBOC, and submit financial and other reports on a regular basis.

INSURANCE COMPANIES

The insurance industry has a long history in China, and prior to 1949, the industry was dominated by foreign insurance companies.[14] In 1835, the Bao An Insurance Co. was established in Hongkong, the first insurance company in China. Later, other insurance companies (including Yang Zhi Insurance Co., Zhong Huang Insurance Co., and Barle Insurance Co.) were established in Shanghai and Guangzhou. The first Chinese insurance company was Ji Ren He Insurance Co., which was established in Shanghai in 1885. By the 1920s, there were more than 30 Chinese insurers, but they were overshadowed by the larger foreign insurance companies and operated near bankruptcy. After liberation in 1949, the assets of foreign insurance companies were confiscated and their privileges were terminated. On October 20, 1949, the People's Insurance Company of China (PICC) was established to take over the insurance business. By the end of 1958, PICC had over 1,300 branches and sub-branches throughout China, employing 4,600 agents and 50,000 staff members.

In 1959, the domestic insurance activities of PICC were terminated because it was argued that losses suffered by enterprises due to accidents, natural disasters, and so forth should be covered by the state. Moreover, there was no need for personal insurance since the state or enterprises should be responsible for the welfare of the people. However, PICC continued to offer foreign insurance services.

With the reforms that started in 1979, PICC resumed its domestic insurance activities and expanded its scope of operations, and by 1990, there were over 2,800 branches and sub-branches across China, employing 80,000 persons. The firm expanded its business activities and currently offers approximately 100 types of insurance at home and abroad. While PICC dominates the insurance industry, other companies have been established to compete with it. In March 1986, the State Council promulgated the "Interim Regulation on Management of Insurance Enterprises," under which several new insurance companies were established, including Agricultural and Husbandry Insurance Co. of Xinjiang, Production and Construction Corps, Ping An Insurance Co., and Sichuan Life Insurance Co., Ltd.

From the viewpoint of the financial market, insurance companies are important "collectors" of funds. These institutions are restricted in their investment activities, and most available funds are held as bank deposits. For example, in 1990, PICC's assets of RMB 23.84 billion were invested as follows: cash in hand and bank, 62.9 percent; investments (mostly in foreign securities), 21.4 percent; fixed assets, 9.2 percent; and other assets, 6.5 percent (China Finance and Banking Association, 1991: 175).

NOTES

1. The assets of a collective are not state owned but rather are owned in common by the group of individuals or households that are members of the collective. The fact that the assets are not state owned led to resentment of the RCCs during the Great Leap (1958–60) and the Cultural Revolution (1966–76), when ultra-leftist policies prevailed.

2. The immediate discussion draws on Chen and Zhao (1990: 81–82).

3. China Finance and Banking Association (1991: 174).

4. The immediate discussion draws on Long (1990: 32–33, 60); Shun (1991: 27–28); Zhou (1991: 25–28); and Guo (1993: 12–14).

5. TICs are small compared to Chinese banks, and the degree of competition should not be exaggerated. In 1989, banking assets were estimated at RMB 2.309 billion, while those for TICs were RMB 77.44 billion.

6. China Handbook Editorial Committee (1990: 370).

7. The discussion follows the format presented in Chen and Zhao (1990: 74–80).

8. In total, CITIC invested in 324 projects, including the 114 Sino-foreign projects.

9. The nature of, and accounting procedures for, leases are discussed in Van Horne, Dipchand, and Hanrahan (1993).

10. "Leasing in the Lead" (1985: 20) and "Japan, China and Korea Agree to Leasing Venture" (1991: 3).

11. In 1985, COLC and Oriental Leasing Co., Ltd., cooperated on China's first export lease: the rental of a Chinese bulk cargo ship to Norway.

12. The following discussion draws on Wang (1992), Chen (1992), and Huang (1991).

13. Joint venture leasing companies are usually highly leveraged, with about 80 debt to 20 percent equity. Therefore, access to low-cost debt capital with the desired maturities is important to their operations.

14. This section draws on several articles, including the following: Huang, Liu, and Zhang (1990: 220–228), Shang (1991: ch. 10), Chen and Zhao (1990: 71–74), Han (1991a, 1991b), and Wei (1988).

REFERENCES

China Finance and Banking Association. 1991. *Almanac of China's Finance and Banking*. Beijing: China's Financial Publishing House.

China Handbook Editorial Committee. 1990. *Economy*. Beijing: Foreign Languages Press.

Chen Guang Xing. 1992. "An Investigative Report about Finance Leasing Industry in Henan Province." *China Finance*, February, 36–37.

Chen Yuan and Zhao Haikuan. 1990. *Almanac of China's Finance and Banking.* Beijing: China's Financial Publishing House.

China State Statistics Bureau. 1989. "The Chinese Economy in 1988." *Beijing Review*, February 6–12, 21–22.

Donnithorne, Audrey. 1967. *China's Economic System.* London: Allen and Unwin.

do Rosario, Louise. 1985. "Time to Pay the Piper." *Far Eastern Economic Review*, April 23, 100–101.

Friedland, Jonathan. 1990. "CITIC Secures Hongkong's Heights at a Discount: The Cadre's Bargain." *Far Eastern Economic Review*, January 11, 95.

———. 1991. "CITIC Phone Home." *Far Eastern Economic Review*, March 1, 8–9.

Guo Qijiang. 1993. "Retrospective and Prospects of China's Trust and Investment Industry." *Shanghai Finance*, March, 12–14.

Han Guojian. 1991a. "Expanding Insurance Coverage for Foreign Firms." *Beijing Review*, July 8–14, 39–41.

———. 1991b. "Life Insurance in China." *Beijing Review*, July 29–August 4, 20–22.

Huang Dang, Liu Hong Yu, and Zhang Xiao, eds. 1990. *The Encyclopaedia of Finance and Banking in China.* Beijing: Economic Management Press.

Huang Yi. 1991. "Some Problems on the Leasing Industry Development." *Financial Studies*, June, 54–56.

"Japan, China and Korea Agree to Leasing Venture." 1991. *Asia Wall Street Journal Weekly*, June 17, 3.

Jia Jian Dong. 1992. "A Brief Analysis of UCC Development in China." *China Finance*, November, 40–42.

Langstron, Nancy. 1985. "Fame is the Spur." *Far Eastern Economic Review*, June 6, 58.

"Leasing in the Lead." *Far Eastern Economic Review*, April 15, 20.

Lee, Mary. 1980. "Leasing Helps in Greasing Business." *Far Eastern Economic Review*, June 6, 64.

Li Junfeng. 1991. "Classified Reform of RCCs." *Financial Studies*, March, 6–12.

Liu Guoguan. 1989. "A Sweet and Sour Decade." *Beijing Review*, January 2–8, 22–28.

Long Zhen Lai. 1990. "On the Issue of Trust and Investment Industry Management." *Financial Studies*, August, 32–33, 60.

Qi Guiling. 1992. "Some Policy Suggestions to Improve the UCC Management." *Financial Studies*, May, 50–51.

Salem, Ellen. 1983. "Slow Boat to China." *Far Eastern Economic Review*, April 23, 51–53.

———. 1987a. "Cooling Off the Economy." *Far Eastern Economic Review*, March 26, 80.

———. 1987b. "Major Hurdles to Revitalization." *Far Eastern Economic Review*, March 19, 62.

Shang Ming, ed. 1991. *Money and Banking.* Beijing: Social Sciences Press.

Shun Yuai. 1991. "The Problems and Correction of China's Trust and Investment Industry." *Financial Studies.* May, 27–28.

Van Horne, James C., Dipchand, Cecil R., and Hanrahan, J. Robert. 1993. *Financial Management and Policy.* 9th ed. Scarborough, Ontario, Canada: Prentice-Hall Canada Inc., ch. 19.

Wang Qujun. 1992. "An Investigative Report about Sino-Foreign Leasing Companies in Shanghai." *Shanghai Finance*, March 26, 28–29.

Wei Runquan. 1988. "The Open Policy and Insurance Industry of China." *Canadian Underwriter*, May, 40–42.

Yue Haitao. 1986. "Leasing Thrives in China." *Beijing Review*, July 27, 28.

———. 1987. "Leasing Invigorates Small Businesses." *Beijing Review*, July, 26–27.

Zhen Yuren and Wu Shiqi. 1993. "Market Oriented Reform of RCCs." *Rural Financial Studies*, January, 41–45.

Zhou Shu Li. 1991. "Retrospect and Prospect of China's Trust and Investment Industry." *Financial Studies*, December, 25–28.

6

The Interbank and Foreign Exchange Markets

The interbank and the foreign exchange markets are two powerful institutions involved in the mobilization of funds in the Chinese financial system. Both institutions have had interesting developments, perform different functions, and will continue to play a significant role in the future development of China's economy. Interbank and foreign exchange activities are conducted through the financial market, as illustrated in Figure 2.2.

DEVELOPMENT OF THE INTERBANK MARKET

As the name implies, the interbank market involves lending and borrowing among banks and other financial institutions. This type of activity became popular in the mid-1980s and was intended to promote the horizontal circulation of funds across banks, industrial sectors, and regions in the country. Prior to 1985, it was common practice for banks with surplus funds to "hold onto" them, while banks in need of funds had very little opportunity to borrow. This attitude resulted from the credit allocation procedures that were implemented after liberation in the early 1950s (discussed in chapter 1). This system of vertical allocation of credit from the State Council through the central bank was rigid and worked reasonably well for a planned economy. The supply of goods and services operated according to plan, demand was reasonably well anticipated, prices were fixed, and the state controlled the purchase and sale of goods among enterprises. Allocated credit could only be used to purchase authorized quantities of raw materials at fixed prices. Moreover, there was no increase in effective demand, and consumer purchasing power and monetary control were forced to work with only a limited amount of cash in circulation. There was little reason for banks to be commercially aggressive.

With the reforms that were started in 1979, the situation began to change and banks were put in a situation where they were subject to credit limits and had to generate funds to extend loans (see chapter 3). In late 1983, it was decided by the State Council that the circulating (or working) capital needs of enterprises should be handled through the banking system and not through government finance departments. With the creation of a central bank to oversee the national credit plan, the specialized banks were forced into an internal planning and allocation system with respect to their mode of operation. PBOC approved the lending plan for each bank, and the head office of each bank approved the credit plan of each major provincial branch, which then set credit plans for branches and sub-branches under their respective jurisdictions. Normally, the credit plan at each branch and sub-branch was based on forecasts of funds that they could generate to maintain loan levels.

With the freeing-up of the economy after 1979, the planned economy started to break down, and some industrial and commercial activities gradually were shifted away from under government control. Some prices moved in response to market or quasi-market forces, production emphasis shifted to more seasonal activities, and state-ownership began to give way to collectives and other forms of enterprise ownership. The resulting outcome was one of changing regional and seasonal patterns of production and demand, which created an increasing demand for credit (Delfs, 1986). The rigid vertical allocation of credit could not adjust to the changes in these regional and seasonal production and demand patterns, as many of these changes could not be well predicted when the credit plans for the respective regions were formulated. Under the vertical circulation of credit, funds allocated to a region or regional sub-system stayed there, whether or not they were used

Matters came to a head in 1985 when PBOC tightened credit to cool a heated economy (Appendix). The efforts of the central bank were relatively successful from a macro viewpoint: industrial growth fell from 23 percent annually in early 1985 to 2 percent annually in late 1985 and 4.4 percent annually in early 1986. However, from the micro level, things were different: enterprises found it difficult to obtain short-term credit, suppliers suffered, and defaults occurred. Pockets of idle funds existed in the national banking system, but they were generally not freed up to help credit-starved regions. These pockets of idle funds created problems for money supply management at the national level. Attempts by the state to alleviate some of these problems through the central bank had some influences on the increases in the money supply (see chapter 1). Regional or subregional shortages of funds created pressures for increases in credit and money supply at the national level, despite the fact that there were idle funds in other regions and subregions. There was need for a mechanism (like an interbank market) to mobilize pockets of idle funds, both vertically and horizontally.

The Interbank Market

The terms *interbank market, money market,* and *debt market* are used interchangeably in China. Unofficially, China's interbank market started in 1983, when the WenZhou Branch of the Agricultural Bank of China (ABC) experimented with horizontal capital accommodation within its own system, among its branches in different counties. Branches with temporary excess funds lent to those in need of funds to meet loan commitments. This practice was quite a radical departure from the vertical allocation system that existed within the ABC network but the benefits of horizontal circulation of funds were quickly recognized. It did not take long to expand the WenZhou interbank market to include the PBOC, ICBC, BOC, and PCBC branches of the city. To this extent, the interbank market encouraged the horizontal circulation of funds across the city's financial institutions.

At the beginning of 1985, when PBOC strengthened its macro control of the economy in an effort to control inflation and tighten the money supply, some banks in certain regions of the country began to run short of funds for working-capital loans. Given this situation, many PBOC branches began to organize an interbank business to equalize funds among specialized banks under their respective administrative controls. Banks throughout China began to operate interbank transactions, and this activity subsequently caught the attention of the state. In January 1986, the State Economic Structure Reform Committee and PBOC held a symposium and agreed to experiment with interbank business in five cities: Guangzhou, Chongqing, Wuhan, Shenyang, and Changzhou. However, in the same month, the State Council published "Provisional Regulation on Management of Banks in PRC" and gave official sanction to the interbank business. In October 1986, PBOC issued a notice to encourage the interbank business:

All financial institutions have the right to handle interbank lending and borrowing. . . . Top banks and local governments should not interfere by any means. . . . [I]nterbank business must be based on the principle of self-willingness and mutual benefits. . . . PBOC should actively support interbank business and help to solve problems for financial institutions dealing with interbank business.

In addition, this notice outlined the rules and regulations that should govern interbank business. Encouraged by the provisional regulations and the notice, interbank markets among financial institutions of China sprang up like mushrooms, and by the end of 1987, most regions in China had set up organized or over-the-counter interbank markets. Currently, there are six well established regional markets: the coastal zone (with Shanghai as the center), middle and south China (with Wuhan as the center), northern China (with Beijing/Tianjin as the center), northeast China (with Shenyang as the center), northwest China (with Xian as the center) and southwest China (with Chongqing as the center). In these regions or centers there are over-the-counter and organized facilities designed to handle the interbank business, as discussed later in this chapter.

Finance Companies

Before discussing the management and regulation of the interbank market, it is instructive to review the impact of finance companies on this market. In 1988, as part of China's economic reform and financial market development, most provinces, municipalities, autonomous regions, and specially listed cities established finance companies with the approval of PBOC. In that year, 38 finance companies were established in an effort to unify diverse and developing components of the financial system and to make the interbank business more convenient. The major business activities of finance companies included: interbank lending and borrowing, the discounting of commercial bills, security transactions for short-term accommodation, the handling of assignments of securities among financial institutions, and financial consultancy.

The establishment of the finance companies was done in haste and without proper regulatory planning. Due to poor business practices (overextensions, the tendency to borrow short and lend long, etc.), poor management, and lax government supervision and control, the operations of some finance companies left certain unfavorable effects on the country's economy. In 1989, in line with the objective of improving the economic environment and consolidating economic order, PBOC decided to abolish all finance companies. This action was not welcomed by sponsors of finance companies, particularly those whose companies were relatively efficient and successful.

In March 1990, in order to standardize the interbank business and consolidate intermediary institutions in the interbank market, PBOC issued "Provisional Measures on the Management of Interbank Business," which formalized the concept of a financial market as a place where interbank business, securities transactions, and other financial activities are conducted in a centralized manner and under centralized supervision and control. Furthermore, a city could have only one financial market, and the choice of cities would depend on its volume of financial business.

Supervision and Operating Principles

PBOC is the administrative organ of China's financial market and is responsible for organizing, managing, supervising, and auditing the interbank business. Consistent with "Provisional Measures on the Management of Interbank Business" (March 1990), financial markets can be established in those cities with comparatively advanced economies and adequate volumes of financial businesses. In principle, one city can set up only one financial market and its establishment must be approved by the appropriate PBOC branch at the provincial level and by the PBOC head office.

Participants in the interbank market must be approved by PBOC, must be representatives of banks and other financial institutions and must abide by the following operating principles:

1. Interbank business should be done on the basis of independence and self-willingness, mutual benefit and equality, integrity of credit, and short-term accommodation.

2. Funds lent by banks and non-bank financial institutions in the interbank business are confined to deposits remaining after required reserves have been met. Funds belonging to correspondent banks and loans from the central bank cannot be used for interbank lending. Borrowed funds can only be used to finance shortages in the clearance of bills, remittances to correspondent banks, and satisfaction of the temporary demand for the borrower's revolving fund. No borrowed funds can be used for on-lending to finance fixed assets.

3. Banks and nonbank financial institutions must control the amount of borrowed funds to maintain acceptable levels of solvency ratios. For banks, the daily average of borrowed funds outstanding should not exceed 5 percent of stipulated deposits taken in by the end of the preceding month. For municipal credit cooperatives, the net daily average of borrowed funds outstanding expressed as a ratio of self-owned capital must not exceed a value of 2. For other financial institutions, the net daily average of borrowed funds outstanding must not exceed self-owned capital.

4. The term and maximum interest rate for interbank lending and borrowing are fixed and are adjusted by PBOC in line with the supply of, and demand for, funds. Usually, the term is four months or less and the interest rate is not to be more than 0.30 percent of the daily lending interest rate offered by PBOC to specialized banks.

5. Payments for interest and service in the interbank business are all settled in accounts instead of in cash. "Withdrawals" and "kindness payments" are not allowed.

6. Management principles for the administration of the financial affairs in the interbank market are set through discussions between the local PBOC branch and the local fiscal and tax authorities. Internal management measures are determined by the local PBOC branch and member banks participating in the interbank market.

7. PBOC branches are authorized to carry out periodical auditing and statistical analysis on interbank activities and participants in the financial markets have specified reporting duties.

Volume of Business and Market Characteristics

The interbank market started out on a modest basis. In the first six months of 1986, the experiment in the five cities handled RMB 13.74 billion; in three months in mid-1986, a newly opened market in Shanghai handled RMB 1.27 billion; and for the year 1986, all centers in China handled RMB 30 billion (Delfs, 1986). Business volume increased to RMB 230 billion in 1987 and to RMB 520 billion in 1988. Thereafter, volume declined to RMB 290 billion in 1989 and to RMB 260 billion in 1990 (Zhao, 1991; Shi and Yan, 1992). The decline in the interbank market reflects, in part, the exit of the finance companies (as noted earlier). These companies had borrowed heavily in the interbank market on behalf of the sponsoring local authorities. More important, the volatility in business volume reflects the fluctuating economic conditions in the country and the effects of

Table 6.1
Movement of Funds in the Interbank Market for Selected Cities and Provinces, December 1990 (Value in Millions of Renminbi)

	Beijing	Shanghai	Wuhan	Chongqing	Hebei Province	Guangdong Province	Hainan Province
Borrowing							
Within the Province							
From Banks	975.00	2,302.82	6.00	1.30	306.56	883.19	152.28
From Non-banks	1,241.55	1,428.60	65.00	199.55	124.92	780.19	192.50
Outside the Province							
From Banks	0.00	0.00	55.00	109.00	0.00	883.30	199.45
From Non-banks	0.00	34.30	40.00	211.89	0.00	421.00	226.50
Total	2,216.55	3,765.72	166.00	521.74	431.48	2,967.68	770.73
Lending							
Within the Province							
To banks	281.30	1,825.14	0.00	1.30	198.64	1,403.70	175.69
To non-banks	435.70	1,938.00	0.00	199.55	134.12	930.62	315.30
Outside the Province							
To banks	467.40	152.00	0.00	105.00	0.00	11.00	4.50
To non-banks	219.00	112.63	0.00	38.40	0.00	50.00	22.00
Total	1,403.40	4,027.77	0.00	344.25	332.76	2,395.32	517.49
Borrowing							
Within the Province							
From Banks	43.99%	61.15%	3.61%	0.25%	71.05%	29.76%	19.76%
From Non-banks	56.01%	37.94%	39.16%	38.25%	28.95%	26.29%	24.98%
Outside the Province							
From Banks	0.00%	0.00%	33.13%	20.89%	0.00%	29.76%	25.88%
From Non-banks	0.00%	0.91%	24.10%	40.61%	0.00%	14.19%	29.39%
Total	100.00%	100.00%	100.00%	100.00%	100.00%	100.00%	100.00%
Lending							
Within the Province							
To banks	20.04%	45.31%	#DIV/0!	0.38%	59.69%	58.60%	33.95%
To non-banks	31.05%	48.12%	#DIV/0!	57.97%	40.31%	38.85%	60.93%
Outside the Province							
To banks	33.30%	3.77%	#DIV/0!	30.50%	0.00%	0.46%	0.87%
To non-banks	15.60%	2.80%	#DIV/0!	11.15%	0.00%	2.09%	4.25%
Total	100.00%'	100.00%	#DIV/0!	100.00%	100.00%	100.00%	100.00%

Source: China Finance and Banking Association (1991: 80–81).

'Actually 99.99%. Rounded to 100%.

government economic policies. The rapid increase in 1987–1988 reflects an economic upturn while the decline in 1989–1990 reflects the austerity measures that were taken to combat inflation and an overheated economy.

Table 6.1 shows data on the movement of funds in the interbank market for selected regions or centers in China for December 1990. Using this database, the following are some highlights of interbank activities.

First, some regions/centers (e.g., Beijing, Shanghai, and Hebei Province) rely almost exclusively on internal (provincial) sources for interbank borrowing. That is, borrowers do not go outside the province to procure funds. On the other hand, some regions/centers (e.g., Wuhan, Chongqing, Guangdong Province, and Hainan Province) have to rely on sources outside the province for some funding. To this extent, the interbank market facilitates the regional mobility of funds.

Second, while some regions/centers (e.g., Beijing and Chongqing) lend to borrowers outside the province, most of the interbank lending is confined to the regions/centers.

Finally, the role of financial institutions in interbank borrowing varies across regions/centers. For example, in Shanghai, banks accounted for 61 percent and other financial institutions, for 39 percent, but in Wuhan, they accounted for 37 percent and 73 percent, respectively. A similar pattern existed for interbank lending. For example, in Guangdong Province, banks accounted for 59 percent of interbank lending and other financial institutions, 41 percent, but in Chongqing, they accounted for 31 percent and 79 percent, respectively. Disregarding the variations in the roles of financial institutions, it is quite clear that there is some mobility of funds across institutions.

Some Characteristics of the Interbank Market

During its brief history, the interbank market has developed some interesting characteristics, including the following:[1]

1. The interbank market is essentially an over-the-counter market. There are five organized Interbank Market Centers (Beijing/Tianjin, Shanghai, Wuhan, Shenyang, and Xian), and they accounted for less than 3 percent of the borrowing and lending activities in the late 1980s (Shi and Yan, 1992).

2. The over-the-counter interbank market lacks an adequate telecommunications system, and while there is some mobility of funds (as discussed above), it operates in somewhat of a segmented environment. The six regional areas identified earlier are segmented, and the degree of segmentation varies with the economic stature of the respective regions/centers. One of the results of segmentation is the existence of interest rate differentials across regions/centers. For example, over 1987–1990, the weighted average interest rate in the coastal zone (with Shanghai as center) was 6.172 percent; in middle and south China (with Wuhan as center), 5.592 percent; in northwest China (with Xian as center), 5.79 percent; and in northern China (with Beijing/Tianjin as center), 5.58 percent. Had there been a higher degree of regional mobilization of funds, there would have been an equalization of lending rates across the regions.

3. During the 1987–1990 period, the distribution of the maturity structure of interbank loans was as follows: 1-day, 10.92 percent of loans; 2-day, 2.81 percent; 3-day, 5.62 percent, 4- to 60-day, 32.24 percent; and over-60-day, 48.41 percent. Thus, about half the interbank loans were for two or more months. The less developed economic regions/centers tend to employ longer maturities than the more developed regions. For example, Wuhan and Xian set most of their maturities at in excess of two months (with some exceeding the statutory four-month limitation), while Shanghai deals mainly with maturities of less than three months.

4. The volume of business in the interbank market is influenced by the economic conditions in the country and the macroeconomic policies of the state (as discussed earlier in this section). However, the volume of business is not influenced by the growth in domestic credit, since financial institutions cannot use interbank funds to "break through" their credit limits.

5. There is a seasonal element in interbank activities, which is mainly associated with activities in the agricultural sector of the economy. July to September is harvest time, and banks hold on to funds to finance this activity and thus avoid the interbank market. This action on the part of banks, the largest group of participants, results in relatively lower interbank business during that period. On the other hand, December to February is the selling period, during which banks are repaid, and at that time they tend to have excess liquidity to participate in the interbank market. Therefore, interbank business tends to peak in these months.

6. While all financial institutions may participate in the interbank market with approval from PBOC, the ICBC dominates. For example, in 1990 in Hebei Province, the branches of ICBC accounted for over 80 percent of the interbank business. This situation exists in the more active regions/centers including Beijing/Tianjin, Shanghai and Guangdong Province.

7. Funds in the interbank market are used more effectively than the circulating (or working) capital funds contained in the state's credit plan. For example, in 1990, the average velocity of interbank funds was 6.5 times, compared to less than 3 times for circulating funds in the credit plan. The higher velocity in the interbank market is partially due to the short maturity structures for interbank loans.

A Typical Organized Interbank Market Center

As indicated earlier, interbank activities are conducted either over-the-counter or at organized centers. Over-the-counter deals are usually done through telecommunications devices by traders approved by PBOC. On the other hand, an organized center has a physical location, and fixed business hours, and lenders and borrowers deal with each other face to face. The following is a summary of some of the details of the Shanghai Short-term Fund Financing Center (SSFFC):[2]

1. SSFFC is run by PBOC, Shanghai Branch, from a physical location in Shanghai. The center accounts for 27 percent of the city's total interbank business, which in 1992 was estimated at RMB 150 billion.

2. SSFFC is a nonprofit organization and operates on a membership system. In November 1992, there were 65 members representing banks and other financial institutions. Only members can conduct business at the center.

3. Lenders present proposals with offering rates and terms, while borrowers present proposals with borrowing rates and terms; transactions are usually settled on a negotiated basis. SSFFC normally lends for one month, with some loans for three months. Lending and borrowing rates have to conform to guidelines set by PBOC.

4. Loan applications are normally used for funds committed to approved projects, while bankers' acceptances are popular for general lending activities.

5. SSFFC is somewhat protectionist since it considers local institutions before

those from outside Shanghai.

6. All transactions are in renminbi, the local currency.

7. SSFFC has never defaulted on a contract governing its operations.

THE FOREIGN EXCHANGE MARKET

Over the 1949–1979 period, foreign exchange control took a back seat in China's national economy while the nation was closed to the outside world. However, with the open door policy and the resulting economic reforms, starting in 1979, China paid increasing attention to its capacity to generate and retain foreign exchange. Attempts are continually being made to maximize foreign reserves while at the same time ensure that foreign trade and other international transactions are adequately financed. Foreign exchange is actively managed in China through a series of regulations, institutions, and control mechanisms.[3]

The Regulatory Environment

Foreign exchange management is a centralized and unified administrative function under the State Administration for Exchange Control (SAEC), which is a division of the central bank, the People's Bank of China (Figure 2.2). SAEC was established in 1980 and derives its authority from the "Provisional Regulations for Exchange Control in the People's Republic of China" (1980).[4] Under these regulations, the Bank of China is the sole institution which was authorized to handle foreign exchange business, but in the late 1980s, this clause was relaxed and all Chinese banks and other financial institutions were accorded the privilege (discussed in chapters 3 through 5). Currently, there is keen competition among Chinese banks and other financial institutions for foreign exchange business.

Some General Foreign Exchange Rules for All Business Firms. To simplify the discussion, the following exposition looks at the position of business firms that are major users of foreign exchange. Generally, the discussion is applicable to most economic units in the Chinese economy. Under the provisional and subsequent regulations, and unless special approval is given, all foreign and domestic firms in China must observe the following general rules:

1. All foreign exchange receipts may be held in foreign currency or renminbi accounts at an approved Chinese bank. (Initially, firms were required to sell all foreign exchange to the Bank of China or another approved Chinese bank and to hold renminbi deposit accounts.)

2. Firms are free, with approval from SAEC, to buy or sell foreign exchange at the foreign exchange swap centers (discussed later in the chapter). (Initially, these transactions could only be done at the Bank of China or other approved Chinese banks.)

3. The use or circulation of foreign currency in China is legally prohibited.

4. Firms must submit to SAEC, on a timely basis, forecasts of foreign exchange receipts and foreign exchange payments for approval and inclusion in the unified state foreign exchange plan for the coming fiscal year. Allocations of foreign exchange to firms are made on the basis of these forecasts.

5. Firms must submit to SAEC, on a timely basis and with supporting documentation, statements for actual foreign exchange receipts and foreign exchange payments for the latest fiscal year.

6. Firms must receive SAEC approval for the purchase of foreign exchange. These are usually required for the payment of imports or the repayment of foreign debt.

The following discussion highlights some major exceptions to the above general rules. The following is a list of Chinese foreign exchange regulations that were promulgated up to 1987 (relevant regulations since 1987 are noted in the notes to this chapter).

Foreign Exchange Control Regulations of the People's Republic of China up to 1987

1. Regulations of the Bank of China for Providing Short-term Foreign Exchange Loans, promulgated by the State Council, 30 March 1980.

2. Provisional Regulations on Foreign Exchange Control of the People's Republic of China, promulgated by the State Council, 18 December 1980.

3. Rules for the Implementation of Foreign Exchange Control Relating to Foreign Representatives in China and their Personnel, promulgated 10 August 1981.

4. Rules Governing the Carrying of Foreign Exchange, Precious Metals and Payment Instruments in Convertible Currency Into or Out of China, promulgated 10 August 1981.

5. Rules for the Implementation of Foreign Exchange Control Relating to Individuals, promulgated by SAEC, 31 December 1981.

6. Rules for the Implementation of the Examination and Approval of Applications by Individuals for Foreign Exchange, promulgated by SAEC, 31 December 1981.

7. Regulations on Foreign Currency Deposits and Special Renminbi deposits by the Bank of China, promulgated by PBOC, January 1983.

8. Rules for the Implementation of Foreign Exchange Control Regulations Relating to Overseas Chinese Enterprises, Foreign Enterprises and Chinese Joint Ventures, promulgated by SAEC, 1 August 1983.

9. Penal Provisions for Violation of Foreign Exchange Control Regulations, promulgated by SAEC, 1 April 1985.

10. Interim Banking Control Regulations of the People's Republic of China, promulgated by the State Council, 7 January 1986.

11. Provisional Rules Concerning Renminbi Loans against Mortgage on Foreign

Exchange by Enterprises with Foreign Investment, promulgated by the PBOC, 26 November 1986.

12. Rules of the Ministry of Foreign Economic Relations and Trade Concerning the Purchase of Domestic Products for Export by Enterprises with Foreign Investment to Balance Foreign Exchange Revenues and Expenditures, promulgated by the Ministry of Foreign Economic Relatioins and Trade (MOFERT), 20 January 1987.

13. Provisional Rules Concerning the Provision of Foreign Exchange Guarantees by Organizations within the Chinese Territory, promulgated by PBOC, 20 February, 1987.

14. Rules of the Bank of China on Loans for Foreign Investment Enterprises, promulgated by BOC, 24 April 1987.

15. Foreign Exchange Control Rules for Non-Banking Financial Institutions, promulgated by PBOC, 1 October 1987.

The Two Currency System. Chinese currency, the renminbi, was first issued in 1948 by the People's Bank of China as the unifying currency for liberated China. A new version of the renminbi was issued on March 1, 1955 and this remains the official currency of China (Xinhua, 1983: 189–191). In April 1980, the Chinese introduced the Foreign Exchange Certificate (FEC) in an effort to capture foreign exchange from foreigners visiting China and to reduce the purchase of imported goods and services by Chinese residents.[5] Foreigners are required to exchange hard currencies at Chinese banks at the spot rate, which is set by the People's Bank of China. A receipt is issued to evidence the exchange, which is required if the FEC is to be converted into hard currency at a later date.

FEC holders may purchase imported goods and services in China, while RMB holders can only buy domestic items. Officially, FEC and RMB have the same value, but because the FEC can be used to buy imported goods, it has a higher value in the black market. Over the years, a thriving black market existed for the FEC despite government efforts to crack down on its activities.[6] The most significant and recent effort to curb black market activities occurred in 1989 (Baralle and Steinert, 1989). On November 29, 1989, SAEC announced new regulations to restrict the convertibility of FEC for foreign individuals and for offices of foreign governments, commercial enterprises, and nonprofit organizations.[7]

Under the new regulations, only 50 percent of the FEC held in cash can be converted into hard currency (upon presentation of a valid FEC receipt). Prior to passage of this regulation, a foreign person or entity could convert 100 percent of FEC. The new regulations were prompted by an illegal practice whereby Chinese individuals or enterprises with FEC made foreign exchange deals with foreigners for hard currencies. Usually, the exchange rates in these private deals are more favorable than those obtainable at Chinese banks and thus more attractive to foreigners.[8]

Foreign Exchange Clawback from Chinese Domestic Enterprises. Domestic enterprises involved in export activities are required to surrender a negotiated percentage of foreign earnings to the government. In 1979, the central government introduced a foreign exchange credit system for domestic Chinese enterprises in a bid to promote exports (Yowell, 1988). Exporting enterprises were allowed to retain 6 to 7 percent of foreign exchange earnings, and the balance was distributed to the central government and local administrative bureaus. Enterprises were required to sell all foreign exchange to the Bank of China, and a foreign exchange credit account was opened for the enterprise with SAEC. In theory, the exporting enterprise could use its approved foreign exchange credit for approved imports, but in practice, the system did not work well. SAEC's reporting, allocation, and approval procedures are tedious and time-consuming, and the foreign exchange credit system lost much of its appeal as an incentive to boost exports.

In 1985, the clawback provisions were liberalized.[9] In most provinces, 75 percent of total foreign export earnings went to the central government and the balance was split equally between the local government and the exporting enterprise. However, there were some exceptions. Provinces that were dominated by minority ethnic groups (such as Xinjiang) retained 50 percent, the special economic zones and Tibet retained 100 percent, and Guangdong and Fujian provinces retained 50 percent. Additionally, some industries received special treatment: tourism-related enterprises kept 30 percent and electrical and machinery enterprises kept 50 percent. Retention rates were further liberalized in 1991, and it is estimated that from 40 to 70 percent of foreign exchange earnings are retained at the local level (Davis and Yi, 1992). The higher foreign exchange retention rates minimized, but did not eliminate, the time involved in getting SAEC's approval.

Direct Foreign Investments. Since 1979, the Chinese have made special efforts to attract direct foreign investments from three well-defined sources: enterprises with overseas Chinese capital, enterprises with foreign capital, and Chinese-and-foreign joint ventures. Enterprises with overseas Chinese capital include units registered in China with capital from overseas Chinese or compatriots from Hong Kong and Macao, while enterprises with foreign capital include units registered in China with capital from foreigners (except for overseas Chinese and compatriots from Hong Kong and Macao). Both these types of business organizations may be managed independently or jointly with Chinese enterprises. Chinese and foreign joint ventures include units registered in China with capital from overseas Chinese, compatriots from Hong Kong and Macao, and foreigners, and are jointly managed with Chinese enterprises.[10] Tax and other developmental incentives have been offered to attract foreign investments to China.[11]

As a matter of policy, foreign investments were encouraged for economic reconstruction in five selected industrial sectors, with the objective that technology would be upgraded and exports enhanced.[12] For most foreign-funded firms, 80 to 100 percent of production was to be exported. With these and other factors in mind, special foreign exchange controls are placed on foreign-funded firms including the following:

1. Firms must register the value of foreign capital (cash and in-kind) remitted to China with the appropriate Chinese authorities.

2. Each firm must open a foreign exchange account with a designated bank in China, and all export earnings and foreign capital must be credited to this account. The bank has the authority to supervise the account on behalf of SAEC.

3. Firms must pay for approved imports, other foreign obligations, and the repatriation of profits and capital from foreign exchange earnings. That is, the foreign-funded firm is required to balance foreign exchange payments with foreign exchange earnings. If firms are short of foreign exchange (as is usually the case), they have acquired (since 1986) some other options.[13]

   a. With the approval of SAEC, renminbi may be sold for foreign exchange at the foreign exchange swap centers.

   b. With the approval of the Ministry of Foreign Economic Relations and Trade (MOFERT), renminbi may be used to buy Chinese products for export to generate foreign exchange.

   c. Renminbi may be used to invest in another foreign-funded firm which is generating foreign exchange and these funds may be remitted.

4. Firms must permit SAEC officials to audit their books when the appropriate request is made.

Foreign Exchange Earnings in Bonded Areas. A bonded area is one in which raw and semifinished materials are imported and processed, and the finished goods exported without being subject to customs duty. The central government has approved bonded area status for Guangzhou, Shenzhen, Shanghai, Tianjin, and Dalian (Wang, 1991). Special foreign exchange controls apply to these bonded areas and imports and exports must be settled in foreign currencies under the supervision of the Chinese customs bureau. Enterprises must transfer foreign exchange earnings to accounts in domestic banks, while Chinese funded enterprises are allowed to retain foreign exchange earnings in cash.

Debt in Foreign Currencies. Chinese domestic (financial and non-financial) enterprises are prohibited from borrowing in foreign currencies without the approval of the People's Bank of China (Xinhua, 1983). The normal practice is for the central bank to approve foreign borrowing by the Chinese banks and other financial institutions for on-lending to domestic nonfinancial enterprises. In a sense, foreign exchange is allocated to domestic enterprises from the unified state foreign exchange budget. On the other hand, firms with foreign capital may borrow overseas, but they are responsible for repayment in the respective foreign currencies. Some foreign-funded firms that have approval to sell in the domestic market may receive foreign exchange allotments from SAEC but even in the best of times, access to these allocations can be time-consuming and frustrating.

Dominant Factors Influencing Foreign Reserves in China

Foreign reserves increased steadily from U.S. $2.5 billion in 1980 to U.S. $42.6 billion in 1991 (China Statistical Yearbook, 1991). This rather dramatic increase is due to several major factors that are summarized (although in no special order of importance) in the following discussion.

Devaluing the Chinese Currency. China devalued its currency several times over the 1980–1991 period, from RMB 1.5303/U.S. $1.00 in 1980 to RMB 5.3234/U.S. $1.00 by the end of 1991. This is the official exchange rate, and it is claimed that it is based on an assortment of international currencies, but the Chinese have never divulged the weighting formula. The official rate is determined by the Bank of China on a daily basis in U.S. dollars, and rates of other currencies are set in terms of cross-rates to the dollar. Prior to the early 1980s, foreign trade was centralized with state foreign trade corporations (FTCs), and the official exchange rate was of little significance. All foreign exchange from exports were sold to the state, and all foreign exchange for imports were bought from the state, so the net impact (in exchange gains or losses) was absorbed by the state.

With the decentralization of foreign trade in the early 1980s, the FTCs and other provincial entities were authorized to engage in foreign trade and to be accountable for their own profits and losses. The state was not prepared to absorb exchange losses for it was readily acknowledged that the RMB was overvalued. Accordingly, an internal settlement rate was introduced in January 1981, under which China employed a two-tiered exchange system, meaning that Chinese exporters exchanged foreign exchange with the Bank of China at an RMB rate that was higher than the official rate. For example, over the 1981–1984 period, the internal settlement rate was RMB 2.80/U.S. $1.00, while the official rate ranged from RMB 1.70/U.S. $1.00, in 1981, to RMB 2.30/U.S. $1.00, in 1984. Thus, the sale of foreign exchange to the Bank of China was attractive to Chinese exporters since they received more RMB.[14] Foreigners had to use the official exchange rate, and they protested the presence of the internal settlement rate. As a consequence, over the years the Chinese attempted, through devaluations, to bring the two rates closer together.

The devaluation strategy promoted exports and restricted imports. The Chinese currency was consistently devalued, from RMB 1.5303/U.S. $1.00 at the end of 1980, to RMB 3.721/U.S. $1.00 in mid-1986. Thereafter, the Chinese were reluctant to devalue until 1989 even though the trade balances were extremely unfavorable (Table A.4). Then in November 1990, the currency was devalued to RMB 4.7221/U.S. $1.00 in an effort to boost exports. Since then, the rate of devaluation has been continuous and gradual, in keeping with changes in the U.S. dollar in the international market.

The foreign exchange rate in the foreign exchange swap centers had an impact on the devaluation strategy. The rates in the swap centers tended to reflect the black-market rates which, some would argue, were the true values of the RMB. The official rate tended to follow the swap rates, and by early 1992, it was about 15 percent below them.

Imports/Exports. Foreign trade increased significantly over the 1980–1991 period (see Appendix). Exports increased from U.S. $22.01 billion in 1981 to U.S. $71.90 billion in 1991, and imports, from U.S. $22.02 billion and U.S. $63.80 billion, respectively (China Statistical Yearbook, 1991). China controls both exports and imports but for different reasons. Exports are encouraged in order to earn foreign exchange, and exporting enterprises are monitored, through Chinese customs and the banking system, to ensure that such earnings are remitted to China. Over the years, the country has attempted to change its export product mix to include higher-valued manufacturing items, and foreign-funded firms have been lured to improve production technology for exports. Domestic firms have been encouraged with various types of export incentives and export subsidies. Recently, the Bank of China started to offer export credits for high-valued items costing more than U.S. $1 million.

With imports, the emphasis is on capital goods for the reconstruction of the economy and raw materials that are not normally available in China. Imported goods are classified into three categories of item: priority, negotiated, and prohibited. Priority items include the capital goods and supplies required for key construction projects, and have first preference to foreign exchange. Negotiated items, which include industrial equipment, raw materials, and supplies for service industries, stand next in line. Import permits and SAEC approval for foreign exchange are usually easy to obtain for these items.

Generally, the trade balance was favorable in the early 1980s, but there were some very unfavorable trade balances over 1985–1989. China's response was to restrict imports in order to restore the favorable balances that had been observed since 1990. Overall, exports were not a net foreign exchange earner over the 1979–1990 period.

Foreign Debt. After 1979, China needed foreign exchange in a hurry and this prompted the country to turn to the international capital market for borrowed funds. In 1980, "China took a fresh step into the world of international high finance . . . when she joined the International Monetary Fund and the World Bank. In addition, she launched herself into such capitalist practices as budgetary deficit and a sizable foreign debt."[15]

China's foreign debt increased from an estimated U.S. $6 billion in the early 1980s to about U.S. $60 billion by the end of 1991. Initially, China was very cautious in its foreign borrowing strategies and utilized IMF/World Bank credits and official export credits (from the U.S. Eximbank, the Japan Export-Import Bank, and equivalent European agencies), which were considerably cheaper than commercial credit. Accordingly, China drew on these sources of funds rather than the larger (and more expensive) lines of credit from commercial banks. It is estimated that by the end of 1986, about 25 to 30 percent of China's foreign debt consisted of these soft loans, and China intends to continue this strategy, as much as possible, in the future.

Usually, loans and assistance from international funding agencies (such as the World Bank and Asian Development Bank) are channeled through the China Investment Bank for on-lending to Chinese enterprises. Commercial loans are syndicated through the Bank of China, CITIC, and other Chinese banks for on-lending in China. These Chinese financial institutions have tapped every major financial center in the global marketplace, looking for competitive borrowing rates, and they are very sensitive to their international credit ratings.[16]

The annual debt service ratio averaged less than 10 percent in the 1980s (an acceptable safe ratio is less than 20 percent). Considering this fact, it is tempting to argue that China has ample foreign debt capacity to meet future financing requirements. A World Bank projection put China's foreign debt by the year 2000 at around U.S. $128 billion; other projections are closer to U.S. $100 billion.[17] These projections generally assume that China's exports and gross domestic product (GDP) will grow at an annual rate of 8 percent and that foreign debt will be used to finance export-oriented, long-term projects. Of course, history has shown that all has not been well with foreign debt management in China.

Over the 1979–1984 period, China enjoyed trade surpluses and added to its foreign reserves. However, over 1984–1985, import levels went out of control and foreign reserves fell rapidly, meaning that drastic measures had to be taken to correct the situation. These remedial actions included a 25 percent devaluation of the RMB from the start of 1985 to July 1986, import controls mainly on consumer goods, cancellation of some key projects, and the curtailment of credit (including foreign currency loans) by the domestic banking system. Foreign reserves fell from U.S. $17 billion in early 1984 to about U.S. $10 billion in early 1986, and the Chinese began to use short-term foreign debt to pay for their monthly trade deficits, which ranged from U.S. $1–$1.5 billion.[18] Depending on the source of the estimates (IMF, World Bank or China), short-term debt as a percent of foreign debt at the end of 1985 ranged from 40 to 55 percent. The economic situation had improved by early 1988.[19]

However, the economy started to overheat by the end of 1988, and an austerity program had to be implemented over the next two years. With inflation running at over 20 percent, growth in money supply at over 40 percent, and industrial production at more than 20 percent, the economy had to be slowed. Price reforms were suspended, some 18,000 key projects were canceled, and import restrictions were again imposed. Allocations of foreign exchange were slowed, if not canceled, in order to preserve foreign reserves.

Japan is a key lender to China, and when China started to receive aid in 1979, the exchange rate was yen 120–130 equals RMB 1. By 1987, when some of the Japanese loans were repaid, the rate was yen 42 equals RMB 1, and currently, the rate is about yen 17 equals RMB 1. China has been borrowing in a currency that has upvalued significantly over the last decade, and it is not known to what extent the borrower took advantages of hedging techniques to protect against the foreign exchange risk. In the mid-1980s, Japanese loans constituted about 40 percent of China's foreign debt.

Then the Tiananmen Square confrontation occurred in June 1989, and this had political overtones. Fortunately, China recovered from the adverse effects and publicity by early 1991 and was able to return to the global capital market for funds.[20]

These events proved difficult for domestic firms, which depend on foreign exchange from a unified state foreign exchange budget to maintain orderly levels of operation. The events are also onerous for foreign-funded firms, which face import cuts on raw materials/equipment, project terminations or delays, and delays in trade settlements, the ability to withdraw foreign exchange from a Chinese bank, and foreign remittances.

Foreign Investments. As stated earlier, China's attempts to attract direct foreign investments are intended to upgrade production technology and boost exports. To facilitate this process, five special economic zones were established in south China, where foreign-funded firms benefit from tax concessions, exemptions from import restrictions, and favorable land and labor policies. In 1984, 14 open coastal cities along the eastern seaboard were allowed to offer incentives similar to those in the special economic zones so as to attract foreign investments. In addition, the state and provincial governments have offered selected development incentives to foreign investors in other industrial zones throughout China.

By the end of 1990, China had approved an estimated 29,000 foreign-funded firms with a total contract value of about U.S. $40.4 billion, of which about U.S. $18.4 billion has been remitted to China for investment.[21] While the remittance rate of foreign capital is less than 50 percent of contract value, foreign investments are a valuable source of foreign exchange to China. The rate of foreign investments in China has accelerated in recent years, as shown by the following statistics:[22]

Year	Number of Contracts	Contract Value (U.S. $billions)	Remitted to China (U.S. $billions)
1986	1,498	2,83	1,87
1987	2.233	3.71	2.31
1988	5,945	5.30	3.19
1989	5,779	5.60	3.39
1990	7,276	6.57	3.41

THE FOREIGN EXCHANGE SWAP CENTERS AND THE NATURE OF OPERATIONS

By 1985–1986, the state began to find it difficult (or at least, became reluctant) to fulfill its role as an allocator of foreign exchange under the unified foreign exchange plan. The economic indicators were bad, and included adverse trade balances, rising foreign debt to finance trade deficits, an overvalued RMB, and falling foreign reserves. Accordingly, the decision was made to introduce some form of market mechanism to assist in the allocation of foreign exchange: this was the primary motive in promoting the foreign exchange swap center. A foreign exchange swap center is an organized trading facility for foreign currencies, and the foreign exchange swap centers in Shenzhen and Shanghai are the most active in China. Shenzhen Foreign Exchange and Regulation Center opened in November 1985, and the Shanghai Foreign Exchange Transaction Center, in the late 1980s.[23] By the end of 1990, there were over 100 foreign exchange swap centers across China.[24] The markets expanded, from the open coastal cities and a few provincial cities to almost every province, autonomous region, municipality, and city with acceptable levels of financial activity.

Business volume in 1990 reached U.S. $13.164 billion, up by 54 percent over 1989, which in turn was two times the 1988 volume.[25] Participants trade in approved foreign currencies and approved volume, subject to supply/demand conditions. The swap exchange rate is usually higher (in terms of RMB) than the official exchange rate at the bank, and this is attractive to sellers. In addition, the swap exchange rate tracks the black-market rate, and the foreign exchange swap center has some influence in reducing black market activities. Details on the organization and operation of a typical foreign exchange swap center are presented in the following paragraphs.

Organization and Operation of a Typical Foreign Exchange Swap Center

The following summary applies to the Shenzhen Foreign Exchange and Regulation Center, as stipulated under "Shenzhen Provisional Management Measures of Foreign Exchange Transaction" of March 1990.

The establishment of the exchange swap center was authorized by SAEC, which also manages and supervises the center. There is a fixed trading location in Shenzhen, with regular hours for trading.

Membership

Dealers and brokers are members of the swap center and have trading privileges. Dealers are enterprise representatives and trade solely for their respective enterprises. Brokers are employees of financial institutions and they trade on behalf of clients on a commission basis. Members must be licensed by SAEC and have a seat on the swap center.

Currencies Traded

The currencies traded are the U.S. dollar, the yen, deutsche mark, pound sterling, Hong Kong dollar in cash, and in the case of allocated foreign exchange quotas from SAEC, the U.S. dollar. All foreign currencies are quoted with reference to the RMB, and cross-conversions are not allowed; that is, U.S. dollars cannot be sold for Hongkong dollars, only RMB.

The Buyers and Sellers

All state-owned enterprises, collectives, government institutions, foreign-funded firms, and private businesses may trade through brokers. The amounts traded must be approved by SAEC and are usually limited to the retained foreign exchange and foreign exchange quotas for domestic firms, foreign exchange quotas for other domestic units, and foreign exchange receipts for foreign-funded firms. The trading activities must relate to approved activities, and all buyers and sellers are required to register with SAEC.

Transaction Price

Generally, the transaction price is determined through a bidding process on the floor of the swap center, based on supply/demand conditions. However, the central bank may intervene as a buyer or seller to stabilize supply/demand conditions.

Settlement

There are margin requirements with each order, with a broker who is responsible for settlement at the end of each trading day. Dealers handle their own settlements daily.

Violations

SAEC has the authority to penalize violators of trading regulations, and penalties can range from critical notices to loss of license.

In an attempt to coordinate and integrate the foreign exchange swap centers across the country, SAEC provides weekly quotations for exchange transactions. For example, a weekly quotation may be RMB 0.50 to RMB 0.53 above the official exchange rate obtained at the bank. In addition, in 1990, a national foreign exchange coordination center was established in Beijing to provide a network system across swap centers (Zhao, 1991). It was estimated that in 1990, the trans-regional volume of business was U.S. $3 billion, and it is hoped that this volume can be increased with a national information system.[26]

NOTES

1. This discussion draws on Shi and Yan (1992: 7–25).
2. This discussion draws from Chen (1992).
3. Foreign exchange includes foreign currencies, securities in foreign currencies, instruments payable in foreign currencies and other foreign exchange funds. There are foreign exchange controls on individuals in China, but these economic

units play a relatively small role in the foreign exchange business and are not discussed here.

4. There are several laws relating to foreign exchange control and they are documented in *The China Investment Guide* (1990, ch. 20).

5. Sillitoe and Delfs (1985) reported on a proposal to issue a third currency in the Shenzhen Special Economic Zone, but this idea was not implemented.

6. Lee (1985) reported on a crackdown of the black market in Beijing.

7. See People's Bank of China, *Regulations on Several Questions Concerning Conversion of Foreign Currencies*, October 30, 1989.

8. Delfs (1986) reported on some Chinese suggestions to abolish the FEC but to date no action has been taken.

9. In 1980, Chinese enterprises were permitted to trade foreign exchange allocations with other domestic enterprises. However, the exchange rate was usually unattractive for the seller, and the market was relatively illiquid.

10. See "Rules for the Implementation of Exchange Control Regulations," *Beijing Review*, No. 34 (August 22, 1983): 25–27. See also *The China Investment Guide* (1990, ch. 17).

11. For a sample of the developmental incentives offered to joint ventures, see "Regulations for the Implementation of the Law of the People's Republic of China on Joint Ventures Using Chinese and Foreign Investment," *Beijing Review*, No. 41, (October 10, 1983): i–xxvi.

12. See Wei (1982: 18). The five industrial sectors are (1) energy; (2) light industry, textile industry, food industry, pharmaceuticals, telecommunications, and electronics; (3) building materials, machinery, iron and steel, as well as the chemical industry; (4) agriculture, animal husbandry, and animal raising and breeding projects; and (5) tourism and the service trades. The Chinese monitor foreign-funded firms to ensure that investments are made as planned. See *Renmin Ribao* (Beijing), 21 February 1990, FBIS CHI 90 035.

13. See *Renmin Ribao Overseas* (Beijing), 23 April 1990, FBIS CHI 9 078.

14. Yowell (1988: 11) argued that the Chinese government could have subsidized foreign trade and provided export incentives without devaluing the currency.

15. "The Need for More Foreign Finance Continues," *Far Eastern Economic Review*, September 26, 1980, 52. For a discussion of the implications of Chinese membership in IMF and the World Bank, particularly as it impacts on loans to less developed countries (LDCs), see "Changing the Power of Balance," *Far Eastern Economic Review*, April 25, 1980, 85.

16. See "China's Grating Ratings," *Far Eastern Economic Review*, September 10, 1987, 58–59.

17. See "High Interest, Low Lending," *Far Eastern Economic Review*, January 7, 1988, 40–41.

18. See "China's Mounting Trade Deficit Forces a Devaluation," *Far Eastern Economic Review*, July 17, 1986, 50–51.

19. See "China's External Accounts Enjoy a Quick Turnaround," *Far Eastern Economic Review*, January 7, 1988, 40–41.

20. See, for example, "Foreign Lending Makes a Comeback in China," *Far Eastern Economic Review*, June 20, 1991, 94–95, and "China Expected to Issue Yen-Denominated Bonds," *Far Eastern Economic Review*, April 18, 1991, 73.

21. See "New Customs Bonded Rules," *Beijing Review*, May 6–12, 1992, 28; China Statistical Bureau (1989), and *Xinhua* (Beijing), March 11, 1991, FBIS CHI 91 047.

22. See *Xinhua* (Beijing), March 11, 1991, FBIS CHI 91 047.

23. See Wang Deshun (1992).

24. See "More Money Changes Hands," *Beijing Review*, August 22–28, 1988, 30, and Wang (1992: 22).

25. See *China Daily* (Beijing), August 17, 1990, FBIS CHI 90 160.

26. See "Foreign Exchange Market Opens Wider," *Beijing Review*, June 3–9, 1991, 27.

REFERENCES

"Auspicious Beginning." 1985. *Far Eastern Economic Review*, December 11, 86–87.

Baralle, Lucille A., and Steinert, A. 1989. "Exchanging Foreign Currency in China: New Rules Issued." *East Asian Executive Reports*, December 15, 9–10.

Chen Weihua. 1992. "Interbank Lending Up 44%." *China Daily*, November 29, 3.

Chen Yuan and Zhao Haikuan. 1990. *Almanac of China's Finance and Banking*. Beijing: China's Financial Publishing House.

China Finance and Banking Association. 1991. *Almanac of China's Finance and Banking*. Beijing: Editing Department, Almanac of China's Finance and Banking.

China State Statistics Bureau. 1989a. "The Utilization of Foreign Capital: 1979–88." *Beijing Review*, March 6–12, 26–29.

———. 1989b. "The Chinese Economy in 1988." *Beijing Review*, February 6–12, 21–22.

"China's Major Cities Join the Interbank Market." 1986. *Far Eastern Economic Review*, December 11, 85–87.

Davis, Virginia and Yi, Carlos. 1992 "Balancing Foreign Exchange." *China Business Review*, March-April, 14–21.

Delfs, Robert. 1986. "Thinking of Alternatives." *Far Eastern Economic Review*, April 11, 104.

Donnithorne, Audrey. 1967. *China's Economic System*. London: Allen and Unwin.

do Rosario, Louise. 1985. "Time to Pay the Piper." *Far Eastern Economic Review*, April 23, 100–101.

Huang Dang, Liu Hong Yu, and Zhang Xiao. 1990. *The Encyclopaedia of Finance and Banking in China*. Beijing: Economic Management Press.

International Monetary Fund. 1987. *International Financial Statistics*. Washington, D.C.: International Monetary Fund.

———. 1988. *International Financial Statistics*. Washington, D.C.: International Monetary Fund.

Lee, Mary. 1985. "Banana Skinners Slip Off." *Far Eastern Economic Review*, April 25, 130–132.

Liu Guoguan. 1989. "A Sweet and Sour Decade." *Beijing Review*, January 2–8, 22–28.

Liu Suinan and Wu Qungan. 1986. *China's Socialist Economy: An Outline History (1949–84)*. Beijing: Beijing Review.

People's Republic of China Year Book 1990/91. Beijing: PRC Year Book Ltd.

Salem, Ellen. 1983. "Slow Boat to China." *Far Eastern Economic Review*, April 23, 51–53.

Shang Ming. 1992. *Money and Banking*. Beijing: Social Sciences Press.

Shi Hui Wen and Yan Rui Ling. 1992. "The Relationship of Interbank Market and National Economic Development." *Financial Services*, January, 7–25.

Sillitoe, Paul, and Delfs, Robert. 1985. "Rate of Exchange." *Far Eastern Economic Review,* March 21, 150–151.

Wang Deshun. 1992. "Shanghai Foreign Exchange Transaction Center." *Beijing Review,* February 24–March 1, 22–23.

Wang Xiangwei. 1991. "Foreign Exchange Regulations for Bonded Areas." *China Daily,* July 5, 2.

Wei Yuming. 1982. "China's Policy on Absorption of Direct Investment from Foreign Countries." *Beijing Review,* July 26), 18–22.

Xinhua. 1983. *A History of Chinese Currency.* Beijing: Xinhua (New China) Publishing House and People's Bank of China.

Yowell Diane. 1988. "Swap Center System to Expand." *China Business Review,* September/October, 10–12.

Zhang Yichun, Dipchand, Cecil R., and Ma Ming Jia. 1992. *China's Financial System and Its Management.* Beijing: Social Sciences Press.

Zhao Xiaojian. 1991. "Economic Change Creates New Market." Beijing Review (June 24–30): 14.

7

Securities Markets

The earliest activity in the securities markets in China can be identified as far back as 1914, when the Shanghai government enacted legislation to permit the trading of securities in Shanghai. Over-the-counter (OTC) trading prevailed until 1920, when China's first securities exchange was established in Shanghai to trade in treasury bonds. Later, exchanges were set up in other cities, including Beijing, in 1918, and Tianjin, in 1921 (China Fund Inc., 1992: 24). With the liberation of China in 1949, all securities were abolished, exchanges were closed, and bureaucratic capital was confiscated (Liu and Wu, 1986: 3–86). While some attempt was made to reopen the Tianjin and Beijing exchanges over 1949–1950, both were again closed by 1953. Securities trading in China came to a halt until the 1980s when, as a result of the open door policy and its associated economic reforms, securities trading resumed in several cities in China.

Five years ago it would have been premature to talk of securities markets in China, much less to devote a chapter in a book to the topic. However, the country's climate is changing, and while political ideology remains intransigent, economic progress is racing ahead. What once seemed a nonevent or an elusive thought is now being promoted with vigor and vitality at even the highest levels of government. The development of China's securities market is in its infancy, and indeed the market may suffer from infant mortality, but it is still instructive at this time to document the progress that has been made in recent years to revive securities activities.

OVERVIEW: UNIFIED FINANCIAL MARKETS

The following statement, which was made in 1989, is still true today (Jin, 1989: 24): "China's stocks and bonds are issued mainly by state-owned businesses under the unified guidance of state planning and subjected to strict control and supervision."

By 1988, China had experimented with securities in the primary and secondary markets (Jin, 1989; "Stock Market Picks Up in China," 1988).

Table 7.1

China: Gross New Bond Issues, 1981–1990 (Value in Billions of Renminbi)

	1981–85	'86	'87	'88	'89	'90	Total (1981–90 RMB	Percent
A. State and Other Government								
State Treasury Bonds	23.72	6.25	6.29	9.23	5.61	9.33	60.43	36.02%
State Finance Dept. Bonds				6.61		7.11	13.72	8.18%
State Construction Bonds				3.07			3.07	1.83%
Key Construction Bonds				0.06			0.06	0.04%
Special State Bonds					4.37	3.24	7.61	4.54%
Value Proof Bonds					8.74	3.74	12.48	7.44%
Infrastructure Bonds				8.00	1.46		9.46	5.64%
Subtotal	23.72	6.25	6.29	26.97	20.18	23.42	106.83	63.68%
B. Enterprises								
Key Enterprise Bonds			3.00	1.00	0.79	0.62	5.41	3.23%
Other Enterprise Bonds		10.00	3.00	3.00	1.48	4.93	22.41	13.36%
Subtotal	0.00	10.00	6.00	4.00	2.27	5.55	27.82	16.58%
C. Financial Institutions								
Finance bonds	0.50	3.00	6.00	6.50	6.07	6.44	28.51	17.00%
Total Bonds	24.22	19.25	18.29	37.47	28.52	35.41	163.16	97.26%
D. Shares			1.00	2.50	0.66	0.43	4.59	2.74%
Total Bonds and Shares	24.22	19.25	19.29	39.97	29.18	35.84	167.75	100.00%

Source: China Finance and Banking Association (1991: 58).

State treasury bonds were issued to the public starting in 1981, and enterprises were given permission to issue bonds and stocks in 1984. By the end of 1988, a total of RMB 99.23 billion worth of bonds had been issued: RMB 45.49 billion of state treasury bonds; RMB 17.74 billion of other government bonds for projects, and similar endeavors; RMB 16 billion of financial bonds; and RMB 20 billion enterprise bonds (Table 7.1). In addition, RMB 3.6 billion of stocks were issued by state-owned enterprises, of which 61 percent were sold to the public. Finally, by February 1989, China had tapped the international markets for foreign currency bonds and loans (discussed in chapter 2).

The secondary market for securities was encouraged when, in 1986, bonds and shares of enterprises were allowed to be traded over the counter in selected cities. This was followed, on April 1, 1988, by state treasury bonds, which were offered for trade on an experimental basis in five cities: Shenyang, Shanghai, Guangzhou, Wuhan and Chongqing. By the end of 1989, more than 90 cities, involving more than 410 financial institutions, had trading counters where individuals and agencies traded on a cash basis. By 1988, the annual volume of trading in the secondary market was RMB 2.5 billion, with state treasury bonds accounting for about 90 percent of the activity. Investors earned 10 to 30 basis points over bank savings rates for comparable maturities in the secondary market; this was permitted by PBOC in compensation for the additional risks involved in investing in securities.

There is no national securities law in China, and bond and stock trading was unregulated and ill defined. Events in Shenzhen (and the Tiananmen Square incident) led the state to temporarily freeze stock trading in 1989. A curbside market outside brokers' offices in Shenzhen had five stocks whose prices and trading volume experienced explosive growth. For example, one stock that was issued for RMB 20 in April 1988, had risen to RMB 118 by early 1990, a speculative trend that was similar for other stocks. Local authorities were forced to take action to control the situation in Shenzhen and, at the same time, in other cities including Shenyang, Chongqing, and Wuhan (Cheng, 1990). In general, the state attempted to control (or recentralize) security market activities.

In a continuing effort to bring "economic order" to the financial system, PBOC decreed that all financial activities should be centralized in approved financial centers and be operated by approved personnel. The "Provisional Regulation of Interbank Business" (March 1990) established the financial market as the place where all financial transactions should be centralized. In chapter 6, we discussed the operations of the interbank and foreign exchange markets; in this chapter the focus will be on the bond and stock markets, which collectively are referred to as the securities markets. The typical securities markets in China deals with four main types of financial instruments: treasury bonds issued by the state, financial bonds issued by financial institutions, enterprise bonds issued by nonfinancial business enterprises, and shares issued by financial and nonfinancial enterprises.

The period 1990–1991 witnessed continuing reforms and consolidation of the securities markets. The Shanghai Securities Exchange (SHSE) opened for business in December 1990, and the Shenzhen Securities Exchange (SZSE), in July 1991. As there was no national securities law at that time, these two organized exchanges operate under rules and regulations promulgated by the local political and financial authorities. The principal regulatory authority for the SHSE is the People's Bank of China, Shanghai, and that for the SZSE is the People's Bank of China, Shenzhen. By the end of 1991, there were 59 securities firms, with 300 affiliates and over 30,000 employees, handling primary and secondary transactions in the securities markets. Over the period 1981–1990, the volume of primary distribution was over RMB 167 billion (Table 7.1) while the secondary trading volume was over RMB 15 billion, or about six times the 1989 levels.

The push to promote securities distribution and trading in China has been influenced by at least four factors:

1. The public is provided more investment opportunities. The traditional bank savings deposit is the primary avenue for savings, but returns are relatively low. While securities have higher risks, they offer higher returns and bolster investor enthusiasm.

2. As far as the state is concerned, it is able to tackle the deficit problem by borrowing, which reduces overdrafts at PBOC and the temptation to print excessive money. Traditionally, state deficit was financed by printing more money, which had inflationary effects. Furthermore, the sale of treasury bonds gives the central bank some experience in open market operations.

3. With the ongoing reform of the banking system, it is necessary to reform the securities markets to give firms greater opportunities to raise funds from the public. The state has reduced its role as a provider of circulating funds to enterprises and for capital construction.

4. China needs foreign exchange, and it has to end its isolationist and self-reliance policies. Participation in the international financial marketplace provides one mechanism by which it can do so.

However, the development of China's securities markets will not be an unregulated capitalistic endeavor. The country's leaders are determined that development must proceed to the benefit of China, and the following guiding principles are in effect:

1. Public ownership of the factors of production will dominate the economy. Consequently, the state, state-owned enterprises, banks, and other financial institutions will own most of the shares, and these units will also be the primary issuers of bonds.

2. The issuance of stocks and bonds by all units must be incorporated in the unified plan for the economy for approval by the State Planning Commission. Through this mechanism, the state hopes to exercise microeconomic control over the economy and to direct funds into desired development activities.

3. Approval for the issuance of bonds and stocks will follow China's industrial policy, as defined by the state. With the passage of time, components of this industrial policy will be incorporated into the unified plan for implementation within a given time frame.

4. PBOC will have unified administration and control of the financial markets. In 1986, the People's Bank of China was named as the regulatory body for the financial market and, by virtue of this mandate, the central bank manages, supervises, guides, and coordinates the activities of the financial system.

Normally, the regional branches of PBOC carry out these four functions. Currently, the main responsibilities of PBOC with regard to the securities markets include the following:

1. Enact, promulgate, and implement regulations governing the securities markets.

2. Supervise the issuance and listing of securities, including the issue price and method of distribution.

3. Register, regulate, and supervise the over-the-counter and organized securities exchanges.

4. Monitor the trading of listed securities on the organized exchanges.

5. License and supervise securities companies, foreign securities agents, and clearing banks.

6. Discipline and penalize violators of regulations relating to the securities markets.

7. Supervise listed companies with respect to dividend distribution, use of proceeds from share issues, and financial and reporting requirements.

THE BOND MARKET

Like most important economic activities in China, the development of the bond markets is under the control of the state through PBOC.[1] The following examples serve to illustrate this point and provide perspective.

1. In 1981, state treasury bonds were issued for the first time, an event that marked the birth of China's bond market in the reform era.

2. Over 1981–1985, RMB 23.7 billion in state treasury bonds were issued, but they were barred from secondary trading by the state. This action was taken mainly to protect the value of the bonds from the vagaries of market forces.

3. In 1984, enterprises were given permission to issue bonds to the public, subject to the approval of PBOC.

4. On April 1, 1988, the state permitted secondary trading of treasury bonds on an experimental basis in five cities, which marked the official beginning of the secondary market.

5. The volume of new bond issues is subject to the unified physical plan for the upcoming year. For example, the forecast for new bond issues for 1989, based on economic activities in the physical plan was RMB 41.9 billion: RMB 5.5 billion in state treasury bonds, RMB 12 billion in value-proof bonds, RMB 5 billion in special state bonds, RMB 5.5 billion in construction bonds, RMB 7 billion in bank bonds, and RMB 6.5 billion in enterprise bonds. (Given the actual economic conditions during that year, only RMB 28.52 billion in bonds was issued, as shown in Table 7.1).

The Primary Bond Market

Primary issues of bonds dominate the new issues market in China and accounted for about 97.26 percent of the total of RMB 167.75 billion worth of new securities issued over the 1981–1990 period (Table 7.1). New bond issues totaled about RMB 163.16 billion, with state treasury bonds accounting for about 36 percent; other government bonds, 30 percent; enterprise bonds, 17 percent; and financial bonds, 17 percent. Technically, the state is responsible or legally liable for all bonds issued since they were issued with state permission. In this respect, there should be no quality differential across bonds of the various issuers.

State Treasury Bonds. Table 7.2 shows the purchasers of the new bonds. Except for the year 1981, sales were about equally split between state-owned enterprises and state-owned financial institutions and individuals until 1984. However, after 1984 individuals accounted for the majority of the purchases, and by 1989, they were the sole buyers. There are some interesting reasons for this sales pattern, as well as some undesirable consequences.

From 1981 to 1991, state treasury bonds were sold through administrative allocations (or quotas) to the various state-owned firms and other employers with orders to further allocate to employees. The normal expectation was that a unit would meet or exceed its quota and that allocations (or sales) to

Table 7.2
Purchases of State Treasury Bonds, by Individuals and Units, 1981–1990
(Value in Billions of Renminbi)

Year	Issued	Number Purchased		Percent Purchased	
		Units	Individuals	Units	Individuals
1981	4.87	4.86	0.01	99.79%	0.21%
1982	4.38	2.41	1.97	55.02%	44.98%
1983	4.16	2.10	2.06	50.48%	49.52%
1984	4.25	2.04	2.21	48.00%	52.00%
1985	6.06	2.18	3.88	35.97%	64.03%
1986	6.25	2.89	3.36	46.24%	53.76%
1987	6.29	2.26	4.03	35.93%	64.07%
1988	9.22	3.49	5.73	37.85%	62.15%
1989	5.61	0.00	5.61	0.00%	100.00%
1990	9.35	0.00	9.35	0.00%	100.00%

Source: China Finance and Banking Association (1991: 246).

workers would be paid through payroll deductions. In the countryside, the household responsibility contract would normally include a clause governing the purchase of, and payment for, bonds. In a sense, purchasing of state bonds was mandatory both for the state-owned firms and individuals: the state treasury bonds were viewed as a form of taxation. As far as individuals are concerned, state treasury bonds are not attractive (Tai, 1991: 42): "workers and farmers had been forced to buy bonds, which were proffered by their work units in lieu of wages. This provoked widespread resentment among the recipients who regarded the practice as a confiscation of income rather than as a long-term investment."

State-owned firms were in a hurry to avoid being forced to purchase state treasury bonds. The quota assigned to a state-owned firm would be based on its extrabudgetary funds and profits after taxes. Loss-making enterprises had more reasons to negotiate zero or lower quotas than profit-making enterprises, and they did so. Considering that about 20 percent of the large- and medium-sized firms were in a loss-making position, the burden was shifted to a smaller base of buyers. Assuming that the data in Table 7.2 is correct, state-owned firms had negotiated away all their allocations by 1989.

The issues of state treasury bonds over 1981–1984 had unattractive terms and were isolated from competition, since no other issuers were allowed in the market. The term to maturity was ten years (too long for the Chinese investor), the coupon was 5 percent (not attractive for an illiquid investment), and the bonds were barred from secondary trading (meaning that the investors had to hold them to maturity). As will be discussed further in this chapter, competition was introduced starting in 1985 and the terms of the issues after 1984 were "sweetened.' The maturity was shortened to three to five years, and yields were increased to partially reflect rising interest rates. However, these measures were not enough to stem investor dissatisfaction, since there were more attractive alternatives in the marketplace. Unfortunately, investors could do nothing, as the state treasury bonds were still sold under the quota system.

In 1991, syndication was used for the first time to supplement the administration allocation system for the sale of state treasury bonds. In April 1991, the Ministry of Finance announced that a syndicate of 58 financial institutions would underwrite RMB 2.5 billion (of a planned annual issue of RMB 10 billion for the year) of state treasury bonds (Tai, 1991). This was a radical departure from the administrative allocation system which caused much uncertainty about market acceptance. The system appeared to be successful in 1991 but ran into trouble in 1992, and in November 1992, it was reported that the majority of the planned bond issues totaling RMB 37 billion, had yet been sold ("Sluggish State Bond Sales Alert," 1992). Competition from financial and enterprise bonds, shares, real estate, and other investment opportunities was keen, which created anxious moments for the state.

In early 1993, the state was forced to cancel the first issue of the 1993 treasury bonds due to lack of interest in the market, especially in Shanghai (Evans, 1993). Inflation was running at about 20 percent in the larger cities and 13 percent in the rest and the coupon on the bonds was expected to be 10 to 11 percent. The expected coupon was unattractive and, moreover, there were also apprehensions about the ability of the state to devise and implement effective macroeconomic policies: the government deficit was about RMB 60 billion in 1991 and about RMB 70 billion in 1992. With the failure of a proposed underwritten issue, the state reverted to the administrative allocation system for the sale of treasury bonds in 1993.

Financial and Enterprise Bonds. The period 1984–1985 witnessed a continuing debate about the need to reform the financial market so as to permit more participants with a diversity of financial instruments to enhance the rational allocation of resources and promote greater market efficiency. As far as the bond market was concerned, permission was given to banks and enterprises to issue bonds, which they did starting in 1985–1986 (Tables 7.1, 7.3). Table 7.3 shows the bonds (and some of their features) issued by the various banks. Financial and enterprise bonds are sold on a voluntary basis to individuals and units, and have more attractive features than state treasury bonds. For example, the ICBC issue in 1985 with a maturity of one year offered a yield of 9 percent compared with the 1985 state treasury bond with a maturity of five years and a yield of 9 percent. In addition, financial bonds may have serial maturities, with interest rates increasing as a function of maturity, as is the case for the 1990 BOC bond. Normally, financial bonds are issued to meet commitments under the credit plan.

Enterprise bonds may be sold to the public or to employees, and in either case, they provide more attractive features than state treasury bonds. Bonds sold to employees are not negotiable, but their short maturities and higher yields make them attractive investments over the intended holding period. Usually, enterprise bonds have had to limit coupon to 20 percent above the bank deposit savings rates of comparable maturities. These bonds must be for approved projects, which should be included in the unified physical plan.

Table 7.3
Some New Bond Issues by Chinese Banks, 1985–1990
(Value in Billions of Renminbi)

	1985	1986	1987	1988	1989	1990
ICBC						
Amount (RMB Millions)	500	1,500	1,500	1,278	2,100	2,700
Maturity (Years)	1	1	1	1–5	1	1–3
Interest Rate	9%	9%	9%	9%–13%	N.A.	N.A.
Amount (RMB Millions)			1,400	181		
Maturity (Years)			1–5	1–3		
Interest Rate			9%–13%	10%		
Amount (RMB Millions)			400			
Maturity			1-3			
Interest Rate			10%			
ABC						
Amount (RMB Millions)	1,340		1,016	1,254	920	806
Maturity (Years)	1		1	1–5	1	1–3
Interest Rate	9%		9%	9%–13%	13.34%	N.A.
BOC						
Amount (RMB Millions)			440	920	990	620
Maturity (Years)			1	1–3	1–3	1–3
Interest Rate			9%	9%-11%	13.34%–14.14%	12.08%–12.8%
PCBC						
Amount (RMB Millions)			1,050	620	1,630	1,230
Maturity (Years)			2	1–3	1–3	1–3
Interest Rate			9%	9%–11%	13.34%–14.14%	12.08%–12.98%
Amount (RMB Millions)				400		
Maturity (Years)				1-3		
Interest Rate				10.3%		
BOCOM						
Amount (RMB Millions)			200	182	420	580

Source: China Finance and Banking Association (1991: 163–164).

Secondary Bond Market

As noted, the secondary market for bonds started on an experimental basis on April 1, 1988, when trading of state treasury bonds was allowed in five cities: Shenyang, Shanghai, Guangzhou, Wuhan, and Chongqing. PBOC permitted individuals to trade in the 1985 and 1986 treasury bond issues at designated financial institutions. However, initial trading was thin and bearish, and complaints of poor service and long lines at the transaction counters were widespread (do Rosario, 1989). In addition, there were profiteers or speculators who would illegally buy the bonds (and any other treasury bonds) at discounts (e.g., RMB 60 for RMB 100) and then cash them for face value at banks, with the help of corrupt clerks. A popular target for profiteers were farmers who were generally ignorant of bond investments and regarded them as "dead" money. Furthermore, profiteers arbitraged: buying in the northern cities and selling in the southern cities, where prices were 5 to 6 percent higher.

Estimates of early secondary bond trading were RMB 6 to 7 billion in 1990, up from RMB 2 to 2.3 billion in 1989 (Cheng, 1990). Shanghai was the main bond trading center accounting for 35 to 40 percent of the business. In December 1990, a Securities Trading Automated Quotation system (STAQ) was introduced by China International Trust and Investment Corporation and a Beijing research institute ("Let Twenty Securities Firms Bloom," 1990). Initially, STAQ linked 20 trading companies in seven cities and traded in state treasury bonds. Now, however, the system has been expanded to other financial centers and deals with most bonds and shares.

The Struggle for Resources

The bond market developed out of at least two competing and conflicting objectives: a laudable desire by the state to reform the financial market and a selfish desire by the state to garner resources to meet mounting annual deficits and key construction projects. As discussed in chapter 2 and the Appendix, the state had experienced rising deficits since 1979 and at the same time had endeavored to finance key construction projects. The money press could not run for long without stirring up inflation from undesirable "money hangovers," but at the same time, fewer funds were remaining with the state. Table A.6 in the Appendix shows the shift in extrabudgetary revenues away from the state to other economic agents. While the state reduced allocations to enterprises and banks, this was not enough to stop the bleeding, and the bond market became quite attractive as an alternative source of funds. For a while, the state cornered the bond market, which was not necessarily bad, as it was practicing some much-needed open market operations and drying up some inflationary funds.

However, financial institutions and enterprises were put in an awkward position: these firms had to fight for some of their funding to meet the demands of the economic development expected (or mandated) by the state. The corporate culture was not one of the management of finance but rather of production to a plan, and it was difficult to adjust. As firms adjusted to their newly allotted function (and freedom) they were prepared to compete with the state to maintain their productive capacities, not to mention their status and privileges. The state had used its position to create some hardships for firms, as in the following two events. First, state-owned firms were paid a lower interest rate than individuals on state treasury bonds. For example, the 1985 treasury bond paid 9 percent to individuals and 5 percent to enterprises. Second, in 1991, the state rolled over treasury bonds to firms but paid cash to individuals, as firms were borrowing at higher rates than they were getting from the state.

Nevertheless, firms needed money and the bond market was accessible to them, providing a good competitive (or quasi-competitive) environment for the state. Maturities were shorter and yields were higher than on state treasury bonds, and very often, the state was forced to adjust coupon rates and maturities. Matters came to a head in early 1987, when central planners became alarmed at the competition for funds on the part of financial institutions and enterprises. Regulations were passed to limit the volume of bonds that these firms could issue under the pretext that solvency was being jeopardized. Enterprises were accused of exceeding safe debt limits and investing in unproductive projects. On the other hand, financial institutions were accused of collusion with local government officials to raise funds for client enterprises in a regional context. With inflation rising in 1987 and 1988, individuals were attracted to some enterprise and bank inflation-indexed bonds.

By early 1989, the state had had enough of the competition and, through regulation and value-proof bond issues, it tried to curb the fund-raising enthusiasm of financial institutions and enterprises. State regulation in early 1989 barred government departments and nonproductive enterprises from issuing bonds, and restricted the issues of others. These measures, and others introduced in 1990, placed a damper on the bond issues of financial and enterprise bonds. Thus, the state continues to dominate.

DEVELOPING A CHINESE SHAREHOLDING SYSTEM

The development of a stock market presupposes that there are common shares in the economy that are tradable. After liberation in 1949, the ownership of enterprises by the public disappeared in China, giving way to state ownership of the productive resources in the economy. This situation started to reverse itself starting in the early 1980s, but for ideological and other reasons, the Chinese continue to wrestle with the adaptation and implementation of a shareholding system that differs from that found in the Western hemisphere. For example, the concept of shares in China is different from that in the Western world. Common shares, as they are called in the West, have at least four essential elements, as follows (Van Horne, Dipchand, and Hanrahan, 1993):[2]

1. The common shareholder has an ownership interest in the enterprise, with the size based on the number of shares held. For example, if an enterprise has 1,000 shares outstanding, an investor with 100 shares owns one-tenth of the firm.

2. There is a separation of ownership and management of the enterprise, and the common shareholder has the right to vote for the board of directors which manages the organization. Usually, one share is entitled to one vote.

3. The common shareholder has a residual interest in the enterprise and bears the ultimate risk of ownership, depending on the profitability of the firm. Dividends are paid from after-tax profits, are uncertain and are paid only if they are declared by the board of directors. If the enterprise is liquidated, the common shareholder is entitled to a liquidating dividend.

4. The common shareholder is free to trade shares held, and a stipulated percentage of the shareholders may vote for the sale of the enterprise.

Preferred shares are a second category of shares normally used in the West. The traditional preferred share has no maturity, is entitled to a dividend when it is declared by the board of directors, is nonvoting, and has no ownership rights in the enterprise.

Common-share ownership, as popularized in the West, is associated with at least the private sector ownership of production facilities and capitalism. The successful adoption and implementation of a Western-style shareholding plan requires political acceptance of this type of ownership/management system in the economy. Historically, China has been a socialist state controlled by the Communist Party of China, and the 14th Party Congress, November 1992, vowed that this situation would continue in the future. Since 1979, the state has permitted Chinese residents to undertake a limited amount of economic activities on a private basis, has encouraged foreign investments, and implemented a number of economic reforms. However, most of the productive assets in China are still owned by the state, and central planning is still a dominant feature of both the Chinese economy and the Chinese political system. Currently, China is trying to plan and implement a shareholding system with Chinese characteristics.

The Concept of Chinese Shares

There are two general categories of shares in China: A shares and B shares. A shares include state shares, enterprise shares, and individual shares, and are held by the Chinese. The state shares are held by the state on behalf of the Chinese people and provide ownership rights in state-owned enterprises. Under Chinese laws, state-owned enterprises are permitted to sell new capital stock and these enterprise shares may be purchased by the enterprises themselves, other enterprises or institutions, or individuals. Unlike state shares, enterprise shares have no ownership rights. Finally, those enterprises that are not state-owned (for example, collectives or a foreign-funded joint stock company) may issue shares to the private sector; these are classified as individual shares.

State shares are not tradable and the return to the state (apart from taxes) may be a negotiated percentage of the profits under the contract responsibility system or of the dividends. With enterprise shares, the characteristics are best illustrated by an example: an issue of RMB 57.56 million of capital stock by Shanghai Electronic Vacuum Device Co.(SEVDC) in August-September 1987 (Yue, 1987).[3]

1. The stock was sold by the Industrial and Commercial Bank of China and the Shanghai Trust and Investment Co. at a commission of 3 percent of the face value of RMB 50 per share. The shares were issued to Chinese nationals and were denominated in the Chinese currency.

2. By law, enterprise shares should not exceed 30 percent of the capital stock of a state enterprise. After the issue, the value of the capital stock of SEVDC was RMB 200 million, and the issue of RMB 57.56 million represented 29 percent of the total capital stock. Therefore, following the issue, 71 percent of the capital stock was in state shares and the remainder in enterprise shares.

3. Private buyers (or individuals) are constrained in the amount of shares they can buy to prevent them from having a significant control over state

enterprises. Under this condition, SEVDC sold 50 percent of the new issue to state-owned and collective enterprises and the rest to individuals who were limited to buying 20 shares each with a maximum value of RMB 2,000.

4. The stock is really a bond or debenture offering a fixed interest and a guaranteed dividend from after-tax profit. The yield on the new stock, taking into account the interest and dividend bonus, was 14.4 percent. Generally, the interest on the share is pegged to the annual fixed deposit rate at the bank and is variable with that rate. Considering that the annual interest rate for a fixed deposit was 7.2 percent at the time of the issue, the share was relatively attractive at 14.4 percent. Most later issues of A shares lack the interest and guarantee features of this issue. By 1990, the trend was toward dividends being paid from after-tax profits and limited in total to after-tax profits ("Overgenerous Share Enterprises to Lose Assets," 1990).

5. The payment of interest and principal is guaranteed by the state. If SEVDC were to default, shareholders would be paid 6 percent interest annually and the shares could be cashed at any time at face value. Again, later issues of shares may not have this state guarantee for interest and principal.

6. The shares are tradable and prices are determined by market forces on the OTC where they are trading.

Individual shares have the income or dividend features of the enterprise shares but may lack the guarantee in case of default and are usually nontradable due to the smaller sizes of the issuing enterprises. Stock market activity in China is mainly concerned with enterprise shares, which have features of several securities available in the West: like debt, they may pay interest; like a preferred or common share, they have a claim to dividends, and like a common share, they have some voting rights to elect members of the management team. While they can be traded as an A share at the discretion of the holder, they have no ownership rights. The state shares have the ownership rights and, to the extent that state shares must be at least 70 percent of the capital stock of an enterprise, management is also state controlled.

Entry of Foreign Investors

A shares are available only to Chinese investors and are traded only in RMB. This strategy was followed to exclude foreign investors and thereby avoid issues relating to the repatriation of profits and the remittance of foreign currency. Later attitudes changed and attention became focused on foreign investors, mainly as a source of hard-currency equity capital. On December 16, 1990, regulations were first enacted to permit the issue of B shares in Shenzhen ("Shenzhen's Special Stock Regulations," 1991). B shares are issued only to foreign investors (including those from Hongkong, Macao, and Taiwan), denominated in RMB, and settled in foreign exchange. The proportion of B shares of the total stock of an enterprise is subject to the approval of PBOC, and they have no voting rights. To this extent, they are like preferred shares.

The Shanghai Vacuum Electronic Component Cell Co., Ltd., issued China's first B share in November 1991, and other enterprises quickly followed ("Shanghai Issues Special Stock," 1992; Cheng, 1992a, 1992b; Chen, 1992). The issue was for RMB 100 million, the lead underwriter was the Chinese securities firm of Shanghai Shenyin Securities Co., and the foreign securities agents were Swiss Bank Corp., Solomon Bros., and Sun Hung Kai Co., Ltd. The issue was sold as a private placement to foreign institutional investors and was rather significant at the time because it was made by a state-owned enterprise. Shortly afterwards, China Southern Glass, a joint venture enterprise in Shenzhen, issued 16 million B shares to raise HK $85 million.

Early Evidence of Chinese Shareholding

By the mid-1980s, a serious academic and political debate ensued over the appropriateness of a (capitalist) share-holding system for Chinese enterprises ("China Tries Out Shareholding System," 1987; Li, 1986, 1990). While this debate was going on, some enterprises found share issues a convenient way to raise much needed capital and were encouraged in this by their respective (sympathetic) political regimes. Available reports indicate that the issue of shares by some Chinese enterprises started in the mid-1980s; and the following is some supporting evidence.

1. In July 1984, the Tianqiao Department Store Co., Ltd., sold over 3 million shares to its workers and 13 state-owned organizations and collective units through the Industrial and Commercial Bank of China, Beijing ("Shares of Stocks in Beijing Store," 1989). This Beijing enterprise had been state owned since the early 1950s, and with this issue, members of the Board of Directors were selected from representatives of the largest shareholders, including the state.

2. In 1984, the municipal government of Shanghai issued a regulation authorizing the issue of shares: "Rules Governing the Issue of Shares." Under these rules, a share issue was made by Fiele Acoustics Company in 1984.[4]

3. By August 1986, about 20 collectives in Shenyang had sold a portion of their capital stock to their staff. For example, the Shenyang Compressor Factory sold shares worth RMB 200,000 to 937 workers and staff ("Stock Exchange Debut in China," 1986). While the amounts involved were not large, they proved useful funding for collectives. They also provide further evidence of the trend in Chinese share holding.

4. Shenyang and four other cities (Guangdong, Chongqing, Wuhan and Changzhou) were allowed to issue shares starting in 1984, and by the end of 1988, enterprises had raised about RMB 200 million in these cities ("Stock Exchange Debut in China," 1986).

5. On September 26, 1986, an OTC market was opened in Shanghai, and two stocks were traded on this exchange: Shanghai Yanzhong Industrial

Corporation and Fiele Acoustics Corporation. These firms were state-owned enterprises, like Tianqiao Department Store Co., Ltd., and their shares were traded through the Shanghai Trust and Investment Company, a subsidiary of the Industrial and Commercial Bank of China, Shanghai. In addition, the People's Bank of China (Shanghai Branch) had approved the share issues of 20 enterprises worth over RMB 20 million (Dai, 1986).

By late 1986, the trend toward share holding appeared to be on the rise, prompting this editorial caption to an article by Li Yining, Professor of Economics at Beijing University: "Shareholding, as a new kind of socialist public ownership, is not just an idea. It is spreading throughout China. Currently there are over 6,000 shareholding enterprises involving more than 6 billion yuan in investment" (Li, 1986: 17).[5]

Moreover, as mentioned, much academic and political debate surfaced and three views emerged regarding share holding in China ("China Tries Out Shareholding System," 1987). The first view advocated an all-around implementation of the share-holding system for the following reasons:

1. Share holding would strengthen, rather than weaken, the state-owned economy, as more funds would be invested to increase social property.

2. The share-holding system could be used to reform state-owned enterprises and eventually lead to a separation of ownership and management. This would lead to a separation of government administration and enterprise management and enable the state to better regulate and control the country's microeconomy.

3. Part of the state's original property would be transferred without charge to collectives and workers, which should help develop the socialist market economy.

4. Individuals would own a relatively small percentage of shares compared to the state, and state-ownership would remain dominant.

The second view advocated experiments with shareholding in selected areas for the following reasons:

1. China should experiment with share holding in the collectives and cooperatives in order to develop a system with Chinese characteristics.

2. China should not rush into share holding but rather should limit it to newly established enterprises with a need for high investment and limited funds.

3. The share-holding system should be applied to certain high-risk projects or sectors; to date, it has been applied to only profitable, low-risk enterprises.

4. Enterprises should be encouraged to buy shares, while individual buying should be limited.

Finally, a third view opposed the share-holding system for the following reasons:

1. Only the state can represent the public, and therefore state ownership of productive factors must continue.

2. The adoption of share-holding is a restoration of capitalism.

3. Under central planning, enterprises and individuals have limited resources; only the state has the resources to finance enterprises.

THE TRADING OF COMMON SHARES

Common shares are traded over the counter and on two organized securities exchanges. As indicated, bonds and shares are traded at the same financial center under centralized management and control, but the volume of bond trading far outweighs that for shares.

Early OTC Stock Market Activity

There are two competing claims concerning establishment of the first OTC stock market in China since 1949 ("Rebuilding China's Securities Markets," 1991). It was reported that on August 5, 1986, a stock market opened in Shenyang, the capital of the province of Liaoning. The market was run by the Shenyang Trust and Investment Corporation with approval from the People's Bank of China, and the objective was to develop the city's money market. Shareholders traded over the counter according to given price quotations or at freely negotiated prices, and commissions ranged from 0.4 percent to 2 percent of the shares' face value ("Stock Exchange Debut in China," 1986). Since the start of 1985, business enterprises in Shenyang had been issuing about RMB 200 million worth of shares, and the shares of two of the largest issuers were traded on the new exchange. The experiment in Shenyang was also carried out in four other cities in China: Guangzhou, Chongqing, Wuhan, and Changzhou. However, a competing claim for the first stock market was made when the Shanghai Stock Market opened on September 26, 1986 (Dai, 1986). The trading was limited to the shares of Shanghai Yanzhong Industrial Corporation and Feile Acoustics Corporation, and prices were determined daily on a floating basis according to market supply/demand conditions. The stock exchange belonged to the Jingan Branch of the Shanghai Trust and Investment Corporation and was run by a single person.

Table 7.4 lists the first 12 public issues of shares in Shanghai and Shenzhen under the caption "Twelve Chinese Pioneers"; and at one time or another, all these stocks were traded over the counter. While OTC trading is not necessarily a bad activity, there can be adverse consequences if the operation is not properly managed. OTC trading in China suffered some bad consequences, and the experience of the curbside market in Shenzhen can be used to illustrate the point. Five stock issues traded on the curbside market outside the brokers' offices in Shenzhen during 1989–1990, causing prices and trading volumes to experience explosive growth for no apparent fundamental reasons. It was pure speculation, and the authorities had to

Table 7.4
Issuing of Shares: Twelve Chinese Pioneers

Name of Company	Type of Business	Date of Listing	Value of Shares Issued (RMB)	Issue Price (RMB)
Public Issues in Shanghai				
1. Shanghai YanZhong Industrial	Photoprinting	Jan. 1985	5.0 million	50
2. Ace	Consultancy in technology applications	1985	0.4 million	50
3. Shanghai Vacuum Electronic Device	Light bulbs, TV tubes	Jan. 1987	200.0 million	100
4. Shanghai Feile	Electrical appliances	July 1987	24.6 million	100
5. Yu Garden	Food stores	Mid-1987	6.5 million	50
6. Shanghai Feile Electro-acoustic	Sound equipment	Dec. 1984	1.65 million	50
7. Shanghai Electric-Engineering	Electrical engineering products	Mar. 1990	1.0 million	n.a.
Public issues in Shenzhen				
8. Shenzhen Development Bank	Finance	Apr. 1988	13.0 million	20
9. Shenzhen Vanke Co.	Consumer products, property	Jan. 1989	38.0 million	1
10. Jiantian Industry	Textiles, property	Feb. 1989	10.7 million	10
11. Anda Transportation	Transport	Dec. 1989	5.0 million	1
12. Shenzhen Champaign Industrial	Textiles, property	Mar. 1990	24.5 million	10

Source: Cheng (1990: 55).

n.a. = not applicable.

step in and take actions to control the trading activities. PBOC, Shenzhen, imposed limits on daily price movements (a maximum of 1 percent up and 5 percent down) and a 6 percent stamp duty on stock transactions. On the other hand, the municipal government decreed that all street trading was illegal and that stocks should be registered only with authorized brokers. Meanwhile, the state placed a temporary freeze on experimental stock trading in other cities (as noted earlier).

In these early trading activities, very little if any distinction was made between primary and secondary market activities. Consequently it was quite acceptable for the same securities company or broker to handle primary and secondary distributions and act as agent on both sides of a transaction. Despite these and other imperfections, the stage was set for further stock market development: investors and enterprises recognized the benefits of equity financing and, putting ideologies aside, the state had to respond.

The Organized Securities Exchanges

By mid-1980, the state apparently had adopted a strategy of, "if you can't beat them, join them." Under the guise of financial market reform, the strategic approach to control the securities market was to unify and centralize trading activities on an experimental basis. Given this strategy, approval was given for the establishment of two organized securities exchanges: SHSE (December 1990) and SZSE (July 1991). With the approval of PBOC, bonds and unlisted stocks may be traded at any of the approved financial centers across the country. However, listed stocks may only be traded on the exchange on which they are listed. The centralization of trading of listed stocks reflects the state's desire to keep a watchful eye on market developments and in particular, to spot and control any speculative stampedes. In many respects, the nature and operations of SHSE and SZSE are similar, so the following detailed account of SHSE will apply to SZSE as well.

The Shanghai Securities Exchange (SHSE)

The SHSE was founded on November 26, 1990, and opened for trading on December 19, 1990. The exchange is a nonprofit legal entity that organizes the trading of listed securities and provides for clearing, settlement, custodial, and registration services. The Assembly of Members is the highest organ of the exchange, and it includes an Executive Council (the decision-making body) and a Supervisory Committee (the regulatory body). A general manager is responsible for day-to-day operations of the exchange. The regulatory framework for the exchange is shown in Figure 7.1.

The following rules and regulations are part of the regulatory framework for the Shanghai Securities Exchange:

1. *Listing Rules for All Kinds of Securities:* Rules for Administration of Securities Trading in Shanghai (issued by the municipal government of Shanghai on November 27, 1990).

2. *The Securities Exchange Rules:* Provisional Operating Rules of the Shanghai Securities Exchange (issued by the Shanghai Securities Exchange on November 26, 1990).

3. *The Additional Listing Rules for B Shares:*

   a. Rules for Administration of Securities in Shanghai (issued by PBOC-Shanghai on November 25, 1991).

   b. Rules for the Implementation of the "Rules for the Regulation of Shanghai Renminbi-Denominated Special Shares" (issued by PBOC-Shanghai on November 25, 1990).

4. The Law of the People's Republic of China on Joint Ventures Using Chinese and Foreign Investment: Listed companies with Sino-foreign joint venture status must abide by the law (issued July 1979).

5. Company Law: Provisional rules on the administration of limited share-holding enterprises in Shanghai (issued by the municipal government of Shanghai on May 18, 1992). This law governs the establishment, operations and management of a limited company in Shanghai. It is similar to the Hongkong company law and covers the following areas:

   a. Principal/legal status of a limited-liability share-holding company;

   b. Articles of association and establishment procedures;

   c. Share capital and shareholders' rights;

Figure 7.1
Regulatory Framework for the Shanghai Securities Exchange

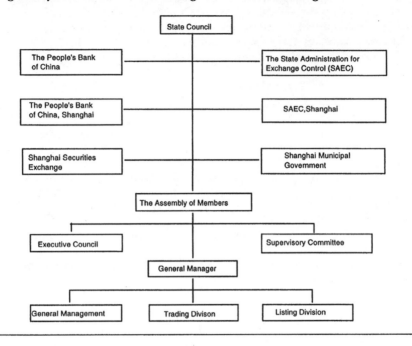

d. Selection of Board of Directors;

e. Financial and reporting requirements;

f. Mergers, winding-up, and liquidation;

g. Penalties for breach of corporate law.

6. *Listing Requirements:* The following criteria must be fulfilled before a company
   is accepted for listing.

   a. The company must be legally registered with the Industrial/Commercial
      Administration Division of the municipal government in Shanghai.

   b. Paid-up capital should not be less than RMB 5 million.

   c. Public shareholding should exceed 25 percent of the total issued share
      capital.

   d. The number of registered shareholders should exceed 500.

   e. There must be two consecutive years of profitability prior to the year of the
      share issue.

   f. The company must be sponsored by at least one exchange member.

   g. The company must report on a timely basis to the public.

7. *Reporting Requirements:* The company must file interim and audited reports to the exchange and PBOC-Shanghai within 45 days of the end of each period. There is a listing of information to be disclosed.[6]

Exchange Membership. Membership on the exchange is limited to securities companies and other financial institutions that are approved for securities trading by the People's Bank of China, Shanghai. Currently, there are about 103 members: 20 from Shanghai, and the rest from cities in other provinces. All members are affiliated with financial institutions, including securities companies, banks, trust and investment companies, and credit associations, and must join the Securities Trade Association, a self-governing trade organization. Members may be classified in one of three groups: those who trade for clients; those who trade for their own accounts, and those who do both types of trades. Present facilities are limited, and not all members have a seat on the exchange. This situation is to be changed in two ways in the future: by the addition of a third trading floor to increase computer terminals from 212 to 1,200, and through new telecommunications facilities to promote electronic trading ("Chinese Exchange," 1990; "Sluggish State Bond Sales Alert," 1992).

Regulation. The SHSE is regulated by PBOC, Shanghai, and the Shanghai Municipal People's Government. By mutual consent, the local government authorized the establishment of SHSE and specified listing requirements, PBOC-Shanghai authorizes the securities to be listed, and SHSE sets the operating rules. PBOC, Shanghai, has overall responsibility for SHSE and is responsible to the State Council (Figure 7.1).

Securities Traded. As of July 1992, there were 57 securities listed on the exchange: 7 treasury bonds, 13 financial bonds, 22 enterprise bonds, and 15 shares. Based on an estimated trading volume of RMB 11 billion for 1991, the trading of shares accounted for about 17 percent. By the end of September 1992, trading volume had reached RMB 41 billion, with shares accounting for 68 percent. This was an exceptionally speculative period for shares on the SHSE and was of great concern to the authorities.

Shares Traded. Table 7.5 is a list of the shares that were traded on the exchange as of July 1, 1992; the following points are worthy of note:

1. An enterprise that seeks to issue and list shares on the exchange must obtain the approval of the People's Bank of China, Shanghai. There are prescribed reporting requirements in preparation for an issue, and subsequent reporting to shareholders. Usually, the reporting requirements for B-share issuers are more extensive than those for A-share issuers. There are special rules governing the mechanism for the sale of new securities, depending on the size of the issue.

2. A and B shares trade on the exchange. By 5ctober 1992, the number of listed shares had increased from 16 (Table 7.5) to 32 (23 A shares and 9 B shares). There are special rules governing the trading and settlement of B shares that involve foreign investors.

3. The capitalization of shares listed on the exchange at the end of 1991 was

Table 7.5
Shanghai Securities Exchange: Listed Companies, July 1, 1992

Company	Industry	No. of shares issued (millions)	1992E Earnings per share (RMB)	1992E Price earnings ratio	Share price (RMB)	Market capitalization (RMB millions)
A-shares						
Ace Electronics	Electronic equipment	0.270	0.296	1,447.9	429.00	115.8
Feile Accoustics	Audio	0.500	1.800	219.4	395.00	197.5
Feile Co.	Electronic/investment	4.866	0.493	360.7	177.90	865.7
Shenhua Electric	Electrical products	0.500	4.000	95.0	380.00	190.0
Vacuum Electron	TV picture tubes	2.000	24.000	90.5	2,172.50	4,345.0
Xinhye Housing	Property	2.000	3.000	120.3	360.75	721.5
Yanzhong Industrial	Investment holdings	1.000	0.610	279.1	170.25	170.3
Yu Yuan Market	Retail	0.065	97.846	89.4	8,750.00	568.8
Zhejiang Phoenix Chem.	Chemicals	2.470	1.486	204.3	303.50	749.6
Jiafeng Cotton Mill	Textiles	7.063	1.494	146.6	219.00	1,546.8
Light Industry Mach	Machinery	16.500	0.824	208.7	172.00	2,838.0
No. 2 Textile Mach	Textile machinery	17.899	2.240	113.8	255.00	4,564.2
Specially-shaped Steel	Steel tubing	3.611	0.828	253.6	210.00	758.3
United Textile	Textiles	10.100	1.485	153.2	227.50	2,297.8
Total			138.400	138.4		19,929.2
B Shares						
Vacuum Electron	TV picture tubes	1,000	24,000	21.6	518.59	518.6
No. 2 Textile Mach.	Textile machinery	12,500	2,240	20.6	46.07	575.9
Total			23,700	23.7		1,094.5

Source: SBC Research (1992: 19).

RMB 2.9 billion; in May 1992, it was RMB 6.6 billion, and in July 1992, RMB 21 billion (Table 7.5).

4. The average price earnings ratio of shares listed in July 1992, was 138, with a range of 89 to 1,447. Again, these unusually high price earnings ratios reflect speculative trading.

5. The Shanghai Securities Exchange Index is based on the weighted market capitalization method, taking into account all listed stocks and using December 19, 1990, as the base day, with an index of 100. The share index rose from 292.7 on December 31, 1991, to 1187.4 on July 1, 1992, peaking to over 1,400 in May 1992.[7]

6. Earlier in 1992, the exchange had limited daily price movements in an effort to curb speculation, but these were removed in May 1992. The removal of price restrictions saw a one-day increase in the stock index of 649 points, or about 105 percent.

Share prices have been very volatile in the brief trading history of the exchange, due mainly to the limited supply of securities, the significant build-up of personal savings in the banking system, and the limited number of attractive alternative investments for Chinese residents. The exchange moved from boom to almost bust conditions, when the stock index fell to 558 on October 23, 1992. Many residents lost money, and there were unconfirmed reports of some related suicides.

Table 7.6
Selected Market and Other Information: SHSE and SZSE

	Shanghai Securities Exchange	Shenzhen Stock Exchange
Trading hours	Monday–Friday 9:30–11:30 a.m. 1:30–3:30 p.m.	Monday–Friday 9:30–11:30 a.m. 1:30–3:30 p.m.
Trading currency	U.S. $	Renminbi
Settlement currency	U.S. $	HK $
Minimum Trading lot	10 shares	2,000 shares
Share registration	Shanghai Securities Exchange	Authorized foreign clearing banks
Trading costs Brokerage fees Transfer fee Stamp duty Transaction levy	 1% transaction value,. min. U.S. $20 0.1% total par value, min. U.S. $1 0.3% transaction value None	 0.7% transaction value 0.3% total par value 0.3% transaction value 0.05% transaction value
Quote sources	Reuters	Telerate
Broking agents	Through authorized overseas brokers only for investors residing overseas.	Through authorized overseas agents or domestic brokers.
Authorized local brokers	Shenyin Securities Haitong Securities International Securities	Shenzhen Securities Trust & Inv. Corp. Shenzhen Securities Ltd. Bank of China, Shenzhen International Securities China Merchant Bank, Shekou
Authorized foreign brokers	Baring Securities (HK) Diawa Securities (HK) Hoare Govett Asia SBCI Finance Asia Sun Hung Kai Inv. Services Yamaichi Securities	Baring Securities (HK) Chin Tung Ltd. Credit Lyonnais Securities Crosby Securities Hoare Govett Asia Jardine Fleming Asia Peregrine Brokerage Sassoon Brokerage SBCI Finance Asia South China Securities Sun Hung Kai Inv. Services Tung Shing Securities Wardley Ltd.

Source: SBC Research (1992: 18).

Securities Companies. Only domestic securities companies are allowed to trade on the exchange. At the end of 1991, there were an estimated 60 specialized securities firms and over 300 financial corporations engaged in market activities, including underwriting and marketing of new issues, trading on their own account, brokerage/counseling services for clients and securities registration, settlement, and transfer and custodian services. It was estimated that in 1991, about 1 million of the 12 million residents in Shanghai had invested in shares, and that in October 1992, individual accounts with brokers exceeded 750,000, up from 400,000 in 1991 ("Chinese Catch the Market Habit," 1991). Three securities firms are authorized local underwriters and brokers for B shares (Table 7.6). Authorized foreign securities companies trade in B shares through these local securities firms and maintain B shares trading accounts of B shares for settlements.

Trading and Settlement. Trading in B shares must take place on the exchange where the shares are listed and through authorized local securities companies. Dividends and bonuses on B shares and gains on B shares may be remitted abroad in U.S. dollars. Trading off the exchange, short selling, and insider trading of B shares are prohibited. The exchange acts as the depository for all B shares listed on it.

Market Information. Market information including share price, volume of trade, and daily high and low prices, is transmitted by computer to local brokers in Shanghai, and improved telecommunications facilities are planned to provide this service nationwide in the near future. Reuters transmits exchange information to foreign subscribers. Additional details on market activities may be reviewed in Tables 7.5 and 7.6 and Figure 7.1.

Shenzhen Securities Exchange

The SZSE was established in April 1991 and opened for business on July 1, 1991. The regulatory framework is similar to that for SHSE (as shown in Figure 7.1), and SZSE is regulated by PBOC, Shenzhen, and the Shenzhen Municipal Government. Like SHSE, the SZSE operates as a nonprofit legal entity under a membership system. As of March 31, 1992, there were 15 members representing banks and other financial institutions, of whom all were from local institutions or local branches of national institutions. All members may join the Joint Meeting of Shenzhen Securities Institutions, a self-regulatory trade organization. The following is a summary of the highlights of the stock trading operations of SZSE.

1. As of July 1, 1992, there were 26 listed shares (18 A shares and 8 B shares), with a total capitalization of RMB 45 billion. At the end of 1991, there were 6 listed shares with a total capitalization of RMB 7.4 billion. Because of the higher listings of B shares, SZSE has attracted more foreign investment than SHSE.

2. The average price/earnings ratio as of July 1992, was 33.7, which was considerably less than that for shares on SHSE.

3. The SZSE Index is based on the weighted market capitalization method and had a base index of 100 on April 3, 1991. The share index rose from 110.4 on April 3, 1991, to 271.8 on July 1, 1992; a high of 305 was reached in May 1992. The exchange experienced significant price and trading volatility during its brief history. In late 1990, speculative trading forced the authorities to take remedial actions, including a stamp duty, a dividend-withholding tax, and daily price limits (*Xinhua*, 1991c, 1991d; "Troubles Reported," 1991). Thereafter, trading activity dropped, and by September 1991, the index hit a low of 46. It subsequently rebounded to 242, on October 23, 1992 (*Xinhua*, 1991e).

ISSUES, PROBLEMS AND THE FUTURE

The state has so far tolerated (and, at times, even encouraged) a Chinese share-holding system, but it is doubtful how far and how fast the state will move to promote it. In planning for the Ten-Year Program (1991–2000) and the Eighth Five-Year Plan (1991–95), priority has been placed on developing the bond and interbank components of the securities market, while experiments with the stock component were to continue (*Xinhua*, 1991a). The vice-mayors of Shanghai and Shenzhen felt it was necessary to visit the Chinese prime minister when it became known that the stock market did not feature prominently in either the Eighth Five-Year Plan or the Ten-Year Program. Earlier indications had been that the stock market was to have top priority in these planning documents ("Stock Ownership System Planned to be Introduced," 1990).

At the 14th Party Congress in November 1992, Party Secretary Jiang Zemin indicated that China would develop a socialist market economy in which the public sector will dominate ("Stock Exchange Becoming National Trading Center," 1992). The socialist market economy lets market forces, under the macro control of the state, serve as a basic means of regulating the flow of resources, subjects economic activity to the law of value and makes it responsive to changing conditions of supply and demand. It is unclear how this position will influence the growth of Chinese share holding. With state enterprises and collectives in dominance, the growth of share holdings should be low as limits will be placed on private sector ownership. Furthermore, joint stock companies in the private sector or for foreign funded businesses would be of small to medium size and may not prove attractive candidates for the secondary stock market.

The Chinese are aware of the benefits of a share holding system, which, they acknowledge, would facilitate at least the following events (*China Daily*, 1990):

1. The savings of Chinese residents will be put to productive uses rather than being kept in potential consumption modes in bank accounts. At the end of 1990, it was estimated that personal savings in banks were RMB 700 billion.

2. Foreigners who are interested in portfolio (rather than direct) investment may find Chinese shares attractive and may provide further funding for economic development. It may be argued that portfolio investments have lower risks.

3. The Chinese feel that a share-holding system can provide some separation of ownership and management, which would help to improve enterprise efficiency.

However, the nagging issue of public ownership remains, and the Chinese do not view a share-holding system as an avenue to private ownership. The state will take action to ensure that public ownership remains dominant in at least one of three ways:

1. The state owns all major enterprises, and a share-holding system (controlled by the state) will ensure that public ownership remains dominant.

2. The state may control the right of listed companies to operate in a manner consistent with the development of a socialist market economy.

3. The state owns and controls the key sectors of the economy. Even if nonessential sectors are relaxed to a share-holding system, the impact on public ownership will not be great enough to be politically unacceptable.

Without any comparable reference points or statistics, it is difficult to assess the achievements of the Chinese shareholding movement over its brief history. However, the following developments should be noted.

1. Toward the end of 1990, China issued about RMB 167 billion worth of bonds and shares, and the latter accounted for about RMB 5 billion, or 3 percent of the total (*Xinhua,* 1991b).

2. The Chinese stock market (SHSE and SZSE) joins well established stock markets in Hongkong and Taiwan and is considered a part of the equity markets in the China Region. At the end of March 1992, the capitalization of the Chinese stock market was 1.1 percent of the total capitalization of U.S. $283 billion of the stock markets in the China Region.

3. Since 1990, there has been keen interest from foreign investors in Chinese shares, and these investors are well aware of the risks involved, including:

   a. Greater social, economic, and political uncertainty;

   b. Greater price volatility, lower liquidity, and smaller capitalizations;

   c. Currency rate fluctuations and higher inflation;

   d. Controls on foreign investment and limitations on the repatriation of funds;

   e. Greater government involvement in, and control of, the economy; and

   f. Limited market information.

Despite these and other risk factors, 18 mutual funds had been established by the end of March 1992, with a total capital of U.S. $800 million ready for investment in the China Region. Notwithstanding these developments, the following problems, issues, and uncertainties existed during the brief history of the Chinese stock markets.

Corporate Law Is Quite Unclear

Share holding implies that there are joint stock companies operating under a clearly defined corporate law. This is not quite true in China. In April 1991, Shenzhen formulated some regulations governing corporations and some joint stock companies were established. Late in May 1992, Shanghai followed with corporate regulations of its own (Figure 7.1). The state released draft national regulations in May 1992, and these are being discussed and debated. Many legal matters need to be clarified to enhance the development of the stock market, including the authority to issue securities, the fiduciary duties of corporate officers and directors, and shareholder protection. Then, there is the concern for the Chinese judiciary, which is inexperienced in corporate law and associated litigation. Finally, the existing bankruptcy laws appear relatively inefficient in investor protection (Bowles and White, 1989).

Securities Regulation Is Exchange Specific

In recent years, much has been done to improve the trading environment of the two organized exchanges, but securities regulation remain exchange specific. While the exchange rules serve to provide good guidelines for the respective exchanges, there are sufficient differences to limit trading between exchanges. This situation should improve in the future as the PBOC, with funding from the Asian Development Bank, is drafting a national securities law.

Unified Control and Supervision are Needed

The state is attempting to establish the central bank, PBOC, as the watchdog of the entire Chinese financial system, which is a monumental assignment. Conflicts of interest and inefficiency are bound to occur as PBOC tries to execute its duties. Consequently, some attention should be given to the creation of a separate regulatory body for the securities markets.

Stock Markets Are Small, Illiquid and Volatile

The primary market for shares is controlled by PBOC, and the growth of the secondary market would not likely be robust enough to promote any significant amount of liquidity in the near future. The price volatility on the exchanges has been of concern to the authorities, and caution is now the watchword. No doubt, PBOC will be very careful in giving permission for new share listings until adequate laws are promulgated.

Market Information is Inadequate

Information on Chinese firms is of relatively poor quality as compared to the types of information obtainable for firms in the West. Accounting and auditing systems are not consistent across firms (or may not exist in an acceptable format). Currently, the state is designing a new finance and accounting system for government departments and enterprises, which, once implemented, should improve the quality and amount of enterprise information.

NOTES

1. This section draws heavily on Bowles and White (1992).
2. There are variations to the features reviewed in this chapter, but their omission does not detract from the discussion.
3 This was one of the earliest common share issues and its terms have been modified over time for new issues.
4. It is unclear if this issue or the issue by Tianqiao Department Store Co., Ltd., was the first share issue in China since 1949.
5. Li (1986: 17). Many of the 6,000 shareholding enterprises were relatively smaller share-holding cooperatives in China's coastal rural areas (Wang, 1992; "Co-op System in Full Revival," 1992). The trend toward share-holding cooperatives in urban areas follows the pattern in Shanghai (Wang, 1992).
6. Summarized from SBC Research (1992: 32–33). Except for some operating details, the regulatory framework for SZSE is similar to that for SHSE.
7. A second index, Jingan Index, is compiled by the Shanghai Shenyin Securities Company. It is an arithmetic average of the daily prices weighted by the daily trading volume of all listed shares, and had a base index of 100 as of November 2, 1987.

REFERENCES

Bowles, Paul and White, Gordon. 1989. "Contradictions in China's Financial Reforms: The Relationship between Banks and Enterprises." *Cambridge Journal of Economics.* 481–495.
———. 1992. "The Dilemmas of Market Socialism: Capital Market Reform in China — Part I: Bonds." *The Journal of Development Studies,* April, 364–385.
Chen, Weihua. 1992. "Share Issue Mystery." *Shanghai Star,* November, 10.
Cheng, Elizabeth. 1990. "Chinese Capital Markets Back on Track: Counters Revolution." *Far Eastern Economic Review,* July 26, 54–56.
———. 1992a. "Bs in the Honey Pot." *Far Eastern Economic Review,* March 26, 40.
———. 1992b. "Welcome Back." *Far Eastern Economic Review,* January 9, 39.
China Daily (Beijing). 1990. January 17, FBIS CHI 90 018.
China Fund Inc. 1992. *Prospectus.* July.
"China's First Share Success." 1989. *Beijing Review,* April 10–16, 25–28.
"China Tries Out Shareholding System." 1987. *Beijing Review,* October 5, 22–24.
"Chinese Catch the Market Habit." 1991. *Independent,* August 27, 21.
"Chinese Exchange." 1990. *Independent,* November 28, 26.
"Co-op System in Full Revival." 1992. *China Daily,* November 3, 4.
Dai Gang. 1986. "Shanghai Tries Stocks and Shares." *Beijing Review,* October 20, 7–8.
do Rosario, Louise. 1989. "Chinese Shun Peking Bond Dealers." *Far Eastern Economic Review,* March 9, 73.
Evans, Richard. 1993. "Bonds That Need a Boost." *Global Finance,* March, 107.
Jin Jiandong. 1989. "China's Stock and Bond Market." *Beijing Review,* October 30–November 5, 24–27.
"Let Twenty Securities Firms Bloom." 1990. *Japan Economic Journal,* December 15, 11.
Li Yining. 1986. "Possibilities for China's Ownership Reform." *Beijing Review,* December 29, 17–19.

————. 1990. "Stock Market Essential to Reform." *Jingji Ribao,* June 23, 40.

Liu Suinian and Wu Qungan. 1986. *China's Socialist Economy: An Outline History (1949–1984).* Beijing: Beijing Review.

"Over-Generous Share Enterprises to Lose Assets." 1990. *Hongkong Standard,* March 7, 12.

"Rebuilding China's Securities Markets." 1991. *China Business Review,* June, 20.

"Shanghai Issues Special Stock." 1992. *Beijing Review,* December 30–January 5, 29–30.

"Shares of Stocks in Beijing Store." 1986. *Beijing Review,* July 14, 5–6.

"Shenzen's Special Stock Regulations." 1991. *Beijing Review,* January 20–26, 38–39.

"Sluggish State Bond Sales Alert." 1992. *China Daily,* November 2, 2.

"Stock Exchange Becoming National Trading Center." 1992. *China Daily,* October 25, 11.

"Stock Exchange Debut in China." 1986. *Beijing Review,* August 18, 7.

"Stock Market Picks Up in China." 1988. *Beijing Review,* December 19–25, 6.

"Stock Ownership System Planned to be Introduced." 1990. *South China Morning Post,* October 2, 39.

Tai Ming Cheung. 1991. "Peking Inches Closer to Reform of Financial System." *Far Eastern Economic Review,* May, 42.

"Troubles Reported." 1991. *China Daily,* May 10, 4.

Van Horne, James C., Dipchand, Cecil R., and Hanrahan, J. Robert. 1993. *Financial Management and Policy.* Scarborough, Ontario: Prentice-Hall of Canada, chs. 20–21.

Wang Wenli. 1992. "Workers Grab Share in Firms." *Shanghai Star,* November 6, 8.

Wang Xiaozong. 1992. "Shareholding System Now Part of Rural Reform." *China Daily,* November 17, 4.

Xinhua (Beijing) 1991a. April 5, FBSI 066.

Xinhua (Beijing) 1991b. April 16, FBSI 073.

Xinhua (Beijing) 1991c. May 10, FBIS 091.

Xinhua (Beijing) 1991d. June 13, FBIS 114.

Xinhua (Beijing) 1991e. June 19, FBIS 118.

Yue Haitao. 1987. "Stock Buying Craze Hits Shanghai." *Beijing Review,* October 5, 24–25.

8

Foreign Banks in China

The topic of foreign banking is very sensitive for the Chinese as they cannot forget the domineering stranglehold that such institutions had on the local economy prior to liberation.[1] The Chinese detest the actions taken by overseas banks in that era and are determined not to have them repeated. As a first step, after the establishment of the People's Republic of China in 1949, the Chinese government limited the scope of operations of the overseas banks and protected their lawful rights and benefits (discussed in chapter 1). The Chinese government authorized the overseas banks to trade as agents for the Bank of China in foreign exchange and to finance businesses in China. At the same time, their operations were supervised and guided by the Bank of China. For example, Bank of China established correspondent relationships with the branches and sub-branches of Hongkong & Shanghai Bank and Standard & Chartered Bank to promote Chinese foreign trade and effect nontrade settlements. This strategy effectively used overseas banks to expand China's foreign trade and increase foreign exchange income while giving the government some control over a bank's profits.

However, the overseas banks were losing money in China, and by 1952 almost all banks had withdrawn from the country. After 1952, the overseas banks that remained in China included the Hongkong & Shanghai Bank, Standard & Chartered Bank, Overseas Chinese Bank, East Asia Bank, and the ChiyuBank in Shanghai, plus the Overseas Chinese Bank in Xiamen. While these foreign banks were not allowed to do any banking business, they maintained offices in the hope that the situation would change for the better, but it was a long wait for these banks—over 30 years. China's finances were under the control of a monobanking system over the 1950–1980 period, as discussed in chapter 1 (Zhang, Dipchand, and Ma, 1992; Donnithorne, 1967).

Despite their prior actions, the Chinese realize that overseas banks are needed to assist in the reconstruction of the economy. However, their entry has to be on China's terms. The banking reforms discussed in this chapter highlight the modes of entry of overseas banks into China since 1979 and the special problems or issues faced by overseas and Chinese banks as foreign banking was being introduced over the reform era.

The term *foreign bank* has a special definition in the Chinese financial system. Foreign banks are (a) the branches established in China by banks with head offices located in foreign countries and in the Hongkong and Macao regions (i.e., overseas banks), and which are registered in accordance with the laws of the People's Republic of China; and (b) banks with foreign capital, the head offices of which are located in China and are registered in accordance with the laws of the People's Republic of China. *Joint Chinese-foreign banks* and *joint venture banks* refer to banks operating in China that are jointly owned by financial institutions with foreign and Chinese capital. In the broad sense, foreign banks also include Overseas-Chinese banks, which are usually from Singapore, Hongkong, Macao, or Taiwan. Therefore, in this chapter, *foreign banks* refers to branches of overseas banks, joint venture banks, and Overseas-Chinese banks.

ENTRY OF OVERSEAS BANKS AFTER 1979

As indicated, it was almost 30 years before China turned its attention to giving overseas banks access to the domestic market. Over that period, China maintained correspondent relationships with overseas banks and even pushed for the expansion of the Bank of China overseas. The entry of overseas banks has been a tentative and somewhat frustrating experience.

Some Reasons for Allowing the Entry of Overseas Banks

The destructive forces of the Cultural Revolution (1966–76) touched every economic, political, and social sector of the country, making economic reconstruction a priority (Liu and Wu, 1986: 412–439). Instead of taking a cautious approach, the "Outline for Ten-Year Planning for the Development of the National Economy (1976–1985)" set unrealistic goals (Appendix). The 11th Party Central Committee (December 1978) noted the flagging performance of the economy until that time and decided to adjust the economic policies.

One of ten adjustment principles approved at that meeting involved the open door policy (see chapter 1). After the policy was adopted in 1979, it became obvious to China's leaders that overseas banks would be needed to help channel foreign funds to China. The state suffered massive budget deficits in 1979 (RMB 17 billion) and 1980 (RMB 18 billion), which had to be heartbreaking to the Chinese, who took pride in balanced budgets (China Finance and Banking Association, 1991: 243–244). China was forced to abandon its resolve of not using foreign debt: as a result, in early 1980, the declared foreign debt was U.S. $3.4 billion (Bonavia, 1980). Moreover, foreign investors were invited to participate in China's economic reconstruction ("Regulations," 1983; Wei, 1982). It would have been quite inconsistent to invite in foreign investors and foreign capital without including the bankers. The problems that the Chinese leaders faced were how and when to permit foreign banking into China. The entry of overseas banks after the 1980s had to be done in a new way and on China's terms: attracting foreign capital to finance China's economic development, promoting the reform and expansion of the Chinese financial system, and fostering the economic and financial relationships between China and other countries.

The overseas banks that would expand into China should be those involved in international banking activities and should be from the industrialized countries or the major financial centers in the world. Such banks have superior modes of operation, management systems, and communications networks compared to those of the Chinese banks. The entry of foreign banks would serve to transfer advanced banking techniques to China and provide models to their Chinese counterparts to learn and master advanced management techniques, introduce advanced equipment, and gradually begin to operate their banking business according to the conventional rules of the international marketplace.[2] Such an approach would promote the modernization of Chinese financial institutions and accelerate the process of Chinese economic development.

One consequence of the entry of these banks is that foreign capital (equity or loans) for the banks will be brought into the country, as well as their worldwide banking connections. These are of value to China, which relies on overseas financing for some of its economic development. On the other hand, the benefits for overseas banks to come to China include the ability to establish branches to expand their businesses in the large Chinese market, support their clients who invest in China, and provide intelligence for their worldwide operations.

Beginning in 1979, China started to develop a planned commodity economy, and it was necessary to introduce some degree of competition. The entry of overseas banks into China puts some competitive pressure on the domestic banking industry, especially the Chinese specialized banks. The overseas banks are viewed as examples of good banking institutions, and local banks may observe them to identify their own shortcomings and take actions to improve their service.

In the international financial industry, there is a reciprocity principle relating to the establishment of banking institutions in foreign countries. Basically, China should allow entry to banks from countries where Chinese banks have been allowed to operate. The reciprocity relationship exists between China and many other nations and the permission to allow overseas banks to operate in China expands the scope of the Chinese international financing business. Reciprocal establishment of financial institutions with different countries promotes economic and trade cooperation between China and other places in the world. At the same time, the entry of overseas banks contributes to raising the image of the Chinese financial industry in the international community and enhances China as a financial center.

Permissible Modes of Entry by Overseas Banks

In December 1979, the State Council permitted overseas banks to establish representative offices in Beijing; the Export-Import Bank of Japan was the first to do so. A representative office only had the authority to represent its head office and could not conduct business in China for profit. Normally, the representative office would provide market information on the Chinese economy, solicit clients for business to be transacted outside China, and provide advisory services to clients in China (Grieves, 1986). These privileges were confirmed in a directive issued by PBOC: "The PBOC Management Methods on Overseas Chinese or Foreign Financial Institutions Establishing Permanent Representative Offices in China" (February 1, 1983). Representative offices were required to be licensed and to seek a renewal of that licence every three years. While this banking strategy was not profitable, overseas banks took up the challenge and, by April 1985, 63 representative offices were opened in Beijing (Langstron, 1985). The rationale of having representative offices in Beijing was naively stated thus (Langstron, 1985: 71): "A superficial advantage for a foreign [overseas] bank would be the opportunity to insinuate itself into the Chinese financial system to be ready if and when the day comes that full branch banking is granted to foreign concerns."

Overseas banks with representative offices in China hoped the Chinese would permit them to undertake a wide array of banking activities at some future date (McGrath, 1992) and, by early 1985, there were growing expectations that the Chinese banking laws would be revised to permit foreign banks. A token gesture was made toward the end of 1984, when the six foreign banks that remained in Shanghai after liberation were given the authority to accept foreign currency deposits and grant foreign currency loans to joint ventures, fully owned foreign enterprises, and Overseas-Chinese concerns. The overseas banking community did not regard this action as real banking reform that would benefit anyone, not even the six foreign banks involved. The overseas banks wanted access to renminbi to make loans to the Chinese (Langstron, 1985).

In any case, the overseas banking community did not have to wait for long. On April 12, 1985, PBOC announced "Regulations Governing Foreign Banks and Joint Chinese-Foreign Banks in SEZs," which was retroactive to April 2, 1985. These regulations contained the reforms that the Chinese were prepared to make at that time; the essential features are summarized in the following paragraphs. Foreign banks were allowed in the SEZs — Shenzhen, Zhuhai, Shantou, and Xiamen (and later, Hainan Island).[3] The foreign banks could deal in foreign exchange (and renminbi) in the SEZs, but only with nonlocal enterprises and individuals. Initially, the regulations provided for foreign banks to take deposits and make loans in renminbi, but this privilege was withdrawn to protect domestic banks from competition. The overseas banking community did not get what it wanted and so rationalized (Lee and Bowring, 1986: 140): "The Chinese know that they are being courted by banks from around the world so they can afford to be difficult."

Selected Provisions on Banking Reforms, 1985

The following summary of selected provisions of PBOC, "Regulations Governing Foreign Banks and Joint Chinese-Foreign Banks in SEZs," April 2, 1985, was derived from information contained in Cheng (1986) and Lee (1985).

I. The regulation specified three types of foreign banks.

    A. Foreign bank branches that are established in the SEZs by banks from foreign countries or from Hongkong and Macao. A branch must have operating funds in foreign currencies equivalent to RMB 40 million.

    B. Foreign bank head office banks that are owned by foreign capital but have a head office in the SEZs. These head office banks must have a minimum paid-up capital of RMB 40 million.

    C. Joint venture banks that are jointly owned by Chinese and foreign capital and which are established in the SEZs. These institutions must have a minimum paid-up capital of RMB 40 million.

II. Foreign banks may be established only in the special economic zones (SEZs).

III. Foreign banks may conduct the following business only with non-local enterprises and individuals in the SEZs:

    A. Accepting deposits in foreign currencies (and renminbi);

    B. Granting of loans in foreign currencies (and renminbi) and discounting of bills;

    C. Handling of inward/outward remittances and foreign exchange collection;

    D. Settlement of export/import transactions and inward/outward documentary bills;

    E. Exchange business in foreign currencies and foreign-currency bills;

    F. Local and foreign currency investment and guarantee;

    G. Buying and selling stocks and securities;

    H. Trust, safe deposit box, credit investigation, and consulting; and

    I. Handling of deposits and loans in foreign countries.

IV. The registered capital for foreign banks in foreign currency must be the equivalent of RMB 80 million of which at least 50 percent must be paid-in capital.

V. Loans to any enterprise in the SEZ must not exceed 30 percent of paid-in capital.

THE GROWTH OF REPRESENTATIVE OFFICES AND FOREIGN BANKS

Despite the setback in the anticipated reform, overseas banks continued to enter China. By the end of 1990, there were an estimated 209

Table 8.1
Representative Offices of Overseas Financial Institutions by Location, October 30, 1990

	Beijing	Dalian	Tianjin	Qingdao	Wuhan	Shanghai	Guanghou	Shenzhen	Xiamen	Nangtong	Fuzhou	Zhuhai	Quanzhou	Hangzhou	Total
USA	12					3	2	1							18
Brazil	1														1
Canada	4					1			1						6
UK	6	1	1				1	1				1			11
Germany	5					1									6
France	7	1	1			5	5	1							20
Italy	7					2									9
Spain	1														1
Switzerland	3														3
Belgium	1					1									2
Austria	1														1
Luxemburg	1														1
Cayman	1					1	1		1						4
Holland	2														2
Sweden	4					1									5
Norway	2														2
Australia	3					1									4
Japan	42	9	2	3		18	11	1		1	1				88
Singapore	2						1	1			1				5
Thailand	1														1
Jordan	1														1
Kuwait	1														1
Pakistan	1														1
Hongkong	3	1	1		1	1	1	1	1		2		1	1	14
Denmark	1														1
USSR	1														1
	114	12	5	3	1	35	22	6	3	1	4	1	1	1	209

Source: China Finance and Banking Association (1991: 634–651).

representative offices in 14 coastal cities, as shown in Table 8.1. There were 114 representative offices (or 55 percent of the total) located in Beijing, 35 (or 17 percent) located in Shanghai, 22 (or 11 percent) located in Guangdong Province (which includes Shenzhen), and 12 (or 6 percent) located in Dalian. Together, these four regions/cities accounted for 182 representative offices (or 87 percent of the total), which reflects a city-level concentration in China. Apart from commercial considerations, Beijing is important for political reasons since it is the capital of China. While most banks maintain an office in Beijing, some have established one or more offices in other locations as well.

Japan accounted for 88 representative offices (or 42 percent of the total); followed by France, with 20 (or 9 percent); the United States, with 18 (or 9 percent); Hongkong, with 14 (or 7 percent); and the United Kingdom, with 11 (or 5 percent). Together, overseas banks from these five countries accounted for 151 representative offices (or 72 percent of the total), which reflects a heavy "country" concentration. The representative offices were established by about 80 international banks from the countries identified in Table 8.1 (Grieves, 1986; Sargent, 1992).

Table 8.2
Foreign Financial Institutions by Location, October 30, 1990

Financial Institutions	Financial Institutions
Shenzhen and Shekou, Guangdong Province	Xiamen, Fujian Province
1. Nanyang Commercial Bank, Shenzhen Branch	1. United Overseas Bank Ltd., Xiamen Branch
2. Nanyang Commercial Bank, Shekou Branch	2. Chiyu Banking Corp., Xiamen Branch
3. Hongkong & Shanghai Banking Corporation, Shenzhen Branch	3. Hongkong & Shanghai Banking Corp., Xiamen Branch
4. Bank Indosuez, Shenzhen Branch	4. Bank of Orient, Xiamen Branch
5. Standard Chartered Bank, Shenzhen	5. Standard and Chartered Bank, Xiamen Branch
6. Societe General, Shenzhen Branch	6. Xiamen International Bank, Xiamen
7. Banque Nationale de Paribas, Shenzhen Branch	7. Credit Lyonnais, Xiamen Branch
8. Bank of Tokyo, Shenzhen Branch	8. Overseas Banking Corporation, Xiamen Branch
9. Sanwa Bank, Shenzhen Branch	9. Bank of East Asia, Xiamen Branch
10. Fuji Bank, Shenzhen Branch	
11. Bank of East Asia, Shenzhen Branch	Zhuhai, Guangdong Province
12. China International Finance Co., Shenzhen*	
13. CitiBank, N.A., Shenzhen Bank	1. Standard and Chartered Bank, Zhuhai Branch
14. Guangdong Province Bank, Shanghai Branch	2. Zhuhai Nantong Bank, Zhuhai Branch
15. Hokkaido Takushoki Bank, Shenzhen Branch	
16. Boashen Bank, Shenzhen	Haikou, Hainan Province
17. Hongkong Mainland Insurance Co., Shenzhen Branch*	
	1. Nanyang Commercial Bank, Haikou Branch
Shanghai	2. Standard Chartered Bank, Haikou Branch
	3. Hongkong Mainland Insurance Co., Haikou Branch*
1. Hongkong and Shanghai Banking Corporation, Shanghai Branch	
2. Standard and Chartered Bank, Shanghai Branch	
3. Overseas Banking Corp., Shanghai Branch	
4. Bank of East Asia, Shanghai Branch	
5. Shanghai International Finance Co., Shanghai Branch*	
6. Shanghai United Finance Co., Shanghai Branch*	

Source: China Finance and Banking Association (1991: 652–653).

*These are nonbanking financial institutions.

Table 8.2 is a listing of foreign banks and other foreign financial institutions that were established by the end of 1991. Of the 37 financial institutions listed in Table 8.2, there were 32 foreign banks and 5 nonbanking enterprises. Of the 32 foreign banks, 15 were located in Shenzhen, 9 in Xiamen, 4 in Shanghai, 2 in Haikou, 2 in Zhuhai, and 1 in Shekou. Events change rapidly in China and, as a matter of update, at the end of 1992 there were 49 foreign financial institutions in China: 17 in Shenzhen, 15 in Shanghai, 9 in Xiamen, 3 in Haikou, 3 in Shantou and 2 in Zhuhai (Shao, 1992; "Abstract from the Symposium on Foreign Bank Management," 1992). It should be noted that all the international banks listed in Table 8.2 have representative offices in other locations in China.

Looking ahead to 1997 and the return of Hongkong to Mainland China, there have emerged some interesting trends with implications for foreign banking in China. Hongkong has developed as an important trading partner of Mainland China, serving as a conduit for Chinese exports and a major exporter to China (Caplan, 1986; Zhenxing, 1993). International banks have noted this development with interest and are adopting location strategies in order to capitalize on trade financing and other opportunities. First, overseas banks with strong financial bases in Hongkong and entry into China are expanding operations on the mainland. For example, by 1992, the British bank Standard and Chartered had six branches and four representative offices, and the Bank of East Asia, four branches and one representative office ("Hong Kong," 1992). In 1992, these two overseas banks accounted for about 20 percent of foreign banks in China. Second, overseas banks in Hongkong and, in particular, those that have not gained entry into China, are expanding operations in Hongkong in order to gain an "avenue to the mainland market" and "have a good listening post and operating base for capital market activities in Asia" (Loong, 1987b: 12).

In general, two notable events prompted the accelerated expansion in foreign banking in China in the early 1990s. The first event relates to economic developments in Shanghai. In the late 1980s, the Shanghai government decided that the city should regain it status as China's main financial center, a position it had held in the 1930s. The approach was to use judicious and rational economic development strategies to lift the municipality out of its malaise. Accordingly, in April 1989, the municipal administrative council announced that it would proceed to develop a Pudong New Development Zone, which radiates to other parts of Shanghai from that center ("Shanghai Announces Plans to Develop Pudong New Area," 1990; Baldinger, 1990). It was estimated that the development in Pudong would probably require U.S. $20 to U.S. $30 billion and would take about 20 years to complete.[4] Funding looked like a problem. However, by January 1990, two financing strategies had been announced: (a) open up the securities markets to attract funds to Shanghai businesses, and (b) permit foreign banking in Shanghai (*China Daily*, 1990). With respect to foreign banking, operational rules were formulated and, by September 1990, PBOC had issued "Administration on Shanghai Foreign and Foreign-Funded Banking Institutions," which codified those rules. Among other things, the directive invited overseas banks to apply for permission to establish foreign banks in Shanghai, and an estimated 30 to 40 did so (Li, 1991; Tai, 1990b).

In March 1991, it was announced that six overseas banks had been selected to open branches in Shanghai: Citibank and Bank of America from the United States, Bank Indosuez and Credit Lyonnais from France, and Sanwa Bank and the Industrial Bank from Japan. This event marked the first time that foreign banks had been established outside the special economic zones.[5] The permission given for the six foreign banks was just the start of a trend for Shanghai, and by November 1992, the city had 12 foreign banks, a joint venture bank, and 2 joint venture finance companies.

The second event occurred concurrently with the banking reforms in Shanghai. Until 1991, an overseas bank could only open a representative office in Beijing under a license which had to be renewed every three years. This condition was changed in June 1991, when overseas banks were allowed to establish representative offices in any of the 14 open cities in China ("Streamlined Rules," 1991). Moreover, the need to renew the license every three years was waived. Overseas banks are now able to choose the location for their representative offices and presumably may decide based on costs and business opportunities.

Joint Venture Bank: Xiamen International Bank (XIB)

The "Regulations Governing Foreign Banks and Joint Chinese-Foreign Banks in SEZs" (April 2, 1985) made provision for a joint venture bank that involved foreign and Chinese capital. The first such institution was the Xiamen International Bank, which was established on November 28, 1985, with an authorized capital of HK $800 million and initial paid-up capital of HK $420 million. Initially, the shareholders were as follows: Industrial and Commercial Bank of China (ICBC), Fujian Provincial Branch, 25 percent; Fujian Investment and Enterprise Corporation, 16 percent; the Construction and Development Corporation of the Xiamen Special Economic Zone, 10 percent; and Kong Min Xin Holdings, Ltd., of Hongkong, 49 percent. Thus, the Chinese partners held 51 percent of the shares.

In October 1991, three new shareholders were introduced: Asian Development Bank (ADB, which acquired 10 percent of the stock; Long-Term Credit Bank of Japan (LCBJ), with 10 percent; and Sino Finance Group Co., Ltd. (SFGC), with 5 percent. The paid-up capital increased from HK $420 million to HK $620 million, and while the four original shareholders maintained their proportionate ownership in XIB, their share of stock was adjusted to 75 percent ("Foreign Banks Invest in Xiamen International Bank," 1991). Consequently, after the entry of the three new shareholders, share ownership was as follows: ICBC (Fujian), 18.75 percent; Fujian Investment and Enterprise Corporation, 12 percent; Construction and Development Corporation of Xiamen SEZ, 7.5 percent; Kong Min Xin Holdings, Ltd., 36.75 percent; ADB, 10 percent; LCBJ, 10 percent; and SFGC, 5 percent. The three Chinese partners retained 38.25 percent of the shares after the entry of the new shareholders.

XIB remained the only joint venture bank until the early 1990s when there were announcements of additional such institutions. In November 1992, the International Bank of Paris and Shanghai announced its opening in Shanghai, making it the second joint venture bank in China ("City Welcomes Its First Joint Venture Bank," 1992). This joint venture bank is owned by ICBC (Shanghai) and Banque Nationale de Paris. There are indications that the trend in joint venture banking may continue. For example, NanYang Commercial Bank from Hongkong has announced a joint venture bank to be located in Ningbo ("NanYang Bank Opens 4th Branch," 1992; Feng, 1992), and the Agricultural Bank of China (Shanghai) is negotiating with foreign interests (including Rabo Bank of Holland) to establish a joint venture bank in Shanghai.[6] Usually, a joint venture bank has more banking privileges and receives better treatment from the relevant Chinese authorities because of the involvement of Chinese interests.

NATURE OF BUSINESS OPERATIONS

As indicated previously, in the section, "Selected Provisions on Banking Reforms, 1985," foreign banks are allowed to conduct foreign currency business with foreign-funded firms, joint ventures and foreign individuals in the special economic zones and in restricted areas in Shanghai.[7] In general, these banks are involved in foreign currency business relating to deposit taking, syndicated loans, project finance, trade finance, corporate finance involving equity issues of B shares, and financial leasing (Grieves, 1986; Sapp and Watne, 1987; Sargent, 1992; Lindorff, 1993).

It is difficult to obtain reliable and consistently compiled statistics on the operations of foreign banks. The available statistics indicate that the 49 foreign banks operating at the end of 1992 had assets of U.S. $4.3 billion ("Abstracts from the Symposium on Foreign Bank Management," 1992). Given this estimate, the average size of a foreign bank was about U.S. $88 million. In addition, some financial information on the operations of financial institutions in Shenzhen in 1991 are available (summarized in Table 8.3), and these business operations are representative of those for other foreign banks. The following are highlights of the operations of foreign banks in Shenzhen.

1. Deposits flowed mainly from outside China: 84.5 percent versus 15.5 percent from firms and individuals in China. Therefore, the foreign banks depended mainly on foreign investors to secure funding for investment in China.

2. Foreign currency loans were a major business activity for foreign banks and about 84 percent of loans were granted to firms in China. In 1991, there was an estimated U.S. $2.8 billion foreign currency loans granted to firms in Shenzhen, of which the foreign banks accounted for U.S. $1.592 billion (or 57 percent of the total). The domestic banks view this competition with displeasure.

3. Loans exceeded deposits, which indicates that foreign banks had provided equity financing as required by the laws of China. However, the data seem to indicate that foreign banks were providing the minimum equity financing (i.e., the foreign currency equivalent of RMB 40 million, as required by law).

4. Next to the activity in foreign currency loans, trade finance is most of importance to foreign banks. International settlements deal mainly with exports, and foreign banks compete vigorously with Chinese banks for this segment of the banking business. Here again, the domestic banks do not like the competition.

5. Overall, the foreign banks were profitable, earning U.S. $16.83 million in 1991, which was up by 39 percent from 1990.

In addition to loans and settlements, foreign banks provide consultancy services and market information for their overseas parent and their foreign and domestic clientele, including the Chinese state and the provincial and municipal governments in China. A common strategy is to link operations with representative offices in other Chinese cities, but the Chinese

Table 8.3

Selected Financial Statistics for Foreign Financial Institutions in Shenzhen, 1991 (Millions of U.S. dollars unless otherwise indicated)

A.	Number of Foreign Financial Institutions	16	
	Foreign Banks	1	
	Sino-Foreign Joint Finance Company		
	Total	17	
B.	Total Deposits	$1,196.29	84.50%
	From Offshore	$219.44	15.50%
	From China		
	Total	$1,415.73	100.00%
C.	Total Loans		
	Offshore Loans	$252.35	15.85%
	Loans in China	$1,339.45	84.15%
	Total	$1,591.80	100.00%
	Loans Exceed deposit by	$176.07	
D.	Settlement Business		
	Imports	$67.11	13.88%
	Exports	$416.28	86.12%
	Total	$483.39	100.00%
E.	Profits after taxes	$16.83	

Source: Estimated from data reported in Shao (1992, 28–31).

authorities tend to take a dim view of such practices since they believe representative offices should not be involved in profit making activities.

Initial Difficulties Facing Overseas Banks

The following discussion is a summary of the difficulties encountered by overseas banks upon entry into China and during the brief period of operation (1979–1992) covered in this study.

1. Initially, the confinement to Beijing inflicted a high cost on the representative offices, as commercial and residential spaces were limited and costly and were confined to designated hotels (including the Jianguo Hotel, the Peking Hotel, and Minzu Hotel). In addition, costly expatriates had to be brought in to handle routine administrative duties, as qualified locals were hard to find. In early 1985, the annual cost of operating an office ranged from U.S. $250,000 to U.S. $300,000, excluding executive salary (Langstron, 1985; "China," 1986). The problem of office space eased somewhat in mid-1985 with the opening of the CITIC office/apartment building and the Noble Tower. Later, in 1991, there was the option to locate in the open cities where space costs are lower.

2. Foreign banks had few opportunities to "carve out" niches in the investment program in the Chinese economy. China is a large country, and the idea of economic restructuring conjures up visions of massive projects requiring large sums of money. While this may be true of China, investment was controlled according to a unified plan. Whatever financing foreign banks had to offer, this had to fit within that unified plan and it normally required close contacts with the Chinese fraternity. Very few foreign banks

had such contacts having been there only for a short time. The second complicating factor was that foreign banks had to compete with the Bank of China (BOC) which had ample foreign exchange to finance projects within the unified plan. This was not an easy task considering that BOC could lend on concessionary terms. The third complicating factor was that the Chinese economy was easy to overheat and when this happened, the state had very little remorse in applying austerity measures which included reduction in investment and even the cancellation of projects. Several other factors contributed to the relatively low level of loans activity of the foreign banks:

a. In 1980, China rejoined the World Bank and as a member of the Third World, it qualified for soft loans. In addition, many industrialized countries offered concessionary export credits. China took advantage of these lower cost financing rather than resort to borrowing at higher cost from commercial lenders.

b. Foreign banks depended heavily on joint ventures or foreign funded enterprises for much of their business. While foreign investors were encouraged through various incentives to invest in China in the early 1980s, there were still enough restrictions and unfavorable influences which limited the business initiatives of foreign banks. The lack of reliable information on borrowers, the lack of adequate accounting rules, the lack of a bankruptcy law and the deliberate action of borrowers not to disclose information impeded the credit assessment process (Gerard, 1989). In addition, the Chinese authorities were slow to liberalize import restrictions, management controls over enterprises and foreign exchange controls, which had adverse effects on the business activities of joint venture firms or foreign funded firms (Sapp and Watne, 1987; Young, 1988a; Gelatt, 1988). With their clienteles operating in a relatively constrained environment, there were less business opportunities for foreign banks.

c. Chinese financial institutions and foreign banks began to set up joint venture leasing and joint venture finance companies in the early 1980s. As discussed in chapter 5, these financial institutions compete with foreign banks in China.

d. China developed its own institutions and used them to raise funds in the international financial markets. Bank of China and CITIC are actively operating overseas on behalf of the state while the larger regions like Shanghai and Guangdong have counterpart institutions performing similar functions. While foreign banks may be involved in syndicates or other deals, they tend to play a secondary role since the Chinese institutions "call the shots."

3. Very often, foreign banks earned low spreads on loans. Generally, the Chinese are tough and skillful negotiators and they shop around for the best deal. With the large influx of foreign banks and other competing sources of financing, the Chinese were able to extract rates which had low premiums above LIBOR. While the normal premium varied between 1.25 to 1.37 percent, it was not unusual to find premiums which ranged from 0.25 to 0.5 percent. Sometimes, there were even requests for negative premiums.

4. Until 1985, there were uncertainties about who had authority to guarantee loans which were extended to Chinese enterprises. Normally, a Chinese parent (for a borrowing subsidiary) or a government ministry under whose jurisdiction the enterprise operated would guarantee a loan. However, it was questionable if such guarantors had the foreign exchange to repay debts in defaulting situations. Technically, BOC had the foreign exchange to repay but it was unclear if BOC would want to guarantee all (the billions worth of) debt. Fortunately, the matter was clarified in 1985 when 23 financial institutions were officially identified as guarantors of Chinese debt by the State General Administration of Exchange Control (Langstron, 1985 and Young, 1988b).

5. The representative office could not engage in profit-making activities in China so it was precluded from signing loan contracts in that country. This restriction entailed additional expenses to have loan contracts signed overseas. Assuming that the contract could be signed in China, things were still not better for a while. In 1983, the Ministry of Finance slapped a 10 percent withholding tax on interest on loans signed in China. Given the tax, offshore signing was still preferable. Fortunately, the tax was abolished in July 1985 (Cheng, 1986).

6. The Chinese have a knack for administratively redefining (or even canceling) regulations, given experience or difficulties with any plan of action. A Westerner will call this a situation of "confusing laws," and rightly so. For example, the regulation permitting foreign banks in the SEZs (April 2, 1985) provided for these institutions to take deposits and make loans in renminbi. However, they were later told that the privilege was canceled in order to protect domestic banks from competition. On the other hand, the regulations may be vague and subsequent clarifications may be done for the benefit of the Chinese. For example, PBOC knew that the foreign banks in the SEZs and those in Shanghai were doing business in areas bordering their respective operating jurisdictions. Staff from the foreign banks held "office hours" in hotel rooms to meet their clients and this practice seemed quite acceptable until PBOC stopped it in 1991. Apparently, BOC complained about the practice since it had lost a significant portion of its business in the areas of concern (Tai, 1990a).[8]

Difficulties for the Chinese

The following discussion is a summary of the issues that the entry of foreign banks have posed for the Chinese.[9]

First, the domestic banks are upset with the competition in the foreign currency loans and the international settlement businesses. For example, BOC (Shenzhen) has lost business to foreign competition: it had control over 85 percent of international activities but this fell to about 70 percent in the early 1990s. The Chinese banks complain about the higher level of efficiency of the foreign banks: "speed," "too quick," and "even quicker."

Second, Chinese banks are losing their more capable employees to the foreign banks which offer higher salaries and better professional and social welfare conditions.

Third, foreign banks have better access to foreign exchange since they deal with joint ventures and foreign funded firms which are foreign exchange earners. The Chinese banks deal with a smaller percentage of the Chinese business community whose access to foreign exchange is limited. Accusations are being leveled at the foreign banks, such as illegal transfer of profit, tax avoidance, and illegal transfer of working capital abroad.

Finally, China has no national or unified law governing foreign banks and regional conflicts have arisen. For example, Shanghai and Shenzhen are typical economic and political rivals which have differing regulations in their bid to attract foreign banks. For example, Shenzhen does not collect a unified industrial and commercial tax from foreign banks but Shanghai does and this practice gives Shenzhen an advantage over Shanghai. In another case, the reserve requirement in Shenzhen is 6 percent but it is lower at 5 percent in Shanghai and this (negotiated) central bank requirement gives Shanghai the advantage.

POLICY ISSUES FOR THE FUTURE

The policy issues which are currently being discussed are not tasteful. On the one hand, there is a strong economic and academic opinion that the "playing field should be level." The proponents of this viewpoint argue that foreign banks should not be restricted in business activities in China and this should surely speed up the efficiency of the Chinese banks. Under this policy, foreign banks would compete "head-on" with Chinese banks for both foreign currency and renminbi business. The foreign banks support this approach which would allow them access to domestic savings which are running about RMB 1 trillion, or U.S. $250 billion (Williamson, 1993).

The industry (and political) opinion is quite the opposite and includes the following suggestions:

1. Restrict the entry of foreign banks both in scale and in speed. Ideally, the entry of foreign banks should be at the speed at which the efficiency of the Chinese banks improve; not the other way around.

2. Restrict international settlements and other selected activities of foreign banks. In recent years, all Chinese banks were given authority to deal in foreign exchange and competition for foreign business has increased significantly (Gelatt, 1988). Chinese banks find that they have to compete among themselves and now, with foreign banks for foreign exchange business.

3. Strengthen the auditing management of foreign banks to ensure high quality in capital adequacy ratios, assets, liquidity, profitability, and so forth. A stricter legal environment for foreign firms would guard against banking abuses as mentioned earlier. Foreign banks and their foreign clientele are viewed with suspicion in that they may not be operating in the best interest of China.

4. Only joint venture banks should be allowed entry as this approach would give the Chinese some control over future development in the banking industry.

5. There is some feeling that the banking industry in the special economic zones may be saturated. In the last decade, the domestic banks expanded into the SEZs, and they compete among themselves across industry lines. Even without the foreign banks to worry about, there may not be enough business for the domestic banks. The option, then, is to restrict the further entry of foreign banks in the SEZs.

The prevailing atmosphere in Beijing appears to support further expansion by overseas banks in China. Recently, overseas banks have been allowed to set up branches in seven additional cities in China: Dalian, Tianjin, Qingdao, Ningbo, Nanjing, Fuzhou and Guangzhou. This privilege may be extended to other cities, including Beijing (Ren, 1993; Kaye, 1992). Moreover, China is making a strong bid to enter the General Agreement on Tariffs and Trades (GATT), under whose rules China should not have barriers to entry in the domestic banking industry. Even if overseas banks continue to enter China, there are questions with respect to permissible business activities. The President of Bank of China is quoted as saying that foreign banks will "get bigger pieces of the pie" if the economy grows at the expected 8 to 9 percent per year in the near future ("Overseas Banking Institutions Pledged 'Thicker Share of Cake'," 1993). Foreign banking in China is still a "waiting game."

NOTES

1. For detailed discussion, technical analyses, and further references, see Tamagna (1942), Donnithorne (1967), King (1969), and Rawski (1989).

2. In an interview with an economist attached to the Municipality of Shanghai, one of the authors was informed that these reasons are probably the most important ones which influenced the decision to allow overseas banks to enter China.

3. Some special privileges were already extended to two banks from Hongkong and Macao. In 1982, NanYang Commercial Bank was permitted to open a branch in the Shenzhen Special Economic Zone. In October of the same year, NanYang Commercial Bank opened another branch in Shekou, Shenzhen, and Nantong Bank of Macao opened a branch in Zhuhai (now renamed Nantong Bank of Zhuhai).

4. These estimates were provided to the author by officials of the Shanghai Municipality in March 1990.

5. Since 1987, there were rumors that Beijing would allow foreign banks to locate outside the SEZs ("China," 1987).

6. The ownership of the former is expected to be divided among NanYang Commercial Bank, Bank of China (Zhejiang), and Ningbo International Trust and Investment Corporation.

7. There were some exceptions. Foreign banks in Shenzhen SEZ were permitted to deal with state-owned enterprises ("Forecast 1987—China," 1986) and those in Shanghai, with state-owned trading corporations (Loong, 1987a). Later, however, these privileges were terminated after domestic banks protested to PBOC.

8. It was estimated that over the two years that this practice prevailed, BOC lost about 90 percent of the business in trade bill discounting and document processing in the areas concerned.

9. The discussions in this section and the one that follows draws on Shao (1992) and "Abstract from the Symposium on Foreign Bank Management" (1992).

REFERENCES

"Abstract from the Symposium on Foreign Bank Management." 1992. *Financial Studies,* October, 63–64.

Baldinger, Pamela. 1990. "Interview: Developing Mutual Understanding." *China Business Review,* September/October, 50–51.

Bonavia, David. 1980. "The Red Ink on China's Ledger." *Far Eastern Economic Review,* September 9, 69.

Caplan, Basil. 1986. "Hong Kong: Ten Years to Go." *Banker,* December, 14–22.

Cheng, Elizabeth. 1986. "More Room to Move—Not So Much to Develop. "*Far Eastern Economic Review,* September 11, 95.

China Daily. 1990. January 26, FBIS CHI 90 018.

China Finance and Banking Association. 1991. *Almanac of China's Finance and Banking.* Beijing: China's Financial Publishing House.

"China: Financial Reforms Will Expand Role of Foreign Banks." 1987. *Asian Finance,* December 15, 53–56.

"City Welcomes Its First Joint Venture Bank." 1992. *China Daily,* November 15–21, 11.

Donnithorne, Audrey. 1967. *China's Economic System.* London: Allen and Unwin.

Feng Jing. 1992. "The First Joint Sino-Foreign Bank." *Beijing Review,* January 27–February 2, 24–26.

"Forecast 1987—China: Business as Usual Despite Measly Reliefs." 1986. *Asian Finance,* December 15, 83,85.

"Foreign Banks Invest in Xiamen International Bank." 1991. Xinhua, July 26, 45.

Gelatt, Timothy A. 1988. "Foreign Exchange Control: Beijing Issues New Measures for Foreign Invested Firms." *East Asian Executive Reports,* October 15, 11–12.

Gerard, Sumner. 1989. "U.S. Banks' Tougher Approach." *China Business Review,* May/June, 24–27.

Grieves, Robert. 1986. "Representative Offices with Very Little to Bank On." *Asian Business,* December, 53–55.

"Hong Kong: Quick Off the Blocks." 1992. *Banker,* December, 56–57. (Cited as "Hong Kong.")

Kaye, Lincoln. 1992. "Banking in Asia—China: Bringing up the Rear-Fast." *Far Eastern Economic Review,* September, 60, 62.

King, Frank H. H. 1969. *A Concise History of Modern China (1840–1961).* New York: Praeger.

Langstron, Nancy. 1985. "Waiting—and Wishing—for Some Action." *Far Eastern Economic Review,* April 25, 71.

Lee, Mary. 1985. "Foreign Bank Freedoms." *Far Eastern Economic Review,* April 25, 130–131.

Lee, Mary and Bowring, Philip. 1986. "Bearing Tribute to China—Once Again." *Far Eastern Economic Review,* March 20, 140.

Li Ming. 1991. "Foreign Banks in Shanghai." *Beijing Review,* March 25–31, 25.

Lindorff, Dave. 1993. "Financing China's Capitalist Revolution." *Global Finance,* February, 42–45

Liu Suinian and Wu Qungun. 1986. *China's Socialist Economy: An Outline History (1949–84).* Beijing: Beijing Review.

Loong, Pauline. 1987a. "China: Japanese Joker in the Pack." *Euromoney,* October, 137–143.

———. 1987b. "Hong Kong—Banking on the China Connection." *Euromoney,* November, 12–15.

McGrath, Neal. 1992. "Waking China's Sleeping Cash." *Asian Business,* November, 62–65.

"NanYang Bank Opens 4th Branch." 1992. *China Daily,* November 24, 2.

"1989 Capital Markets Scoreboard: US $137.7 Billion Raised in 1989." 1990. *Asian Finance,* January 15, 43–51.

"Overseas Banking Institutions Pledged 'Thicker Share of Cake'." 1993. *China Daily,* March 25, 4.

Rawski, Thomas C. 1989. *Economic Growth in Prewar China.* Berkeley: University of California Press.

"Regulations for the Implementation of the Law of the People's Republic of China on Joint Ventures Using Chinese and Foreign Investment." 1983. *Beijing Review,* October 10, i–xxvi. (Cited as "Regulations.")

Ren Kan. 1993. "Foreign Banks Sizing Up Beijing." *China Daily,* April 11–17, 1.

Sapp, Richard W., and Watne, Donald A. 1987. "Strategical and Tactical Issues Facing U.S. Banks Entering Mainland China." *World of Banking,* November/December, 20–25.

Sargent, Sarah. 1992. "China's Market Takes Shape: The Bird Flies Out of the Cage; the Buzz of the B Shares." *Euromoney,* June, 551–556.

"Shanghai Announces Plans to Develop Pudong New Area." 1990. *East Asian Executive Reports,* May 15, 9–13.

Shao Hai. 1992. "Problems and Policy Suggestions of Foreign Banks in Shenzen SEZ." *Studies of International Finance,* August, 28–31.

"Streamlined Rules Will Allow Foreign Banks to Have Representative Office in Any Open City." 1991. *American Banker,* June 14, 11. (Cited as "Streamlined Rules.")

Tai Ming Cheung. 1990a. "Back to Basics." *Far Eastern Economic Review,* June 28, 27–28.

———. 1990b. "Pudong's Investment Lures." *Far Eastern Economic Review,* October 4, 68–69.

Tamagna, Frank M. 1942. *Banking and Finance in China.* New York: Institute of Pacific Relations.

Wei Yuming. 1982. "China's Policy on the Absorption of Direct Investment from Foreign Countries." *Beijing Review,* July 26, 18–22.

Williamson, Malcolm. 1993. "Follow the Leader." *Banker,* March, 18–19.

Xinhua. 1983. *A History of the Chinese Currency.* Beijing: Xinhua and People's Bank of China.

Young, Jack C. 1988a. "Foreign Exchange Control: Beijing Issues New Measures for Foreign Invested Firms." *East Asian Executive Reports,* October 15, 11–12.

———. 1988b. "Foreign Exchange Guarantee—A Chinese Puzzle." *International Financial Law Review,* April, 26–29.

Zhang Yichun; Dipchand, Cecil R.; and Ma Ming Jia. 1992. *The Chinese Financial*

    System and its Management. Beijing: Social Science Press.
Zhenxing Zhou. 1993. "All Eyes on the China Factor." *Banker,* March, 16–17.

9

The Outlook for China's Financial System

From 1979 to the early 1990s, China had moved from a monobanking system (Figure 1.2) to a financial system that is typical of that in an industrialized country (Figure 2.2). Considering the political, economic, and social environment that prevailed prior to 1979 (chapter 1), China's achievements in reforming the financial system are quite commendable. With political ideology in check, or even liberalized to some extent, China's rulers focused on economic and social reforms following the 11th Party Central Committee held in December 1978 (Appendix). Concurrently, the focus was also on reforming the financial system, since China's rulers recognized that economic, social, and financial system reforms are an interactive and integrated process (Liu, 1993). Chapters 2 through 8 review the essential achievements of reforms in the financial sector.

It is not an easy task to be prescriptive about the future of the Chinese financial system. In the past, reforms to the financial sector have been successful because economic and social reforms were successfully implemented. The Chinese population were content (except for the Tiananmen Square incident) to await political reforms. However, in the near future, it is expected that heightened political awareness by the masses would have a greater impact on the course of development in China. The liberal economic policies of the aging Deng Xiaoping may or may not continue depending on the emerging successor regime. Promises to let Hongkong continue with its capitalist economy may be broken. Social unrest and criminal incidents in China may escalate to the point where foreign investors may avoid the country. Regional political, economic and social conflicts and discontent may reach a point where national unity may be threatened. These and other similar events point to the uncertainties which face the future of China's financial system.

In addition, China is in the midst of transition from the traditional planned economy to a socialist market economy where market forces should play an important role in the allocation of resources. The coexistence of these two systems are creating further problems in an already confusing political, economic and social environment including the following ("Agencies Set up to Strengthen Securities Sector," 1993: 4):

1. There is a relative lack of fair and free competition in the dominant sectors of the economy and interest groups go to any length to protect their "empires."

2. Administrative decrees (under the planned economy) and market regulations (under the socialist market economy) are at best mixed-up, and may be giving erroneous or conflicting signals about the future directions of reforms.

3. Market trade is in relative chaos. Illegal activities abound even at the upper levels of the CCP hierarchy, contracts are being broken with impunity, market regulations are routinely ignored, and regional conflicts and jealousies abound.

4. While over 300 economic laws and regulations have been passed unto the early 1990s, many of them contain loopholes which are used by unscrupulous market operators to their advantage.

This chapter is a cautious and reserved review of the immediate future of China's financial system. The discussion reflects the position of the official (or semiofficial) circles in Beijing and is probably the best scenario to present to conclude this book. This position may not be what is best for the long-term in China but at least, readers are presented with the realities of the current situation and their likely impact on the immediate future. Because of rigidities and imbalances in the Chinese political, economic and social system, it is wishful thinking to expect radical changes to the financial system in the near future.

THE SOCIALIST MARKET ECONOMY

At the 14th CCP National Congress in October, 1992, the Chinese Premier Jiang Zemin announced that the country will develop a socialist market economy. He attempted to define the concept as follows ("Deng Blazes Path to Socialism," 1992: 4):

By establishing the structure of a socialist market economy we mean to let market forces, under the macro-economic control of the state, serve as a basic means of regulating the flow of resources, to subject economic activity to the law of value and to make it responsive to changing relations between supply and demand.

By itself, the statement is complex, defies an easy interpretation and has generated a multitude of contradictory and inconsistent commentaries as to the future political ideology of the Chinese Communist Party. While the debate continues, at least three elements appear to be clear. First, China will continue to build socialism with Chinese characteristics under the people's democratic dictatorship, leadership by the CCP and Marxism-Leninism and Mao Zedong thought. This political ideology is a continuation of a process that started after liberation in 1949. Second, the state will allow market forces to play some role in the allocation of resources in the country. However, the extent of this role in the immediate future is debatable. Finally, the state will intervene to marshal or control the direction and impact of market forces on the country's economic development. This attitude flows from a keen desire to channel resources (profitably or otherwise) to enhance the economic reconstruction of the country.

The development of the financial market system is tied closely to reforms in the economic and social structures of China and it is instructive to have an appreciation of why China's rulers have opted for a socialist market economy as the planned commodity economy is being phased out. Wang Jiye (1989) offered seven major reasons:

1. China has a large and growing population: 1.2 billion in 1991 and growing at about 15 to 20 million a year. The ability to feed the nation is of major concern to the state and productivity in and availability of land for the agricultural sector are important variables in this context. Since 1984, the productivity in the agricultural sector has declined or at least stagnated and public funding is needed to upgrade the industry. In addition, the agricultural sector faces competition for land from residential, industrial and commercial developments. The state is very much concerned with the competition for land and the negative effects which may occur in the agricultural sector. Accordingly, the state wants some control over market forces relating to real estate in the country to preserve the vitality of the agricultural sector.

2. It is estimated that by the year 2000, there will be about 160 to 180 million displaced agricultural workers. The state needs access to funds to provide for alternative employment opportunities for these people mainly in the industrial, commercial and service sectors of small and medium-sized cities. That is, the state is encouraging alternative employment opportunities in the rural areas, and is actively dissuading the mobility of the displaced agricultural workers to the industrialized coastal regions, as they are usually not trained for available employment in those areas (Gao, 1993).

3. China faces an aging population. In 1982, 4.9 percent of the population was over 65 years old, and by the year 2000, this figure is expected to rise to 7 percent. Given Chinese culture and customs, the state may have an important role to play in caring for the aged and this would require large amounts of funding until alternatives (e.g., private pension funds and unemployment insurance) are in place in the economy.

4. There is low productivity and uneven economic development across regions and industrial sectors. The state feels compelled to be the "guardian and protector of the weak" and funds would be needed to bolster productivity in selected industry sectors and to correct for regional disparities in economic development. Traditionally, the state experimented with rural (or major) reforms in selected locations or activities and if successful, the practices are extended across the country (Grieves, 1987; Zweig, 1992). This experimentation process and the transfer of knowledge and technology to other locations in China take time to implement.

5. There are changes in the ownership structure of the productive forces in the economy. A nonstate sector has been encouraged and is currently accounting for about 50 percent of the national output (Tanzer, 1992). However, the state-owned enterprises continue to operate in the main industrial sectors of the economy and account for the majority of employment. The state readily admits that its enterprises are relatively inefficient compared to enterprises in the nonstate sector and reforms are needed in their ownership, management, and operations. However, such reforms take time and money. Whatever their shortcomings, the state feels it has an obligation to "stick with" and reform state-owned enterprises, at least to prevent massive retrenchment and to safeguard employee welfare in the immediate future.

6. The commodity economy is relatively underdeveloped and should remain in this status unto the year 2000. This is particularly true for the agricultural sector where about 50 percent of commodity production are consumed by the producers rather than be subject to market forces. Then, there are bottlenecks in the market system (e.g., lack of adequate transportation, energy, etc.) that impede market development. The state feels it has to play a direct role in helping to expand the commodity market since the resources of individual producers are limited.

7. The state feels it must have direct control over foreign exchange since this is crucial for economic reconstruction. While the process of globalization is leading to worldwide liberalization in the product and services markets, as a Third World country, the state is proceeding cautiously in this direction. There is a need for foreign exchange to pay for approved imports and to repay the foreign debt.

The mechanism for the development of a socialist market economy is perplexing but again, Wang (1989) offered a possible explanation. The state would continue to be the primary planning organ for the country and would regulate the market by administrative means. However, in the setting of administrative decrees, the state would pay attention to trends in the marketplace to observe the performance in existing markets, developing markets and new technological information and developments. The expectation is to use market information to maintain a balance between supply and demand and at the same time to encourage expansion and improvement in the economic structure of the country. Hopefully, this approach would enable the state to move away from hard-line central planning to management of the economy through appropriate macroeconomic policies.

The state is expected to achieve the development of a socialist market economy by demonstrating its ability to perform several functions including the following (Wang, 1989):

1. The state should curb inflation through stable monetary and pricing policies.

2. The state should be concerned with the rapid growth of the economy in recent years and should slow economic growth within sustainable targets.

3. The state should control the growth of the money supply at some rate equal to less than the economic growth rate plus a premium for structural price increases, which reflects price increases for controlled commodities.

4. The state should allow interest rates to play a greater role in the allocation of credit in the economy. One popular interest rate policy being suggested is to have differential interest rates depending on the use of funds. For example, there should be different interest rates on loans for capital projects and for working capital, for productive projects and for nonproductive projects, and for industrial projects and for non-essential ones.

5. Although it may be difficult to achieve, the state should link income, consumption, production and investment in a more meaningful manner for the economy as a whole. This would involve the generation of more alternative investment opportunities for the Chinese people who should channel more funds to investment rather than consumption.

The market has to guide enterprises and as such it should be open and competitive to establish realistic prices. Currently, there are three markets: commodity, technology and labor service markets. The consumer goods market is relatively competitive and the capital goods market (relating to technology) is developing at a reasonable pace but still lags in openness and competition. However, the capital (to acquire technology) and labor service markets need serious attention in order for them to play a greater role as guides to enterprises.

Over the reform period, three distinct geographical markets have emerged and they collectively impact on economic developments in China: the developed coastal regions in China, the lesser developed inner regions in China, and the international market. Initially, the idea was to let the market forces in the coastal regions provide signals for "the state to regulate the market, the market to regulate the enterprise." However, the price signals from the coastal regions to the early 1990s have been somewhat distorting due to speculation and overzealous investment and production and may not be used by the state to regulate the market in other regions in China. Under such circumstances, prices have to be controlled administratively to avoid hardships in the undeveloped areas. The international marketplace is expected to provide signals for trading opportunities, pricing of products and services and technological developments.

Economic reforms in China in the 1990s are likely to continue as a gradual process where the state-controlled economy would dominate. Under this scenario, it is almost certain that the development of a market economy (or any version of it) would be a slow process (Fan, 1992). The crux of the matter is the role of the state in the economy and associated property rights. The state has a dual role as an administrator of the country and as the boss of the country (Bian, 1992). As an administrator, the state would agree that adequate macroeconomic policies would go a long way in reforming the economy. However, as a boss, economic management faces some serious hurdles which need to be removed.

As the boss of the country, the state has exclusive control over the productive elements such as capital, labor, and land and other fixed assets. With its control over capital and since the start of reform in 1979, the economy has changed from "the big rice-pot of fiscal fund mechanism" to the "big rice-pot of credit fund mechanism" (Zhou, 1992). The state, through its control over the financial system, has been able to draw funds from the domestic economy and abroad but much of these funds went to the financing of fiscal deficits of governments and losses of state-owned enterprises. The more productive (i.e., the nonstate) sector has limited access or no access to credit and have to survive on minimal state assistance (Chen Xiao, 1993). It is estimated that in 1991, the nonstate sector accounted for 50 percent of the output value of the nation and 47 percent of the value of national industrial output (Fan, 1992; "China Approaches Market Economy," 1992). This contradiction in capital allocation should be changed but it will take time to do so.

With respect to land and other fixed assets, property rights are held by the state on behalf of the Chinese people. In theory, the assets belong to the people. However, nobody bothers about the care and maintenance of assets because management is preoccupied with meeting mandatory productive quotas set by the state, employees are on fixed salaries and compensation schemes and enterprises are not responsible for profits and losses (Fan, 1992; Bian, 1992; Qiao, 1992). It is argued that until there is an effective separation of ownership and responsibility in the state-owned enterprises, there will be very little hope for the development of a market economy. There is considerable ongoing debate on how this could be achieved and the process is sure to be a long one (Ni , 1991; Zhou, 1992; Yu, 1992; Zheng, 1992).

With respect to labor, the state's control appears to be slipping over time. Normally, the state assigned people to jobs, but this general practice is gradually changing. The development of the nonstate sector has provided attractive employment opportunities to China's incremental labor force and to retrenched workers. On the other hand, the lure of higher incomes in the special economic zones and coastal cities have promoted the (voluntary and unauthorized) mobility of labor sometimes with unpleasant consequences (Cheng and Mosher, 1992). Finally, even the state-owned enterprises are recognizing the need for better compensation for employees. Over 1979–90, through direct salaries and bonus schemes, the annual increase in salaries and wages averaged 14.8 percent (Table 2.8).

Ideas for Reform of the Financial System

Within the context of the socialist market economy, there are three dominant ideas for the reform of China's financial system and they flow mainly from academics and practitioners who have been involved in the reform process.

Break Monopoly of Specialized Banks. This opinion holds that at present, China's financial system is dominated by a small number of specialized banks which control the banking industry in terms of business volume and employment (chapter 3). This monopoly (or oligopoly) situation should be broken for several reasons including the following:

1. The specialized banks, under the State Council, possess too much power, which makes it difficult for the central bank to exercise effective macroeconomic control of the economy.

2. The specialized banks have shown very little initiative in promoting the horizontal circulation of funds in the economy. Basically, they have stuck with tradition and stressed the vertical transfer of funds and even interfered with horizontal accomodation to protect their own interests. In short, the specialized banks have still not become commercially agressive after over a decade of reforms.

3. The specialized banks must be managed as profitable entities for financial reform to succeed but the structure of their organizations make this difficult. They are too large, overstaffed and adhere to too much government red-tape to be run as effective enterprises.

The proponents of the idea call for a break up of the specialized banks into independent banks on a regional basis. Furthermore, other financial institutions (of a nonbank nature) should be allowed to coexist with the banking sector and that all financial institutions should be under the general leadership of the central bank. Fair and free competition should dominate in the financial sector.

Dual-Track Banking Sector. Currently, the banking sector allocates funds based on administrative decisions through the unified credit plan and hopefully, on commercial decisions based on risk-return considerations. It is estimated that about 30 percent of loans of specialized banks are based on administrative decisions or are policy based (Yu, 1993). This very often leads to conflict as the political and commercial motives for granting credit may not be consistent. Furthermore, the political motive generally overrides the commercial motive and this creates problems for the central bank in its macroeconomic management of the economy ("Major Expansion in the Cards at Shenyin," 1993). The opinion relating to the dual-track banking sector argues that the specialized banks should be split in two groups: one group to handle policy-based credit and the other, commercial credit.

The banks which should handle policy-based credit (i.e., the political banks) should carry out the state's policies and be of a national character. They may be established to handle business in specific industries (and remain as specialized banks) or in specific regions (and become comprehensive banks). In a sense, these political banks would be "glorified" development banks with deposit-taking functions. On the other hand, the commercial banks should operate as independent units at the grass-roots level and be responsible for profits and losses. Proponents of this view support the existence of nonbanking financial institutions and fair and free competition.

Proper Adjustments to Existing Financial System. The third opinion argues for maintaining the existing financial system but with proper adjustments to correct for apparent weaknesses. This opinions holds that the present financial system with the central bank in the leading position, the specialized banks as the mainstay and the various nonbank financial institutions, is suitable to China's present condition. Accordingly, there is no need for any radical change to the financial system as reflected in Figure 2.2. However, there is need for some adjustments to correct for obvious weaknesses including the following:

1. The powers of the central bank should be increased to enhance its ability at macroeconomic management of the economy. The State Council (and the State Planning Commission) should let PBOC have more powers to use adequate and reasonable direct and indirect levers in its efforts to achieve monetary and price stability.

2. Eventually, the specialized banks should operate like enterprises and be responsible for profits and losses. This position presupposes that specialized banks will be converted to comprehensive banks to handle commercial credit.

3. The financial markets should provide a greater diversity of financial instruments to meet the demands of the socialist market economy. The list includes short-term state debt instruments to enhance open market operations, derivative securities (futures and options), forward contracts in currencies, and more enterprise bonds and shares.

Principles for Improving the Financial System

Considering the tasks ahead and the operating environment, the state has recognized at least eight operating principles or guidelines that should be followed in future financial reforms. These principles are "nothing new" and have been around for a long time. However, the fact that they have resurfaced, appears to indicate that the state would, at last, inject a greater degree of rationalism in reforming the financial system.

The Economic Principle. The establishment of new financial institutions should be done to meet the needs of economic development of the country as a whole or of specific regions, where required. Applications for new financial institutions must demonstrate (through feasibility studies and other reports) that there would be sufficient business to assure profitability. Additionally, new financial institutions should have sufficient capital to maintain solvency and protect depositors.

The Open Principle. Under a socialist market economy there should be an open financial system. In particular, openness refers to China's relationship with the outside world and implies that more leeway should be given to foreign financial institutions operating in China. The state recognizes the need for China's financial system to be a part of the global marketplace.

The Coordinating Principle. Reforms in the financial system should be coordinated with those in other areas, including taxation, public finance, economic planning, and social welfare, to promote orderly development.

The Control Principle. The financial system should be controlled by direct means (e.g., administrative degrees) or indirectly through relevant laws and regulation.

The Competition Principle. The operating environment for the financial system should be fair and competitive. Financial institutions should engage in fair competition, which could be partially promoted by relevant laws and regulations.

The Independence Principle. Financial institutions should be independent and be responsible for profits and losses and bear business risks. In particular, the central bank should have greater independence from the State Council to render it more effective.

The Creative Principle. Financial institutions should be creative to promote new products and services to enhance business opportunities.

The Moderation Principle. Further reform to the financial system would be done in moderation in response to the needs of economic development.

Possible Institutional Changes

The prevailing "official" posture appears to embrace elements of the opinions relating to the dual-track banking sector and proper adjustments to the existing financial system. In fact, the dual-track banking sector is regarded as a subset of the opinion relating to proper adjustments to the existing financial system. Figure 9.1 shows the financial system as it may develop in the immediate future. Relatively major reforms are planned for the state-owned banking sector and the financial markets and these are discussed before presenting an overall view of the future of the financial system.

Reforming the State-owned Banking Sector. There are expected to be at least four major reforms or adjustments which should impact on the state-owned banking sector, as follows:

1. Policy-based credit is likely to be separated from commercial credit.

2. State-owned banks would be independent, involved in fair and free competition, and responsible for profits and losses.

3. State-owned banks would emerge as the dominant national financial institutions in China.

4. State-owned enterprises would be independent, involved in fair and free competition, and responsible for profits and losses.

While all domestic banks have policy-based loans in their respective portfolios, the holdings of some are greater than others. The state-owned specialized banks (BOC, PCBC, ABC, and CIB; see chapter 3) have more involvement in policy-based loans than the state-owned comprehensive bank (BOCOM, see chapter 4). The immediate issue is one of devising a separation mechanism for the two types of credit and associated administrative structures. There are at least three distinct approaches or

Figure 9.1
Conception of the Future of the Chinese Financial System

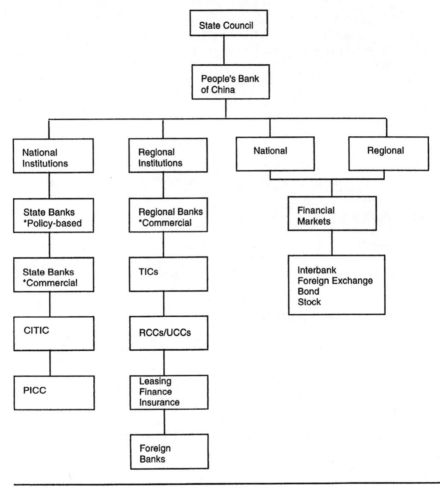

options with related problems.

First, each bank may separate policy-based from commercial loans, and administer them within their existing administrative structures. However, if a bank would be responsible for profits and losses then it has to absorb losses on policy-based loans which it was literally forced to grant by some higher authority in the past. More important, new loans would have to be granted, at least in the near future. As in the past, these new loans may not be based on quality of credit considerations, and the conflicts that now exist may not disappear. A bank would continue to face conflicts between policy-based and commercial credit. Neither of the above two situations would be desirable in the spirit of reforms.

The second approach would be to designate one domestic bank to take over and administer all existing and new policy-based loans to the satisfaction of the State Council. However, the choice of a bank is problematic. The task would require a well capitalized bank with an adequate national infrastructure but none of the likely candidates appear to be available. BOC has a defined role as a foreign exchange and foreign trade bank, ABC is crucially involved with agriculture and rural commerce and industry while ICBC operates in the urban areas. CIB is relatively too small to take on this role and BOCOM has a reasonable comprehensive banking business which it would be reluctant to relinquish.

The third possible approach is to establish a new bank which would be involved with existing and new policy-based loans. Here again, the problems would be capital requirements for the establishment of a national institution and the need for specialized labor. Moreover, the timing of the establishment of a national institution would be of concern.

Considering the difficulties involved, the Chinese have opted to experiment with the issue. Selected branches of the various state-owned banks are used to test the first approach noted above. The argument is that the separation of policy-based and commercial credit would not be an indefinite activity. Eventually, the state-owned banks would all have to be commercially viable and all loans would have to pass reasonable credit screens. Under this scenario, the separation would not last for long.

However, if there should be no separation between policy-based and commercial loans, state-owned enterprises must be independent and be responsible for profits and losses. Under the socialist doctrine, this condition is not likely to be a 100 percent objective as there would continue to be state-owned (loss making) enterprises. The solution to the matter is not an easy one nor would it be done in a hurry. Therefore, it is expected that there may be one or more state-owned banks which would be involved with policy-based credit, as illustrated in Figure 9.1. These institutions may be reflective of approach three above working effectively through the state-owned commercial banks located throughout the country.

Promoting a National Securities Market. The supervision and control of the entire financial system has been a monumental task for PBOC. In addition, rivalries in Shenzhen, Shanghai and other financial centers have created anxious moments for Beijing. Finally, the riot in Shenzhen in August 1992, and the volatility of both the Shanghai and Shenzhen stock exchanges have highlighted the concerns of the investing public in China. For these and other reasons, the State Council has decided to play a direct role in promoting a national securities market and several initiatives have been taken to achieve this goal.

In October 1992, the Securities Committee of the State Council (SCOSC) was established to exercise macro control of the securities market throughout the country. Essentially, this task involves the unification and coordination of policies, the improvement or establishment of adequate supervisory systems, the protection of the interests of investors and the assurance of a healthy environment in the securities markets. SCOCC works in close cooperation with the State Commission for Restructuring the Economy and the securities authorities of the local governments. Concurrently, the China Securities Supervision and Control Committee (CSSCC), an organ of SCOCC, was established to supervise and implement the policies of SCOCC ("Agencies Set up to Strengthen Securities Sector," 1993, 4).

In May, 1993, the State Council released draft regulations governing the issuing and trading of stocks in China and these regulations are considered as the most comprehensive measures issued to date. Consistent with the mandate of SCOCC, the regulations seek to unify stock markets, protect investors and to regulate the issue of shares consistent with the development objectives of the country. A national securities law covering all securities is expected in early 1994 ("Securities Business Now Made More Secure," 1993, 1).

Securities firms (which are largely owned and controlled by state-owned banks) are encouraged to expand nationwide or are established on a nationwide basis to permit easier access to market intermediaries. For example, The Shanghai Shenyin Securities Co. has approval to establish offices in key cities across China ("Major Expansion in the Cards at Shenyin," 1993, 3). As another example, three securities firms (Guotai, Nanfang, and Huaxia) were established in October 1992, in Beijing, Shanghai and Shenzhen with adequate capital for national operations (Ren, 1993a; "National Investment Company," 1993, 2).

The telecommunications system for national trading of securities is being improved with funding from state-owned banks. For example, four state-owned banks are the major source of funds for "The Nets," which would link about 300 cities with the Shanghai and Shenzhen stock exchanges by the end of 1993 (Xiao Liu, 1993).

Under the guidance of SCOSC, regulations are being drafted to promote the trading of state shares (Ren, 1993b). Currently, these shares are not traded and account for 50 to 80 percent of the outstanding shares of listed companies. Assuming that the shares are allowed on the market, this would improve market liquidity. However, several obstacles have to be overcome including the valuation of the shares, the method of releasing them on the market and the pacification of the conservative elements of the CCP who still adhere to the principle of public ownership.

Through SCOSC, the state controls the flotation of new stock issues. For example, in 1993, it was decided that provinces should have some participation in the stock market. Accordingly, each province was required to select two well-run shareholding companies to issue shares to be listed on the stock exchanges in Shanghai and Shenzhen. The total value of new issues was projected at RMB 5 billion ("Prospects Bright for Securities Business," 1993, 1).

In addition, the state is encouraging firms to list shares on overseas stock exchanges. In October, 1992, China Brillance Automotive Co. had a successful listing on the New York Stock Exchange and this was encouraging for the Chinese. Accordingly, it was decided to select ten firms for listing overseas in Singapore, New York, London and Zurich. A 45-member committee under SCOSC has authority to make the selection (Chen Weihua, 1993).

CONCEPTION OF THE FUTURE FINANCIAL SYSTEM

It is not clear at this time what the Chinese financial system would look like in the immediate future. However, Figure 9.1 ventures to present one viewpoint.

The Central Bank

PBOC will continue as the central bank and have control and supervision of the financial system. The State Council (and the State Planning Commission) may continue to have tight control over macroeconomic policies through the central bank. It is not likely that PBOC may have increased leeway to use, on its own, direct and indirect levers, to achieve monetary and price stability.

National versus Regional Financial Institutions

Four dominant groups of national financial institutions should emerge as follows:

1. The state-owned banks that deal with policy-based credit may operate nationally, using the distribution network of the state-owned commercial banks.
2. The state-owned banks that deal with commercial credit would operate nationally, be independent, and be responsible for profits and losses. They are expected to operate as comprehensive banks and to engage in fair and free competition.   ‘
3. CITIC is expected to continue national operations (as described in chapter 5).
4. PICC is expected to dominate the domestic insurance market and to continue to operate nationally (as described in chapter 5). However, the state is encouraging some competition in the industry. In October 1992, American International Group was allowed to establish an office in China (Otis, 1992). Also, domestic insurance firms have been established but they operate on a regional basis.

The decision to operate nationally or on a regional basis may be determined by PBOC as an administrative decree or by the financial institutions taking into account capital requirements for expansion and market opportunities. The four groups listed above are currently operating nationally and the maintenance of the status quo should not present problems. However, new entrants to the national market may have difficulties: high cost, existing competition, and deliberate exclusion from the market by the state. The regional financial institutions would include regional banks, trust and investment corporations, credit cooperatives, foreign banks, and leasing, finance, and insurance companies.

Regional Banks. These institutions would include the specialized Housing Savings Banks (chapter 3), the regional comprehensive banks (chapter 4), new share-holding banks, and new cooperative share holding banks. As discussed in chapter 5, planned reforms for RCCs and UCCs include the upgrading of some of the larger credit cooperatives to share holding and cooperative share-holding banks to serve specific regions and clienteles.

Trust and Investment Corporations. These institutions (discussed in chapter 5) are not expected to undergo any major reforms in the near future. They would continue their role and functions as regional financial institutions.

RCCs and UCCs. Except for those institutions which would be elevated to bank status, no major reforms are expected and they should continue their role and functions as described in chapter 5.

Foreign Banks. The number of foreign banks (i.e., branches of overseas banks and joint venture banks) should not experience any spectacular rise above current levels (discussed in chapter 8). The Chinese have indicated that further entry of foreign banks would be based on the performance of the economy. Furthermore, permissible business activities in China may not be liberalized further in an effort to protect the domestic banking sector which is expected to undergo further reforms in the 1990s.

Other Financial Institutions. Leasing, finance, and insurance companies should continue to maintain their existing roles and functions as no major reforms are planned for these institutions. The state would continue to promote joint venture efforts, but the trend in numbers of institutions is not expected to result in any dramatic increase.

National versus Regional Financial Markets

The major emphasis appears to be the promotion of a national securities market for the flotation and trading of bonds and shares. The initiatives of the state have been noted. In addition, initiatives are being taken by the two stock exchanges, including the following:

1. Shanghai and Shenzhen are actively soliciting membership on their respective exchanges from other provinces in China (Chen, 1992).

2. The prominent financial centers across China are taking measures to ensure that the securities business develops in an orderly fashion in the local area. For example, Guangdong Province has two watchdog organizations to regulate the securities business in that area (Zheng, 1992). The Guangdong Security Committee has overall control of the stock industry including the carrying out of policies, the drafting of regulations and decisions relating to the size and operations of the SZSE. In addition, the Guangdong Security

Supervision and Management Committee directs the flotation and trading of securities and supervises the market participants. These provincial units work closely with their counterparts at the state level.

3. Both Shanghai and Shenzhen pursue independent policies to attract foreign investors. In early 1993, each exchange had nine B shares which have been attractive to foreign investors including China Fund Inc., Greater China Fund Inc. and Jardine China Region Fund (Soares, 1992; Potter, 1992; Woolley and Barnathan, 1992).

Other components of the financial markets are receiving some modest attention. The Shanghai Foreign Exchange Transaction Center introduced currency futures in June 1992, and by May 1993, the cumulative trading volume was U.S. $430 million (Xiao Chen, 1993). The effort is viewed as an experiment to test the market and the results have not been encouraging, due to a low volume of spot transactions and the lack of adequate regulations governing the trading of futures. Nevertheless, the experience may be useful at some future date and the activity continues.

Guangdong has taken another approach to educate its citizens about currency futures: residents are allowed to trade in Hongkong through Hongkong brokers. Currency futures include the British pound, the deutsche mark, Japanese yen, Swiss franc, and U.S. dollar. In the meantime, the Guangdong authorities are learning the trade from their Hongkong counterparts (Li, 1993).

Finally, the interbank market is relatively quiet, and there is not much hope for further development until the reforms in the banking sector have been put into effect. It is hoped that interbank activities will become national once the appropriate infrastructure has been put into place. The telecommunications system for the securities business should improve interbank market activities.

REFERENCES

"Agencies Set up to Strengthen Securities Sector." 1993. *China Daily*, January 18, 4.
"Bankers to help Prevent Overheating Economy." 1993. *China Daily*, January 17–23, 3.
Bian Yi. 1992. "Poor Management of State Assets Must Be Stopped." *China Daily*, November 9, 4.
Chen Fan. 1992. "Stock Exchange Becoming National Trading Center." *China Daily*, October 11–17, II.
Chen Weihua. 1993. "Ten Firms Selected to Raise Funds Overseas." *China Daily*, January 11, 2.
Chen Xiao. 1993. "Private Business Taps Advantages of State Firms." *China Daily*, January 3–9, 2.
Cheng, Elizabeth, and Mosher, Stacy. 1992. "Deng's Distant Vision." *Far Eastern Economic Review*, May 14, 23–24.
"China Approaches Market Economy, Bank Official Says." 1992. *Wall Street Journal*, March 30, B15D.
"Deng Blazes Path to Socialism." 1992. *China Daily*, October 13, 4.

Fan Gang. 1992. "Non-State Sector 'Key to Effective Gradual Reform.'" *China Daily*, November 4, 4.

Gao Jin'an. 1993. "New Measures Will Help Labor Reform to Work Efficiently." *China Daily*, May 5, 1.

Grieves, Robert. 1987. "China Focus: Economic Reforms Given Trial Run in Interior City." *Asian Business*, January, 42–44.

Li Zhuoyan. 1993. "Black Market Money Gets Green Light." *China Daily*, January 3–9, 2.

Liu Guixian. 1993. "Speech to the Managers of National Banks and Insurance Companies: China's Financial Future." *Chinese Finance*, March 12, 4–13.

"Major Expansion in the Cards at Shenyin." 1993. *China Daily*, January 17–23, 3.

"National Investment Company Making a 16-Branch Network." 1993. *China Daily*, January 3–9, 2. (Cited as "National Investment Company.")

Ni Jixing. 1991. "Economic Restructuring in the 1990s." *Beijing Review*, March 11–17, 20–21.

Otis, L. H. 1992. "China's Insurance Industry Facing Radical Change." *National Underwriter*, October 19, 9–10.

Potter, Pitman B. 1992. "Securities Markets Opening to Foreign Participation." *East Asian Executive Reports*, April 14, 7–9.

"Prospects Bright for Securities Business." 1993. *China Daily*, January 4, 1.

Qiao Gang. 1992. "Too Much Government Interference: The Main Block to Develop China's Market Economy." *Financial Times*, November 9, 3.

Ren Kan. 1993a. "The State of the State Shares." *China Daily*, May 2–8, 3.

———. 1993b. "Stock Investors Seek Maturity in '93." *China Daily*, January 3–9, 2.

"Securities Business Now Made More Secure." 1993. *China Daily*, October 13, 4

Soares, Richard. 1992. "China: B-Shares Fever Grips Foreign Equity Investors." *Global Finance*, August, 18–20.

Tanzer, Andrew. 1992. "The Chinese Way." *Forbes*, September 28, 42–43.

Wang Jiye. 1989. "The State, the Market and the Enterprise." *Beijing Review*, April 10–16, 20–25.

Woolley, Suzanne, and Barnathan, Joyce. 1992. "Bulls in the China Shop." *Business Week*, September 28, 9–10.

Xiao Chen. 1993. "Futures Trading Still on Trial." *China Daily*, May 2–8, 4.

Xiao Liu. 1993. "Computers to Provide Broader Access to Market." *China Daily*, January 31, 2.

Yu Nai. 1993. "Bank's Lending Policies to Favor Sound Firms." *China Daily*, February 1, 4.

Yu Tian Yi. 1992. "Market Economy Needs Credit Market." *Financial Times*, December 21, 3.

Zheng Caixiong. 1993. "Stock Watchdog Set Up in Guangdong." *China Daily*, January 17–23, 3.

Zheng Kang Ling. 1992. "Market Economy and Capital Circulation." *Financial Times*, September 21, 3.

Zhou Zhe Qing. 1992. "Socialist Market Economy and Deepening the Financial Reform." *Financial Times*, November 23, 3.

Zweig, David. 1992. "Reaping Rural Rewards." *China Business Review*, November/December, 12–17.

Appendix

A Summary of the Chinese Economy, 1980–1990

In chapter 1, there is a brief discussion of the Chinese economy up to 1980. The following review is a follow-up to that discussion and provides background information for chapter 2. Unless stated otherwise, the statistics in this Appendix are in current monetary values or in nominal rates of return, and these statistics may not be consistent with those presented in chapter 1. However, this should not pose a problem.

The Chinese started the decade with caution and reassessment of priorities. The wasteful and countereconomic policies of the Fifth Five-Year Plan (1976-80), the cost of the Vietnam War (1979), a drop in oil production and associated export revenues, and a poor grain harvest in 1980 exacted a heavy penalty on the Chinese economy. In the early 1980s, the growth of the national economy slowed, industrial output followed a similar pattern, and the budget deficits of 1979 and 1980 proved heartbreaking for the Chinese, who took pride in balanced budgets. The Sixth Five-Year Plan (1981–85) was drafted to embody the various reform packages approved at the Eleventh Party Central Committee (December 1978).

THE GROSS NATIONAL PRODUCT (GNP)

The GNP increased from RMB 399.81 billion in 1979 to RMB 1,768,61 billion in 1990 reflecting an annual growth rate of 14.47 percent (Table A.1). However, the economy did not grow at an even and consistent rate. Initially, the optimism of the Ten-Year Plan (1976–85), as discussed in chapter 1, was unattainable, and the Sixth Five-Year Plan (1981–85) was geared for lower national economic growth. Chinese policymakers were content to live with a "buyers' market," where national supply would marginally exceed national demand and there would be minimal price pressures (Liu, 1989: 22–28). Unfortunately, these expectations were not met.

In the early 1980s, the state relaxed import controls on selected consumer goods, decentralized the export/import trading system, given more autonomy and spending authority over investments to local authorities, and relaxed credit policies through the banking system. Over 1981–1982, the GNP grew less than 9 percent, but thereafter the economy started to heat up: the GNP increased from 8.80 percent in 1982 to 22.92 percent in 1985. Local governments and enterprises used their new freedoms to spend: industrial output exceeded targets, investments exceeded budgets, and imports outstripped exports. The demands which were pent up since liberation created an insatiable appetite for selected consumer goods and once controls were relaxed, these goods suddenly became available. By 1985, China had suddenly become a "sellers' market" where national demand exceeded national supply (do Rosario, 1985:100-101). There were shortages in such crucial resources as energy, materials and capital for various construction activities.

Beginning in early 1985, austerity measures (discussed later in this chapter) were taken to correct the situation and the growth in GNP declined from 22.92 percent in 1985 to 13.31 percent in 1986 (Table A.1). Apart from the austerity measures, which were temporary, there were at least three major factors that appeared to hinder the long-term growth of the economy (Salem, 1983: 51–53, 1987a: 62, 1987b: 80). First, about 17 to 20 percent of the large to medium-sized state-owned enterprises were loss-making units and required subsidies. This was a drain on the economy. Second, in a number of respects, commodities produced were not matching the changing demand in the marketplace and stockpiles were the natural result. Working (or circulating) capital was turning over slowly in the economy putting additional pressures on the credit system to maintain continuous production (of unsalable goods). Third, industrial development, particularly in heavy industries, was impeded by shortages of energy, raw materials for construction and capital, and the lack of adequate and efficient transport and communications networks.

Further austerity measures were introduced in the budget for 1987, including a projected lower growth rate for state expenditures and the delay or cancellation of some key projects. The combined impact of austerity measures implemented over 1985–1987 resulted in slower growth in the national economy over 1986-1987 (Table A.1). The state sector (which accounted for about 75 percent of national output) was adversely affected as the growth of agricultural and industrial output in 1986 had slowed to 6.2 percent compared to 12.9 percent in 1985. Moreover, the growth of output of collectives had slowed to 16.7 percent in 1986 compared to 30.9 percent in 1985. The slowdown in these two sectors could not be allowed to continue, as it involved a retrenchment that was politically unacceptable. The state was pressured into relaxing austerity measures and the spending spree started all over again. The growth of GNP increased from 13.31 percent in 1986 to 23.74 in 1988 (Table A.1) and prices "hit the roof." Austerity measures were again introduced in 1989 to cool the economy, and these remained in place into the early 1990s.

Relatively speaking, inflation was not a serious problem in the early 1980s, but it was of concern in the latter half of the decade reaching as high as 18.5 percent per annum in 1988 (Table 2.8). Controlling for inflation, the real

Table A.1
Gross National Product and Associated Indices (Value in Billions of Renminbi)

Year	Gross National Product		By Type of Industry				Indices 1978=100			Percent of GNP		
	Total	Annual Growth (%)	Primary	Secondary	Tertiary	Total	Primary	Secondary	Tertiary	Primary	Secondary	Tertiary
1978	358.81		101.84	174.52	82.45	100.00	100.00	100.00	100.00	28.38%	48.64%	22.98%
1979	399.81	11.43%	125.89	191.35	82.57	107.6	106.1	108.2	107.8	31.49%	47.86%	20.65%
1980	447.00	11.80%	135.94	219.20	91.86	116.0	104.6	122.9	114.3	30.41%	49.04%	20.55%
1981	477.30	6.78%	154.56	225.55	97.19	121.2	111.9	125.2	122.2	32.38%	47.26%	20.36%
1982	519.30	8.80%	176.16	238.30	104.84	131.8	124.8	132.1	135.2	33.92%	45.89%	20.19%
1983	580.90	11.86%	196.08	264.62	120.20	145.4	135.1	145.8	152.3	33.75%	45.55%	20.69%
1984	696.20	19.85%	229.55	310.57	156.08	166.6	152.6	166.9	178.3	32.97%	44.61%	22.42%
1985	855.76	22.92%	254.16	386.66	214.94	187.8	155.4	197.9	207.9	29.70%	45.18%	25.12%
1986	969.63	13.31%	276.39	449.27	243.97	203.4	160.5	218.2	231.0	28.50%	46.33%	25.16%
1987	1,130.10	16.55%	320.43	525.16	284.51	225.8	168.1	248.1	260.8	28.35%	46.47%	25.18%
1988	1,398.42	23.74%	383.10	658.72	356.60	250.4	172.3	284.1	292.4	27.40%	47.10%	25.50%
1989	1,578.87	12.90%	422.80	738.10	417.97	259.3	177.7	295.5	301.0	26.78%	46.75%	26.47%
1990	1,768.61	12.02%	502.40	782.90	483.31	274.1	190.9	310.5	314.9	28.41%	44.27%	27.33%
r*	14.47%		13.41%	13.66%	17.43%	8.87%	5.48%	10.06%	10.24%			

Source: China Finance and Banking Association (1991:239).

r* = annual growth rate over 1979–1990

annual growth rates of the economy after 1986 were as follows (SBC Research, 1992: 11):

Year	Real GNP (RMB Billion)	Real Growth Rate	Inflation
1987	810	11.0%	7.3%
1988	898	10.9%	18.5%
1989	981	3.6%	17.8%
1990	981	5.5%	2.1%
1991	1,050	7.0%	4.0%

Looking at the industrial composition of GNP, tertiary industries experienced the fastest growth rate at 17.43 percent per annum and by 1990 accounted for 27.3 percent of GNP compared to 20.6 percent in 1979 (Table A.1). This gain in tertiary industries came mainly at the expense of secondary industries which grew at 13.66 percent annually. In 1979, secondary industries accounted for 48 percent of GNP but this fell to 44.3 percent by 1990. Primary industries (agriculture, mining and forestry) had the slowest growth rate at 13.41 percent and fell marginally from 30.4 percent of GNP in 1978 to 28.4 percent in 1990 (Table A.1).

AGRICULTURAL AND INDUSTRIAL OUTPUT

Much of the state's efforts were directed at economic reconstruction in the agricultural and industrial sectors of the economy. Considering the gross industrial output, agriculture continued to decline to the benefit of light industries as is reflected in the following statistics (China Finance and Banking Association, 1991: 236–237):

Year	Percent of National Output		
	Agriculture	Light Industries	Heavy Industries
1980	27.2%	34.3%	38.5%
1985	27.1	34.6	38.3
1990	24.3	37.3	38.3

From the start (1979), China was determined to promote the light industrial sector as opposed to heavy industries because of potential energy and capital shortages and the lack of adequate transport and communications networks (do Rosario, 1985: 100–101; Bonavia, 1980: 69). Significant credit (about RMB 3 billion) was made available to light industries over 1980–1981, and by 1984, the growth in light industries had reached or surpassed that for heavy industries. This trend continued throughout the decade. Overall, actual industrial output tended to overshoot targets by 10 to 25 percent during the decade. For example, in 1983, the actual industrial output grew by 10.3 percent while the target growth for the year was 4 percent; for 1986, the figures were 11.1 and 8.8 percent, respectively. Table A.2 shows the value of output for all industry

Table A.2
Total Output Value of Society (Value in Billions of Renminbi)

Year	Total Value	Industry & Agriculture	Agriculture	Industrial Total	Industrial Light	Industrial Heavy	Total Value	Industry & Agriculture	Agriculture	Industrial Total	Industrial Light	Industrial Heavy
									Annual Growth Rate		Industrial	
1978	685	563	140	424	183	241						
1979	764	638	170	468	205	264	11.63%	13.22%	21.55%	10.48%	11.99%	9.33%
1980	854	708	192	516	243	272	11.69%	10.96%	13.25%	10.13%	18.88%	3.34%
1981	908	758	218	540	278	262	6.33%	7.11%	13.42%	4.75%	14.40%	-3.85%
1982	997	829	248	581	292	289	9.82%	9.41%	13.85%	7.61%	4.96%	10.42%
1983	1,113	821	275	546	314	233	11.69%	-1.00%	10.75%	-6.02%	7.40%	-19.57%
1984	1,317	1,083	321	762	361	401	18.33%	31.91%	16.87%	39.48%	15.09%	72.36%
1985	1,658	1,334	362	972	458	514	25.90%	23.12%	12.60%	27.56%	26.80%	28.24%
1986	1,905	1,521	401	1,119	533	586	14.85%	14.04%	10.89%	15.21%	16.50%	14.06%
1987	2,303	1,849	468	1,381	666	716	20.95%	21.58%	16.52%	23.40%	24.88%	22.05%
1988	2,981	2,409	587	1,822	898	925	29.40%	30.29%	25.43%	31.93%	34.90%	29.17%
1989	3,452	2,855	654	2,202	1,076	1,126	15.81%	18.53%	11.42%	20.81%	19.85%	21.75%
1990	3,800	3,159	766	2,392	1,181	1,211	10.07%	10.63%	17.25%	8.66%	9.78%	7.60%
r*	15.70%	15.65%	14.68%	15.99%	17.28%	14.87%						

Source: China Finance and Banking Association (1991: 238).

r* = annual growth rate over 1979–1990.

Table A.3
Investment in Fixed Assets (Value in Billions of Renminbi)

Investment in Fixed Assets

Year	Total (RMB)	Annual Growth (%)	State-Owned Firms (RMB)	Collectives (RMB)	Households (RMB)	Major Sources of Financing				Types of Assets	
						State Budget (RMB)	Financial Insts. (RMB)	Foreign Capital (RMB)	Local Govt. & Others (RMB)	Productive (RMB)	Nonproductive (RMB)
1979	66.94		66.94								
1980	74.59	11.43%	74.59								
1981	96.10	28.84%	66.75	11.52	17.83						
1982	120.04	24.91%	84.53	17.43	18.08						
1983	136.91	14.05%	95.20	15.63	26.08	33.97	17.55	6.66	78.73	82.91	54.00
1984	183.29	33.88%	118.52	23.87	40.90	42.10	25.85	7.07	108.27	110.37	72.92
1985	254.32	38.75%	168.05	32.75	53.52	40.78	51.03	9.15	153.36	154.41	99.91
1986	301.96	18.73%	197.85	39.17	64.94	44.06	63.83	13.22	180.85	183.93	118.03
1987	364.09	20.58%	229.80	54.70	79.59	47.55	83.59	17.54	215.41	229.18	134.91
1988	449.65	23.50%	276.28	71.17	102.20	40.27	91.46	25.45	292.47	282.87	166.78
1989	413.77	−7.98%	253.55	57.00	103.22	34.16	71.64	27.42	280.55	257.20	156.57
1990	445.11	7.57%	292.68	55.00	97.43	38.77	87.09	27.83	291.42	276.83	168.28
r*	18.80%		14.35%	18.97%	20.77%	1.91%	25.71%	22.66%	20.56%	18.80%	17.63%
Selected Percentage Distributions											
1983	100.00%		69.53%	11.42%	19.05%	24.81%	12.82%	4.86%	57.50%	60.56%	39.44%
1985	100.00%		66.08%	12.88%	21.04%	16.03%	20.07%	3.60%	60.30%	60.71%	39.29%
1990	100.00%		65.75%	12.36%	21.89%	8.71%	19.57%	6.25%	65.47%	62.19%	37.81%

Source: China Finance and Banking Association (1991: 249–50).

r* = annual growth rate.

sectors of the economy. Total value increased at an annual rate of 15.7 percent which is higher than that for the GNP. The annual growth rates for the boom years, 1984–1985 and 1987–1988, were relatively high and contributed to the creation, starting in the mid-1980s, of a "sellers' market," with shortages in energy, construction materials, and capital.

INVESTMENT IN FIXED ASSETS AND ACCUMULATION

Investment in fixed assets increased from RMB 66.94 billion in 1979 to RMB 445.11 billion in 1990 reflecting an annual growth rate of 18.8 percent (Table A.3). This growth rate was much higher than the 14.47 percent observed for GNP. Starting in 1981, the investment for collectives and individuals were included in the statistics; by 1990, these two groups accounted for about one-third of investments. In the early 1980s, the state delegated much of the investment decisions to the local governments and enterprises and, through fiscal and other reforms, more money was in the hands of these units. The state relied on macroeconomic management through the unified physical and credit plans to control investments. Unfortunately, the system did not work well.

Actual investments tended to exceed budgets by 15 to 25 percent, particularly in the boom years, putting pressure on prices. For example, in 1985, actual construction expenditures exceeded the state-approved budget by 31 percent. In addition, there was a tendency for local authorities to undertake projects and to import capital goods which were outside of the unified budget. These actions helped to create unfavorable trade balances. More importantly, the economy might not have had the capacity to handle the scale of construction which was undertaken as is reflected in the following statement:

At present, more than 100,000 projects are under construction, far beyond the state's economic and managerial capabilities. The results [have] . . . been prolonged construction projects, less-than-anticipated returns and loss of some key energy and transport projects. It has also had negative effects on the government's control of the economy, structural reform and steady economic development.[1]

As far as the state was concerned, another disturbing trend was the relatively high percentage of investments (about 40 percent) that flowed to nonproductive projects, including hotels, restaurants, office towers, and convention centers (Table A.3). In the absence of direct state intervention, these decisions were controlled by local governments and enterprises, much to the dislike of state planners. The abuse of construction budgets was so irritating that the state at one time toyed with the idea of slapping a tax on unauthorized projects.

The two primary sources of funding were local governments and direct loans from financial institutions. It is interesting to note that allocations from the state budget played a relatively minor role. In 1979, the state decided that budget allocations to enterprises for investments should be

Table A.4
Exports, Imports, and the Trade Balance (Value in Billions of U.S. Dollars

Year	Total Foreign Trade ($US)	Exports ($US)	Imports ($US)	Trade Balance ($US)	Total	Annual Growth Exports	Imports	Current Account Balance ($US)
1979	29.33	13.66	15.67	−2.01				
1980	37.82	18.27	19.55	−1.28	28.95%	33.75%	24.76%	
1981	44.02	22.01	22.01	0.00	16.39%	20.47%	12.58%	
1982	41.6	22.32	19.28	3.04	−5.50%	1.41%	−12.40%	5.67
1983	43.62	22.23	21.39	0.84	4.86%	−0.40%	10.94%	4.24
1984	53.55	26.14	27.41	−1.27	22.76%	17.59%	28.14%	2.03
1985	69.6	27.35	42.25	−14.90	29.97%	4.63%	54.14%	−11.42
1986	73.85	30.94	42.91	−11.97	6.11%	13.13%	1.56%	−7.03
1987	82.65	39.44	43.21	−3.77	11.92%	27.47%	0.70%	0.03
1988	102.79	47.52	55.27	−7.75	24.37%	20.49%	27.91%	−3.80
1989	111.68	52.54	59.14	−6.60	8.65%	10.56%	7.00%	−4.32
1990	115.44	62.09	53.35	8.74	3.37%	18.18%	−9.79%	12.00
r*	13.26%	14.76%	11.78%					

Source: China Finance and Banking Association (1991: 38, 251). The current account balances for 1982–1984 are from "China's Balance of Payments, 1982–86," *Beijing Review,* September 7, 1987, 28.

r* = annual growth rate over 1979–1990.

reclassified as loans under the supervision of the People's Construction Bank of China. Furthermore, local governments were given authority to establish trust and investment corporations and to issue bonds to raise funds for investments. Enterprises were given a clawback on foreign exchange and were allowed to keep profits after taxes to boost investment capabilities. The decentralization of the investment decision gave new freedoms to local governments and enterprises which, in some respects, abused the privileges.

EXPORTS AND IMPORTS

China's foreign trade (exports and imports combined) increased from U.S. $29.33 billion in 1979 to U.S. $115.44 billion in 1990 reflecting an annual growth rate of 13.26 percent (Table A.4). While exports experienced a higher growth rate than imports (14.76 versus 11.79 percent), it may be argued that China had an alarming adverse trade balance over 1979–1990. Cumulatively, the trade deficits (for 1979–1980 and 1984–1989) totaled U.S. $49.55 billion, compared with a trade surplus of U.S. $12.62 billion for 1981–1983 and 1990 (Table A.4). This adverse trade balance may not be necessarily bad since much of it was caused by the importation of industrial goods (raw materials and intermediate and capital goods) that were needed for the reconstruction of the economy. There are import controls on durable and nondurable consumer goods and nonessential intermediate and capital goods for industry and commerce. The adverse trade balance may be temporary and may be eliminated once exports from the restructured economy pick up. However, controls have not always worked as intended and may furthermore prove ineffective in the face of unscrupulous operators. This happened in China.

In the early 1980s, local governments were allowed to establish foreign trading corporations (FTCs) to handle export/import business. These FTCs were supposed to be independent units which were responsible for their profits and losses including those on foreign exchange transactions. Hundreds of FTCs sprang up across the country and in a frenzy, started to import consumer and industrial goods without due care as to whether they were allowable under existing plans or whether there was foreign exchange to pay for the import bills. Moreover, local authorities were given authority to spend their foreign exchange allocations as they desired without direct state intervention. Imports rose by 11 percent in 1983, 28 percent in 1984, and 54 percent in 1985 (Table A.4). As the import bills were coming in, the local authorities realized that they lacked the money to pay, and there was a run on the State Treasury. Foreign reserves dropped from U.S. $16.3 billion, in September 1984, to U.S. $11.3 billion, in March 1985; there was a further drop to U.S. $8 billion by the end of 1985. The state took stern austerity actions starting in early 1985 and continuing to the end of 1986: high import duties/taxes were levied, some imports were banned, foreign exchange payments for expensive projects were delayed or canceled, spending powers of local governments were curbed, PBOC increased surveillance on foreign exchange borrowing and exports were pushed through an export subsidy program (Salem, 1987b: 80).

With austerity, the growth in imports was controlled for 1986–1987 at less than 2 percent per annum, while exports increased at considerably higher rates (Table A.4). However, after austerity measures were relaxed in 1987, imports increased rather dramatically in 1988, by 27 percent above 1987. Once again, it was time for more austerity measures and by 1990, China had a positive trade balance.

In the meantime, "invisibles" helped to offset some of the adverse trade balances. Over the 1982–1990 period, the total of positive current account balances (U.S. $23.97 billion) provided some cushion for the negative current account balances (U.S. $26.57 billion; see Table A.4). The positive current account balances over 1982–1984 resulted in increased foreign reserves which were used to repay loans to international monetary organizations. However, the negative balances after 1984 added to China's growing foreign debt.

STATE REVENUES AND EXPENDITURES

State revenues increased from RMB 110.33 billion in 1979 to RMB 331.25 billion in 1990 reflecting an annual growth rate of 10.51 percent (Table A.5). The source of state revenues have changed over the years with taxes accounting for almost 90 percent by 1990. State expenditures have increased from RMB 127.33 billion in 1979 to RMB 345.22 billion in 1990, reflecting an annual growth rate of 9.49 percent. The Chinese budget system follows that for the Soviets, which treats debt financing as revenue. Following this approach, there was a budget deficit in each year over 1979–1990, except for a small surplus in 1985. If the debt financing is excluded, the deficit is

Table A.5
State Revenues and Expenditures (Value in Billions of Renminbi)

Year	Total (RMB)	Annual Growth (%)	State Revenues Sources					State Expenditures Total (RMB)	Budget Deficit		Deficit as % GNP	
			Taxes (RMB)	State-Owned Firms (RMB)	Debt (RMB)	Others (RMB)	Subsidies (RMB)		With Debt (RMB)	Without Debt (RMB)	With Debt	Without Debt
1978	112.11		51.93	57.20		2.98		111.10	1.01	1.01	0.28%	0.28%
1979	110.33	-1.59%	53.78	49.29	3.53	3.73		127.39	-17.06	-20.59	-4.27%	-5.15%
1980	108.52	-1.64%	57.17	43.52	4.30	3.53		121.27	-12.75	-17.05	-2.85%	-3.81%
1981	108.95	0.40%	62.99	35.37	7.31	3.28		111.50	-2.55	-9.86	-0.53%	-2.07%
1982	112.40	3.17%	70.00	29.65	8.39	4.36		115.33	-2.93	-11.32	-0.56%	-2.18%
1983	124.90	11.12%	77.56	24.05	7.94	15.35		129.25	-4.35	-12.29	-0.75%	-2.12%
1984	150.19	20.25%	94.74	27.68	7.73	20.04		154.64	-4.45	-12.18	-0.64%	-1.75%
1985	186.64	24.27%	204.08	4.38	8.99	19.89	(50.70)	184.48	2.16	-6.83	0.25%	-0.80%
1986	226.03	21.10%	209.07	4.20	13.83	31.41	(32.48)	233.08	-7.05	-20.88	-0.73%	-2.15%
1987	236.89	4.80%	214.04	4.29	16.96	39.24	(37.64)	244.85	-7.96	-24.92	-0.70%	-2.21%
1988	262.80	10.94%	239.05	5.11	27.08	36.21	(44.65)	270.66	-7.86	-34.94	-0.56%	-2.50%
1989	294.79	12.17%	272.74	6.36	28.30	47.28	(59.89)	304.02	-9.23	-37.53	-0.58%	-2.38%
1990	331.25	12.37%	282.19	7.83	37.55	61.26	(57.58)	345.22	-13.97	-51.52	-0.79%	-2.91%
r*	10.51%		16.26%	-15.40%	23.98%	28.97%	2.58%	9.49%				
Selected Percentage Distribution												
1983	100.00%		62.10%	19.26%	6.36%	12.29%	0.00%					
1984	100.00%		63.08%	18.43%	5.15%	13.34%	0.00%					
1985	100.00%		109.34%	2.35%	4.82%	10.66%	-27.16%					
1986	100.00%		92.50%	1.86%	6.12%	13.90%	-14.37%					
1987	100.00%		90.35%	1.81%	7.16%	16.56%	-15.89%					
1988	100.00%		90.96%	1.94%	10.30%	13.78%	-16.99%					
1989	100.00%		92.52%	2.16%	9.60%	16.04%	-20.32%					
1990	100.00%		85.19%	2.36%	11.34%	18.49%	-17.38%					

Source: China Finance and Banking Association (1991:243–244).

r* is the annual growth rate over 1979–90

significantly larger (Table A.5). Viewed using either method, the budget deficit is getting larger in monetary terms. However, if viewed as a percentage of GNP, the deficit remained at below 1 percent if debt financing is considered, and 3 percent if debt financing is not taken into account. Usually, a budget deficit of 3 to 4 percent of GNP (or national income) is considered acceptable in macroeconomic management.

The shift to taxation as a source of funds was initiated in 1979 on a trial basis with 456 state-owned firms and in 1984, for the entire economy (Han, 1989: 20–23; China, 1989: 21–22). Prior to the start of this system, state-owned enterprises handed over profits and depreciation funds to the state. As a new system in the Chinese fiscal arsenal, there are problems with its implementation. First, it is estimated that state-owned enterprises have devised ways to shield about 50 percent of profits from the full brunt of taxation. The situation is worse for individuals: about 80 percent either do not pay or evade taxes. Second, while taxing powers are with the state, local authorities very often give tax exemptions/reductions to promote economic development in their respective jurisdiction without state authority. Third, the Chinese judicial system is relatively imperfect and prosecutions for tax evasion are a difficult task; consequently, enforcement of the tax system has presented some challenges for the authorities. Considering these and other problems, it was estimated that in 1989, the state was failing to collect about RMB 10 billion in taxes, funds it would welcome to reduce the budget deficit.

Another nagging issue for the state is the question of subsidies. As indicated earlier, about 17 to 20 percent of the large and medium-size state-owned firms are losing money, and with a taxation system in place, they are being subsidized. Close to 20 percent of state revenues have been paid as subsidies to these firms (Table A.5). Then there is the question of price subsidies on such commodities as oil, grain and meat in the domestic market. These subsidies are included in state expenditures and over 1980–1990, they accounted for about 10 percent of such expenditures. Price reforms are being considered to reduce these subsidies but they are meeting with resistance. Finally, there is the issue of export subsidies which exist but are difficult to quantify. Taken together, subsidies exact a heavy burden on the state budget.

Over the years, the state has found it necessary to compete with other economic units for resources. Fiscal and monetary reforms have served to channel more extrabudgetary funds away from the state. In 1952, the state had access to about 92 percent of extrabudgetary funds; other economic units, 8 percent (Table A.6). By 1989, the reverse was true: the other economic units, particularly the state-owned enterprises, had access to 95 percent of extrabudgetary funds; the state, 5 percent.

Table A.6
State Budgetary and Extrabudgetary Income (Value in Billions of Renminbi)

		Extrabudgetary		Distribution of Extrabudgetary		
Year	State Budgetary	Total	Percent of Budgetary	Provinces	Admin. Units	State-owned Enterprises
1952	17.39	1.36	7.82%	1.25		0.11
1957	21.00	2.63	12.52%	0.57	0.38	1.68
1962	31.36	6.36	20.28%	2.05	1.52	2.79
1970	66.29	10.09	15.22%	1.35	2.80	5.94
1975	81.56	25.15	30.84%	2.79	4.23	18.13
1980	104.22	55.74	53.48%	4.09	7.44	44.21
1985	183.72	153.00	83.28%	4.41	23.32	125.27
1986	218.45	173.73	79.53%	4.32	29.42	139.99
1987	226.24	202.88	89.67%	4.46	35.84	162.58
1988	248.94	227.00	91.19%	4.89	43.89	178.22
1989	280.38	265.88	94.83%	5.44	50.07	210.37

Source: China Finance and Banking Association (1991: 245).

NOTE

1. Salem (1987b: 64).

REFERENCES

Bonavia, David. 1980. "The Red Ink on China's Ledger." *Far Eastern Economic Review,* September 9, 69.

China. State Statistics Bureau. 1989. "The Chinese Economy in 1988." *Beijing Review,* February 6–12, 21–22.

China Finance and Banking Association. 1991. *Almanac of China's Finance and Banking.* Beijing: China's Financial Publishing House.

China Handbook Editorial Committee. 1990. *Economy.* Beijing: Foreign Languages Press.

do Rosario, Louise. 1985. "Time to Pay the Piper." *Far Eastern Economic Review,* August 22, 100–101.

Han Guojian, 1989. "Strengthening Taxation's Role as an Economic Lever." *Beijing Review,* August 7–13, 21.

Liu Guoguan. 1989. "A Sweet and Sour Decade." *Beijing Review,* January 2–8, 22–28.

Salem, Ellen. 1983. "Slow Boat to China." *Far Eastern Economic Review,* April 23, 51–53.

———. 1987a. "Cooling Off the Economy." *Far Eastern Economic Review,* March 26, 80.

———. 1987b. "Major Hurdles to Revitalization." *Far Eastern Economic Review,* March 19, 62.

SBC Research. 1992. *China Stock Market Overview,* July.

INDEX

About the Authors

CECIL R. DIPCHAND is Professor of Finance in the School of Business Administration at Dalhousie University. He is the Project Director of the Dalhousie/Xiamen University Linkage Program and is widely published in periodical literature and in books.

ZHANG YICHUN is Professor of Money and Banking and Dean of Economics College of Xiamen University, P.R.C. Professor Zhang has published 14 books, including *Socialist Money and Banking*, and over 60 articles in China of which 4 books and 5 papers were awarded prizes for excellence.

MA MINGJIA is the Vice Head of the Department of Financial Administration of the Bank of China, P.R.C. He has published more than 140 articles on finance, has participated in the compilation of *The Encyclopedia of the Banking of China*, and is chief editor of the Stock Knowledge Series and 12 books on finance which have a considerable influence on financial circles of China.

ISBN 0-313-29282-5

HARDCOVER BAR CODE